THE PSYCHOLOGY
of
CONSUMER BEHAVIOR

THE PSYCHOLOGY
of
CONSUMER BEHAVIOR

Brian Mullen
Craig Johnson
Syracuse University

 LAWRENCE ERLBAUM ASSOCIATES, PUBLISHERS
1990 Hillsdale, New Jersey   Hove and London

Lawrence Erlbaum Associates, Inc., Publishers
365 Broadway
Hillsdale, New Jersey 07642

Library of Congress Cataloging-in-Publication Data

Mullen, Brian and Johnson, Craig.
The psychology of consumer behavior.

Includes index.
1. Consumers.   I. Title.
HF5415.3.M85   1990   658.8′342   87-15601
ISBN 0-89859-857-5

Printed in the United States of America
10   9   8   7   6   5   4   3   2   1

For Terry and Sophie
and
For Curtis and Elaine

Contents

Preface

As conveyed in the title, this book presents an overview of theory and research on the psychology of consumer behavior. After several years of studying, teaching, talking about, and engaging in consumer behavior, we have tried to bring together a representative and broad survey of small answers to the big question: "Why do consumers do what they do?"

It should be recognized that there are at least three different types of books about consumers. One type of textbook about consumers is devoted to an attempt to manipulate and influence consumers' use of products, goods, and services. Another type of textbook about consumers is devoted to an attempt to protect, and to serve as an advocate for, consumers in their interactions with producers in the marketplace. The third type of textbook about consumers is devoted to an attempt to understand the behavior of consumers. It is this third type of textbook that the reader is holding now.

Our goal has been to provide a broad, accessible presentation of current theory and research as it illuminates fundamental issues regarding consumer behavior. The goal of understanding may seem less ambitious than either the goal of influencing consumers or the goal of protecting consumers. However, as the reader delves into the research literature of consumer psychology, it should become apparent that the task of understanding consumer behavior is not a simple task. In addition, there is always the distinct possibility that an improved understanding of consumer behavior might be used to more successfully manipulate and influence consumers' use of products, goods, and services. At the same time, an enhanced appreciation for the complexities of consumer behavior might be used to more successfully serve as an advocate for consumers in their interactions in the marketplace. Regardless of the direction in which the interested reader is heading, a firm understanding of the theory and research that illuminates consumer behavior is an excellent place to start.

Many people must be thanked for their contributions throughout the various stages of development of this text. At the top of the list, the many students who have worked through earlier versions of this text have provided innumerable suggestions, comments, and encouragements. Kelly Shaver and John Nezlak have provided detailed, thoughtful, and extremely helpful comments on earlier versions of this text. The staff at Lawrence Erlbaum Associates, especially Jack Burton and Carol Lachman, have extended the patience and support that helped to transform this book from an idea into a reality. Lou Mullen deserves special thanks for her tolerance, her encouragement, her insightful comments, and her good cups of tea during the many late nights and interrupted vacations. Finally, thanks go to our parents, to whom this book is dedicated, for teaching us the first things we knew about consumers.

Brian Mullen
Craig Johnson

1 | Introduction

Recall the last time you purchased a beverage in a grocery store. You located the beverage aisle, examined the various available brands, selected the chosen beverage brand, and paid for it on your way out: This seems to be an unremarkable and everyday sort of event. However, upon closer examination, there is a host of questions that are raised by this everyday behavior. How did you first become aware of the chosen beverage brand: through commercial advertisements on television, through your friends, or at the point of decision in the beverage aisle? How did you develop a positive evaluation of this brand: was it the price? Has this brand been recommended in the media by one of your favorite celebrities? Does this brand have something unique, making it stand out from the others? What made you want this brand in particular?

These are the type of questions asked within the field of consumer psychology, and this volume attempts to answer these questions in terms of current psychological theory and research. *Consumer psychology* can be defined as the scientific study of the behavior of consumers. A *consumer* is an individual who uses the products, goods, or services of some organization.

As Howell (1976) pointed out, each organization provides some product that is used by some consumers, even though we may not always recognize the products or the consumers as such. For example, it seems fairly obvious that the college students who drink a cola produced by a specific beverage company are the consumers of that beverage product. However, in a sense, we can think of public high school students as the consumers of a state's educational product; voters can be thought of as consumers of a political candidate's leadership and administration product; and, the members of a religious group might be viewed as consumers of a church's spiritual product. Thus, the study of the behavior of consumers involves examination of a wide range of everyday human behavior.

This textbook is structured around a general model of consumer behavior, presented in Fig. 1.1. This model helps the student of consumer behavior consider and deal with the variables and relationships that can affect consumer behavior. Generally, a model is a simple representation of something that is in fact more

1

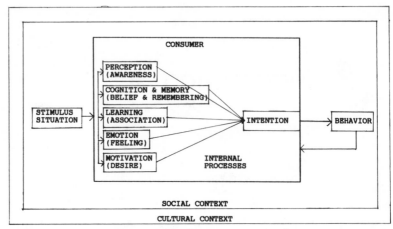

FIG. 1.1. A general model of consumer behavior.

complicated. The model in Fig. 1.1 leaves out some of the complexity of consumer behavior. Nonetheless, this model contains the most fundamental and the most important elements found in other common models of consumer behavior. In a sense, Fig. 1.1 is a simplified schematic illustration of the theory and research that we call consumer psychology. In this chapter we begin our study of consumer behavior by establishing some preliminary definitions of the variables and processes presented in Fig. 1.1. Before moving on to more detailed examinations of these variables and processes in subsequent chapters, we briefly examine some other representative models of consumer behavior, and we consider some basic issues regarding measurement.

A GENERAL MODEL OF CONSUMER BEHAVIOR

Beginning at the left side of the model, notice that a box labelled "stimulus situation" is shown to influence the consumer. The stimulus situation is the complex of conditions that collectively act as a stimulus to elicit responses from the consumer. This suggests that consumer behavior is not typically thought of as being elicited by a single stimulus. Rather, consumer behavior is considered to be the consequence of patterns or constellations of stimuli. For example, when the consumer purchases a can of "Loca-cola" brand beverage, that consumer behavior was not merely the result of the cost of the product. Instead, we would have to consider the cost of the product, the characteristics of the advertisement of the product, the packaging of the product, the individual's past experiences with the product, the placement of the product on the shelf, and so on.

At first glance, this might appear frustrating to the budding consumer psychologist; the stimulus situation that impacts upon the consumer seems to be unmanageably complex. However, it is important to recognize that the world in which consumers behave is, in reality, extremely complex, filled with continual commercials, pretty packaging, and confusing choices. The little box in Fig. 1.1 labelled "stimulus situation" is very full and busy.

Next, the model specifies a number of internal processes. These internal processes are a related series of changes that occur within the individual. Internal processes can be viewed as consequents that are caused by something else, or as antecedents that cause something else. When viewed as consequents, internal processes are thought of as the result of the stimulus situation, the individual's own behavior, the social context, the cultural context, other internal processes, and the interactions between these sets of variables. Research that views a given internal process as a consequent treats it as a dependent variable that is influenced by some independent variable(s). When viewed as antecedents, internal processes can be considered the cause of intentions, behavior, or some other internal processes. Research that views a given internal process as an antecedent treats it as an independent variable that influences some dependent variable(s). One special case of the use of internal processes as independent variables is the concept of psychographics. This refers to the use of individual differences in the internal processes to predict consumer behavior. As discussed in chapter 8, individual consumers who are especially likely to engage in a particular internal process may be more receptive to certain types of messages.

Each of the internal processes are discussed in detail in the chapters that follow. The internal processes are considered from both the perspective of consequents that are caused by something else (i.e., dependent variables) and the perspective of antecedents that cause something else (i.e., independent variables).

Perception is typically defined as the psychological processing of information received by the senses. The result of the internal process of perception is awareness of the product, or awareness of attributes of the product. Cognition refers to the processes of knowing or thought. The result of cognition is a collection of beliefs about or evaluations of the product. Memory refers to the retention of information regarding past events or ideas. The result of this process is the acquisition, retention, and remembering of product information. Learning describes a relatively permanent change in responses as a result of practice or experience. The result of this internal process is the formation of associations between stimuli or between stimuli and responses. Emotion is a state of arousal involving conscious experience and visceral changes. The result of this internal process is feelings about the product. Motivation is a state of tension within the individual that arouses, directs, and maintains behavior toward a goal. The result of this internal process is desire or need for the product.

Note that these internal processes were defined as a related series of changes. Discussing each process separately requires the establishment of somewhat arbitrary distinctions between interdependent events. For example, after the college student first sees a commercial for Loca-cola, he or she might express an interest in the product, and a desire to buy it. Perception seems to have occurred, because the consumer is aware of the product; cognition has taken place, insofar as the consumer has evaluated Loca-cola as being worthy of consideration; motivation may have been engaged, if the student really wants to try the product; and so on. This is to emphasize that, although we can conceptualize these internal processes as separate entities, we must address their interrelationships in order to obtain a full appreciation for their effects on subsequent events (specifically, their effects on other internal processes, intentions, and behavior). Another important thing to recognize about this model is the lack of any predetermined sequencing of the internal processes. That is, the model does not assume that some internal process(es) must occur before other internal processes can occur. Thus, any internal process might come before, and influence, any other internal process.

Intention refers to a plan to perform some specific behavior. Behavior is typically defined as an act or a response. Within the context of consumer behavior, intention refers to the plan to purchase or use the product, and behavior refers to the actual purchase or use of the product. Bear in mind that this applies whether the product is a brand of toothpaste, a course in school, or a political candidate. Both intention and behavior are characterized in Fig. 1.1 as resulting from the direct and interactive effects of the internal processes. Note that behavior may influence the internal processes of the consumer. This type of *feedback* can have very important implications, and is considered in detail later in the book.

Social context refers to the totality of social stimulation that influences the individual. This can include friends, family, or sales personnel. The *cultural context* refers to the totality of cultural stimulation that influences the individual and his or her social context. This can include the individual's culture (e.g., late 20th-century America), subculture (e.g., rural southeastern United States university students), social class (e.g., middle class), and so on. Note that the individual (with his or her internal processes, intentions, and behavior) exists within, and is influenced by, a social context. Further, the individual's social context exists within, and is influenced by, a cultural context.

OTHER MODELS OF CONSUMER BEHAVIOR

Kover (1967) reviewed the use of models in consumer and marketing research. He noted that: "All models have one thing in common: they describe some basic behaviors, needs or situations and make the assumption that 'this is really what man is like'. Then, the particular study builds on this model and usually ignores behavior not included in the model" (p. 129). The intrinsic value of the model presented in Fig. 1.1 is that studies built upon or interpreted within this model will be able to ignore very little, if any, behavior. This is because the model is structured to incorporate the range of variables that have been examined previously in research on consumer behavior.

However, the reader should realize that this model is not some new theoretical breakthrough, "cut out of whole cloth." In actuality, this model is an extension and integration of many previous models of consumer behavior. These models of consumer behavior can be categorized into three types: undifferentiated, unilineal, and cybernetic. These three categories roughly correspond to the three time periods identified by Engel, Blackwell, and Kollat (1978) as pre-1960, 1960 to 1967, and 1967 to present.

Undifferentiated Models

The undifferentiated models of consumer behavior (pre-1960) amounted to lists of variables suspected to influence consumer behavior. However, these lists of variables seldom had any integrative framework (or, any substantiating empirical

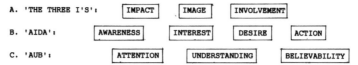

FIG. 1.2. *Examples of undifferentiated models of consumer behavior (pre-1960) (Leavitt, 1961).*

evidence) to justify their serious consideration by researchers. Leavitt (1961) described a number of these early models of consumer behavior, derived from the "folk wisdom" of advertising and marketing. Some of these undifferentiated models of consumer behavior, conveyed in Fig. 1.2, are The Three I's (Impact, Image, Involvement), AIDA (Awareness, Interest, Desire, Action), and AUB (Attention, Understanding, Believability).

For example, consider an application of the AUB model to the consumer considering Loca-cola beverage. The AUB model suggests that three things must occur if the consumer is to purchase Loca-cola: The consumer must become aware of Loca-cola (attention); the consumer must understand that Loca-cola is described as a cola beverage that quenches thirst for 50¢ a can (comprehension); and, the consumer must believe that Loca-cola is a 50¢, thirst-quenching cola beverage (believability). If these three things can occur, according to the undifferentiated AUB model, the consumer should purchase Loca-cola. These undifferentiated models of consumer behavior may be useful if they suggest variables that are important to understanding consumer behavior. However, simply listing these variables, without any consideration for how the processes occur or how they interact, does not take us very far toward explaining why people will buy or use a particular product.

Unilineal Models

The next general trend in models of consumer behavior led to the unilineal models (1960 to 1967). These models went a step beyond the simpler undifferentiated models by arranging the list of variables in some preestablished sequence. For example, Lavidge and Steiner (1961) proposed, and Palda (1966) developed, a "hierarchy of effects" model. Similarly, McGuire (1969) proposed an "information processing model of advertising effectiveness." These models assume a single, one-way ("unilineal") flow of influence among the variables included in the model. These two unilineal models are illustrated in Fig. 1.3.

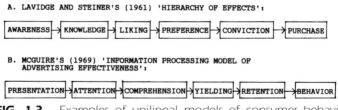

FIG. 1.3. *Examples of unilineal models of consumer behavior (1960 to 1967).*

For example, consider the application of Lavidge and Steiner's Hierarchy of Effects model to the consumer considering Loca-cola. The Hierarchy of Effects model suggests that the following events must occur, in this sequence, if the consumer is to purchase Loca-cola: the consumer must become aware of Loca-cola (Awareness); then, the consumer must know that Loca-cola is a 50¢, thirst-quenching cola beverage (Knowledge); next, the consumer must come to evaluate positively these attributes of 'cola', 'thirst-quenching', and '50¢ a can' (Liking); then, the consumer must come to prefer Loca-cola over all other competing brands (Preference); finally, if the consumer can commit to a specific plan to obtain Loca-cola (Conviction), then, the consumer will actually buy a can of Loca-cola (Purchase). These unilineal models begin to characterize some of the interdependence of the processes involved in consumer behavior. However, as it turns out, human behavior is seldom as simple and as rigid as these unilineal models seem to suggest.

Cybernetic Models

The latest phase in the development of models of consumer behavior is the cybernetic models (1967 to present). The term *cybernetic* refers to recent developments in information science and the understanding of how systems operate; cybernetics often implies the complicated type of information transmission and utilization that we associate with modern computers. The cybernetic models have gone beyond the simpler unilineal models in a number of ways. First, the cybernetic models are generally more complex, listing a larger number of variables than the earlier types of models. Second, although the cybernetic models generally incorporate a one-way flow of influence from one variable to the next, they typically allow for exceptions to this (previously unassailable) unilineal assumption. Finally, true to the term *cybernetic,* these models usually incorporate the process of feedback into the model. For example, if one variable (behavior) is influenced by another variable (perception), behavior might now "feed back" to influence perception. We consider this type of effect in chapter 9. Examples of cybernetic models are Howard's (Howard & Sheth, 1969) model of buyer behavior, and the Engel, Blackwell, and Kollat (1978) model. These cybernetic models are illustrated in Fig. 1.4.

For example, consider the application of Howard's Model of Buyer Behavior to the consumer considering Loca-cola beverage. As a function of whatever newspaper and magazines to which the consumer is exposed (Information Available), the consumer's tendencies to read such newspapers and magazines (Media Habits), and any thirst-(Arousal-) initiated searching for beverage information (Overt Search), the consumer may become exposed to information about Loca-cola (Information Exposed). Especially if thirst (Arousal) had stimulated an increased Attention, the consumer may be better able to retain and retrieve information about Loca-cola (Information Recalled). This recalled information about Loca-cola will contribute to the consumer's knowledge and understanding of Loca-cola as a thirst-quenching cola beverage that sells for 50¢ a can (Brand Comprehension). If this understanding of Loca-cola indicates that it is a close

a. Howard's (1974) "Model of Buyer Behavior":

b. Engel, Kollat, & Blackwell's (1978) Model:

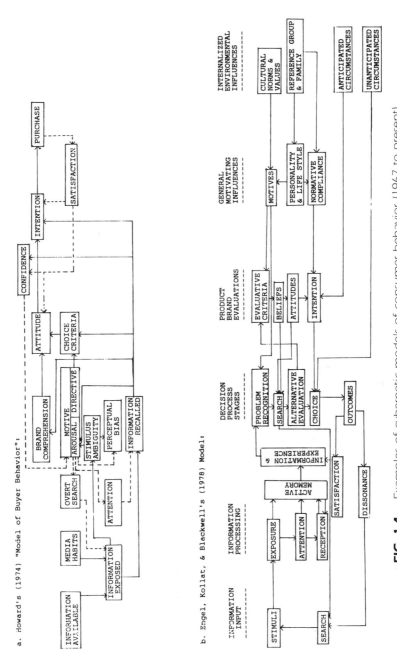

FIG. 1.4. Examples of cybernetic models of consumer behavior (1967 to present).

7

approximation of what a good beverage should be (Choice Criteria), this will lead to a positive evaluation of Loca-cola (Attitude), that may in turn lead to a plan to buy Loca-cola (Intention), that may in turn lead to the behavior of actually buying a can of Loca-cola (Purchase). Note that the retained and retrieved information about Loca-cola may influence this progression from brand comprehension to purchase in complex ways. Moreover, the purchase and use of Loca-cola will then feedback and influence how the consumer feels about Loca-cola (Satisfaction), future plans to buy Loca-cola (Intention), and certainty about Loca-cola and its attributes (Confidence), which may then in turn feedback and influence the motive that may have started the overt search for beverage relevant information in the first place. Even this partial and brief application of the cybernetic Model of Buyer Behavior illustrates the complexity and sophistication of this type of approach.

You have probably noticed the similarity between these cybernetic models (illustrated in Fig. 1.4) and the General Model proposed earlier (illustrated in Fig. 1.1). Note that the fundamental processes presented in the General Model of Fig. 1.1 are found in the various forms of the undifferentiated, unilineal, and cybernetic models presented in Fig. 1.2 through 1.4. This overlap is demonstrated in Table 1.1, in which the variables presented in each of the undifferentiated, unilineal, and cybernetic models are placed in the context of the General Model.

For example, consider the AUB model presented in Fig. 1.2. The three elements of the AUB model directly correspond to particular elements of the General Model of Fig. 1.1. Attention is included in the General Model as Perception; Understanding and Believability are included in the General Model as Cognition and Memory. Similarly, consider the Hierarchy of Effects model presented in Fig. 1.3. The seven elements of the Hierarchy of Effects directly correspond to particular elements of the General Model of Fig. 1.1. Awareness is included in the General Model as Perception; Knowledge, Liking, and Preference are included in the General Model as Cognition and Memory; Liking also involves elements that are included in the General Model as Emotion; Conviction corresponds to Intention; and, of course, Purchase is included in the General Model as Behavior. The reader can see from Table 1.1 that even the complicated and sophisticated cybernetic models presented in Fig. 1.4 are incorporated into the General Model.

The point is that the General Model of Fig. 1.1 is a relatively simple extension and integration of many previous models of consumer behavior. This book tends to rely on this General Model to provide an integrative framework in our consideration of the psychology of consumer behavior. Bear in mind that our task throughout the rest of this book is to understand the various links and connections suggested by the General Model presented in Fig. 1.1.

OPERATIONALIZATION, RESEARCH, AND LOCA-COLA

Before moving away from general, introductory issues, it is important to devote some attention to measurement issues. In the conduct of any science, theoretically important concepts and variables must be defined with extreme precision. One way of accomplishing this is through careful attention to measurement. Operation-alization refers to the assumption that the meaning of a concept or variable is determined by the procedures or operations used to measure it (or, in some instances, to manipulate it). In other words, our definition of a *concept* is the procedure of measurement we use.

For example, consider the seemingly simple issue of gauging Lou's liking for Loca-cola. We might simply ask Lou if she likes Loca-cola. This would yield a dichotomous (yes/no) measure of her liking the product. We might seek a little bit more detail, and ask her to circle a number from 1 to 10, where 1 = "I dislike it immensely" and 10 = "I love it immensely." Alternatively, we might be more interested in Lou's nonverbal, gut-level reaction toward Loca-cola. In this case, we might try to measure changes in some physiological responses that occur whenever Lou is exposed to Loca-cola (e.g., heart rate). It becomes apparent that the meaning of "Lou likes Loca-cola" varies as a function of the operationaliza-tions. That is, the meaning of "Lou likes Loca-cola" changes as we change the measurement procedure from a dichotomous self-report to a physiological measurement.

Most of the chapters in this book start out with a section examining common measurements, or common operational definitions, of the relevant concepts or variables. This consideration of measurement is intended to accomplish two goals. First, it should facilitate our understanding of the research and theory devoted to each particular facet of the General Model being discussed in each chapter. For example, if we understand how "perception" has been operationa-lized, we will have a better appreciation for what is meant by the statement that, expectation influences perception. We will know precisely what is being influenced by expectation. Second, a concern with measurement issues often leads one to be more critical and more demanding in the evaluation of theory and research. If we understand precisely how perception has been operationalized, we immediately become sensitive to the strengths and weaknesses, the generaliz-ability and the limitations, of a piece of evidence regarding the influence of the stimulus situation on perception. The reader is, in a very real sense, a consumer of the theory and research product produced by the field of consumer psychology. A careful concern for measurement will make the reader a more informed con-sumer of this product.

TABLE 1.1. Illustration of the Overlap Between the Various Models of Consumer Behavior

General Model (Fig. 1.1)	Undifferentiated Models			Unilineal Models		Howard's Model of Buyer Behavior (Fig. 1.4a)	Engel, Kollat, & Blackwell's Model (Fig. 1.4b)
	Three 'I's (Fig. 1.2a)	AIDA (Fig. 1.2b)	AUB (Fig. 1.2c)	Hierarchy of Effects (Fig. 1.3a)	Information Processing (Fig. 1.3b)		
Stimulus situation	—	—	—	—	Presentation	Information available Information exposed Stimulus ambiguity	Stimuli
Perception	Impact	Awareness	Attention	Awareness	Attention	Overt search Attention Perceptual bias	Search Exposure Attention Reception
Cognition & memory	Image	Interest	Understanding Believability	Knowledge Liking Preference	Comprehension Yielding Retention	Information recalled Brand comprehension Attitude Choice criteria Confidence	Problem recognition Alternative evaluation Evaluative criteria Beliefs Attitudes Active memory
Learning	—	—	—	—	—	Media habits Satisfaction	Information & experience

Emotion	Involvement	Interest	Liking	—	—	—
Motivation	—	Desire	—	—	Motive (arousal, directive) Satisfaction	Satisfaction Motives Dissonance
Intention	—	—	Conviction	—	Intention	Intention
Behavior	—	Action	Purchase	Behavior	Purchase	Choice Outcomes
Social context	—	—	—	—	—	Normative compliance Reference group, family
Cultural context	—	—	—	—	—	Cultural norms and values
(variables not directly addressed in the General Model)	—	—	—	—	—	Anticipated circumstances Unanticipated circumstances Personality & lifestyle*

* The effects of personality and lifestyle are considered in the context of this General Model in terms of the use of internal processes as psychographics (chapter 8).

2 | Perception

Perception is defined as the psychological processing of information received by the senses. Our emphasis in this chapter is on the process by which the consumer becomes aware of the product. Often, *perception* is used to refer to the content of the consumer's beliefs about a product; for example, it is sometimes said that an advertisement led the consumer to develop a favorable perception of the product. This use of the term *perception* is really inappropriate, and refers to processes we consider later when we discuss cognition and memory in chapter 3.

First, we examine some of the approaches to the measurement of perception. Next, we examine the characteristics of the stimulus situation that affect the individual's awareness of the product and product characteristics. Note that this approach treats perception as a consequent of events occurring in the stimulus situation. Next, we consider the characteristics of the human perceptual process that affect the individual's awareness of the product. Following this, we consider the effects of other internal processes on the individual's awareness of the product. Finally, we examine the fascinating and complicated notion of subliminal perception. Bear in mind that our task in this chapter is to understand how consumers become aware of a given product.

MEASUREMENT OF AWARENESS

There have been a variety of approaches taken to the measurement of awareness. The most common approach has been to measure some aspect of retention (i.e., the persistence of an experience during an interval of no practice). Retention is more directly a measure of memory. However, it is reasoned that if the person remembers information about the product, he or she must have perceived that information. This raises the question of the accuracy of the retention that is supposed to indicate perception.

Marder and David (1961) demonstrated that subject recognition of information presented in commercial advertisements was surprisingly inaccurate. In their procedure, subjects were shown incomplete advertisements that had some combination of illustration, headline, cartoons, and three sections of copy. Later they were presented with the complete advertisement and asked to indicate whether they recognized portions of this complete advertisement (parts of which they had never seen before). For example, 35% of the subjects in one group reported having seen the headline before (when in fact their initial advertisement had shown no headline). Similarly, 24% of the subjects in another group reported having seen the cartoons before (when in fact their initial advertisement had shown no cartoons). Apparently, subjects in these groups were "projecting" into their memory of the advertisements those elements of the final test advertisement that seemed like they might have been in the original advertisement. This type of research suggests that relying on measures of consumers' retention may tell us about things other than awareness of the product (such as distortions in memory processes: see chapter 3). However, as indicated previously, the most common measures of awareness involve some aspect of retention; many of the studies reviewed in this chapter used this type of operationalization of awareness.

Other approaches to the measurement of perception and awareness are sometimes described as "process tracing measures." This refers to the measurement of intermediate responses that are presumed to reflect ongoing perceptual, information processing activity. Measurement of these events is taken during performance of some task (rather than after, as in the case of retention measures).

For example, pupil size has been used to index people's reactions to various types of stimulus situations. Pupil dilation (enlargement of the pupil) reflects a response to a pleasant, desirable stimulus. Pupil contraction (decrease in the size of the pupil) reflects a response to an undesirable, negative stimulus. Thus, Hess (1965) reported that subjects exhibited the greatest pupil dilation while tasting the orange beverage for which they later reported the most preference. Similarly, Halpern (1967) observed pupil dilation in response to explanations about convenience advantages that one package-type had over another package-type. Current research using pupil size as a measure of consumer behavior indicates that this measure may also be relevant to emotion and motivation, in addition to perception (cf. Arch, 1979).

Another way to try to operationalize the consumer's awareness is to study the individual's eye fixations. Russo (1978) observed that about 5% of the time is spent in eye movement, and the remaining 95% of the time the eyes are fixated (i.e., "looking at something"). Eye fixation data can be obtained using very elaborate, computer-controlled eye position sensors, or using a simple videotape recording of the individual's face (which is then coded into eye fixations based on a knowledge of the stimulus display presented to the individual). For example, Russo (1978) reported that eye fixation patterns in response to a simulated supermarket display occurred in three stages: Overview (characterized by the general absence of repeated fixations, typically necessary for establishing the identity of the present brands); Comparison (characterized by repeated pair comparisons, typically involving the usual or preferred brand); and, Checking (absence of repeated fixations, typically looking at the unselected alternatives one last time).

Another approach to the measurement of perception involves the notion of Conjugate Lateral Eye Movement (CLEM). This approach amounts to tabulating the number of times the person's gaze shifts to the left or to the right. This measurement is based upon psychophysiological research that suggests that the left and right hemispheres of the cerebral cortex can be characterized by different specialized capabilities. The left hemisphere is argued to be responsible for verbal, analytic, and sequential behaviors; this type of behavior is associated with the CLEM of looking to the right. Alternatively, the right hemisphere is argued to be responsible for emotional, imaginative, and spatial behaviors; this type of behavior is associated with the CLEM of looking to the left (Katz, 1983; Nebes, 1974; Sperry, 1951). Thus, different CLEMs may reflect different types of processing styles. For example, left-looking CLEMs may be associated with right-brain, emotional information processing; right-looking CLEMs may be associated with left-brain, rational information processing. It is interesting to note that King (1972) found that subjects preferred photographs of models depicting a gaze-direction that coincided with their own tendencies. For example, subjects with a predisposition for left-looking CLEMs (and, presumably, right-brain, emotional tendencies) preferred photographs of left-looking models. Similarly, subjects with a predisposition for right-looking CLEMs (and, presumably, left-brain, rational tendencies) preferred photographs of right-looking models.

At first glance, there may seem to be a discrepancy between the CLEM approach and the eye fixation approach. The direction of the individual's gaze is used to determine what the individual is examining (in terms of eye fixation), or to determine the type of information processing in which the individual is engaged (in terms of CLEM). It remains for future research to compare and integrate these two approaches, and to identify those contexts where one or the other approach can be most informative regarding consumers' perception processes.

Horowitz and Kaye (1975) proposed an interesting application of the CLEM research to consumer behavior. Consider the following line of inference: gazing to the left is associated with right-brain, emotional processing, while gazing to the right is associated with left-brain, rational processing. However, an organization might be interested in engaging both emotional and rational processing among consumers. Therefore, an organization might best construct a printed advertisement such that the rational, factual elements of the advertisement fall on the right side of the page, and the emotional, affective elements fall on the left side of the page. Illustration of this "recommended advertisement" is found in Fig. 2.1. An advertisement of this format would be presenting the emotional information and the rational information where each type of information would be most effectively processed.

A final index of consumer perception that we might consider is Leavitt's (1961) "index of communication effectiveness." This index is calculated by determining the amount of time spent looking at an advertisement while browsing through a magazine, and dividing this time by the tachistoscopic threshold (i.e., the duration of exposure to a picture of the advertisement that is needed for the subject to recognize the product). If this index were very large (e.g., the consumer

Nature is wise. When time pulls the calcium from our bones, nature provides a fresh source. Dairy foods. To enjoy their benefits, we can simply enjoy the variety of dairy foods.

Three servings from a variety of cheese, cottage cheese, yogurt and milk can give you all the calcium you need every day.* A single ounce of cheddar cheese will give you more than 25%. A cup of plain yogurt provides more than 50%. And a cup of cottage cheese is 17%. A glass of milk is over 35%.

And dairy foods fit naturally into a balanced diet. Milk with your cereal at breakfast; a yogurt shake for lunch; cheese enchiladas for dinner. That will satisfy your daily need for calcium.

Or a yogurt dressing for your salad. Or a buttermilk dressing. Or bleu cheese.

Or a quiche or a cheese casserole.

How about creamy chowder on a cold day? Or cottage cheese and fruit on a warm one.

Nature will pay you additional rewards for enjoying dairy calcium. You will receive high quality protein. And the phosphorus that is so important to a woman's chemistry. And the magnesium. Dairy foods are also a good source of vitamin A, riboflavin and other essential vitamins.

That's why dairy calcium is calcium the way nature intended. And time can't change that.

Dairy Calcium.

HOW NATURE REPLACES WHAT TIME TAKES AWAY.

DAIRY CALCIUM. CALCIUM THE WAY NATURE INTENDED.™

FIG. 2.1. *Illustration of advertisement recommended by Horowitz and Kaye (1975).*

spent a long time looking at the advertisement, and was later able to recognize the product after a very brief exposure to a picture of the advertisement), it would be a reasonable inference that the consumer had actually perceived the product advertisement. If this index were very low (e.g., if the consumer had spent very little time looking at the advertisement while browsing, and later took a very long time to recognize the product when presented with a picture of the advertisement), it would be a reasonable inference that the consumer had not perceived the product advertisement.

CHARACTERISTICS OF THE STIMULUS SITUATION: "PERCEPTION BY EXCEPTION"

It has been estimated that the average American household is exposed to about 1 hour of television advertising per day (an estimated 7 hours of television per day times 9 to 16 minutes of nonprogram material per hour (Reed & Coalson, 1977)). The typical full service American supermarket contains over 8,000 different items on its shelves (Twedt, 1961). Advertising folklore (Bauer & Greyser, 1968) holds that the average consumer is exposed to over 1,500 radio, television, newspaper, magazine, and/or billboard advertisements per day. With so much information, with such a complicated and busy stimulus situation, how does the consumer become aware of Product "X"?

Attention refers to the process of selecting, and focusing upon, only a portion of the available stimulation, while ignoring, suppressing, or inhibiting reactions to other stimuli. Psychological research has indicated a number of conditions that affect attention. Many of these can be seen as specific examples of the general principle of contrast. As noted by Myers and Reynolds (1967), the principle of contrast suggests that people tend to perceive by exception, attending predominantly to those stimulus events that represent some difference or some change.

Color

Examples of the application of the principle of contrast can easily be found; these involve such things as color, ambiguity, intensity, size, and movement. For example, Rosberg (1956) observed that color advertisements in the trade publication Industrial Marketing produced more attention than black and white advertisements. It is an interesting historical sidelight to note that the color advertisements in Rosberg's study were considerably more expensive to run than corresponding black and white advertisements. Although the color advertisements did produce more attention, they did not attract as many readers per dollar as the black and white advertisements. Today, the technology, economy, and efficiency of printing has progressed to the point where color advertisements are no longer so rare. As a result, color advertisements may no longer be an "exception." In some color, glossy magazines, or on television, color advertisements may be so common that the rare black and white advertisement now attracts attention due to contrast.

Ambiguity

Another variable that exemplifies the principle of contrast is ambiguity. Ambiguity refers to uncertainty, novelty, or lack of clarity in a stimulus event. For example, Heller (1956) demonstrated that people remembered significantly more when presented with a product slogan that had every seventh letter missing than when presented with complete, unambiguous slogans. A well-known illustration of the use of ambiguity to attract attention to a product is found in Campari's double entendre "first time" advertisements. These advertisements invariably presented an interview with some glamorous, well-known actress, where she detailed how much she didn't enjoy her "first time," and how she had to learn to like "it." The reader did not learn until the end of the advertisement that "it" referred to drinking Campari (a bitter-tasting aperitif).

Intensity

With reference to the variable of intensity, it is almost stating the obvious to say that bright lights or loud sounds can attract our attention. We have all been exposed to countless examples of commercial advertisements that seem to be based solely upon this premise. One unusual example of the use of intensity in advertising contexts is the practice of time-compressed speech in radio commercials. LaBarbera and MacLachlan (1979) exposed people to five radio commercials that were either normal or time-compressed on the order of 130%. These time-compressed commercials were not "sped up" by making the tape run faster; that would also increase the frequency of the auditory signal, and make the announcer sound like a high-pitched Mickey Mouse. Rather, the time-compression technique involves the shortening of pauses between words, and the reduction of the length of vowel sounds. This results in a message that runs more quickly, without changing the pitch of the announcer's voice. These researchers found that the time-compressed advertisements elicited more interest and better recall than the normal ads. Note that the time-compressed commercials are probably more economical, because the advertiser can convey more information in less time. You may be familiar with a less precise version of this type of application of intensity: if you have ever watched late-night television, you have probably seen the proverbial "used car salesman" deliver a 2-minute message within a 30-second television commercial.

Movement

Another attribute of the stimulus situation that attracts our attention is movement. We have all seen rotating outdoor display signs, liquor store promotional displays, and neon lights arranged to turn on and off in sequence to produce an attention-attracting motion. Some commercial advertisements in newspapers and magazines will attempt to simulate movement on a printed page using waving lines (reminiscent of the "op art" fad of the 1960s). Teuber (1974) has discussed how these printed patterns can produce a sensation of apparent movement. Some behavioral neural scientists have proposed "feature detection" mechanisms in cerebral cortex neural pathways. These mechanisms respond to visual stimulation of movement. Apparently, certain repetitive patterns of lines can cause these feature detection mechanisms to respond in the absence of any actual movement. Thus, some printed advertisements can generate an apparent movement that attracts the viewer's attention as effectively as if an actual movement occurred (see also interest box, opposite).

Size

It has almost become a truism that "large produces more attention than small." Although this is generally accurate, we should recognize that size and attention are not perfectly, directly related. For instance, Rudolph (1947) discussed the relationship between the size of advertisements in printed form and the resulting amount of attention. Generally, it seems that attention increases roughly as a function of the square root of the area of the printed advertisement (Rudolph, 1947; Stevens, 1975). For example, if advertisement A is twice as large as advertisement B, then advertisement A will elicit ($\sqrt{2}$ =) 1.41 times as much attention as advertisement B. If advertisement A is 4 times as large as advertisement C, A will elicit ($\sqrt{4}$ =) 2 times as much attention as C.

We should remember that each of these applications of the principle of contrast will probably be affected by a broader context. As mentioned before, color may attract more attention due to contrast if most of the surrounding stimulus situation is colorless. However, if the surrounding stimulus situation is vividly colorful, black and white may attract more attention due to contrast.

With reference to size, the absolute size of a commercial advertisement may not be as important as its relative size (i.e., its size relative to other advertisements in the same source). For example, Ulin (1962) created two identical magazines, with 29 identical advertisements. One magazine was large (the size of *Life* magazine) and the other was small (the size of *Reader's Digest*). A simplistic view of size and the principle of contrast would lead one to expect that the advertisements in the large magazine attracted more attention than advertisements in the small magazine. However, this was not the case. People who looked at the large magazine did not remember advertisements any better than people who looked at the small magazine. A given advertisement (in either the small magazine or the large magazine) was the same relative size as all of the other advertisements in that magazine. Therefore, none of the advertisements in the large magazine were relatively larger than any other advertisements in that magazine, and people paid no more attention to those advertisements than they did to advertisements in the smaller magazine. Thus, on the one hand, factors like color, size, intensity, and so on can be demonstrated to determine which products or product characteristics consumers will become aware of, but on the other hand, it must be understood that color, size, intensity, and so on exist in a context that might modify their effects.

Interest Box

SALES PROMOTIONS

Pepsi keeps sales moving

With price wars in the soft-drink industry growing increasingly intense, Pepsi needed a way to promote sales without giving away the store. Its answer: three moving point-of-purchase displays. The "pouring bottle" and "pouring can" use a rotating acrylic rod to give the impression of Pepsi being poured from its container. The "tipping can" is a mock six-pack that appears to be falling off the shelf, but stops just in

time and then rights itself. The three motion displays, conceived by Dyment, a Cincinnati mounter and finisher of displays, were tested in varying combinations in Safeway, Kroger, and Gerlands supermarkets in Houston during two five-week periods in June and July. Nancy Lucas, associate manager of sales planning in the trade development department of the Pepsi Cola Bottling Group, says that sales increased an average of 12 cases per display. As a result, the motion displays are now being offered to all Pepsi bottlers in the U.S., Canada, and the company's international group.

(*Sales & Marketing Management, 131,* 1983, p. 21. Reprinted with permission of *Sales and Marketing Management.*)

Position

Another attribute of the stimulus situation that may influence attention is position. Position, or location in space, does not seem to involve contrast, or perception by exception. Rather, there simply seem to be particular locations or spatial positions that are more likely to catch the consumer's eye. The location of a commercial advertisement on the printed page may affect the extent to which consumers notice it. For example, Adams (1920) observed that the upper left corner of a page receives the most attention. It should be recognized that this effect is most likely due to culture and not to some type of contrast effect. The upper left corner of a page is where consumers living in most western cultures would begin to read the printed page. Thus, Yamanake (1962) was able to demonstrate that the right side of the page attracted more attention than the left among Japanese subjects (who begin to read Japanese from the upper right corner of a page). Similarly, certain positions on the shelves in a supermarket are more likely to be perceived. For example, the shelves at about eye level are located just where we can most easily look. For this reason, the Campbell soup company tends to put the more popular canned soups (e.g., cream of mushroom, tomato) on the bottom shelves, and the more unusual, slower selling soups (e.g., shrimp bisque, cheese soup) at eye level. This is done in the hopes that consumers will become aware of these alternative types of soup (Merriam, 1955).

Some examples of these characteristics of the stimulus situation that affect attention are presented in Fig. 2.2.

CHARACTERISTICS OF THE HUMAN PERCEPTION PROCESS: GESTALT PRINCIPLES

A number of fundamental principles characterizing the perceptual process were developed by German psychologists near the turn of the century. These researchers emphasized the innate organizing processes that seem to direct perception. The term *gestalt* refers to form, pattern, or configuration. These early experimental psychologists studied the processes by which separate, distinct stimulus elements were perceptually merged into forms or configurations (Koffka, 1935). A number of these fundamental principles of perceptual organization are considered next.

Figure-Ground

A primary gestalt principle is that of figure-ground. This principle holds that our perceptions are fundamentally patterned into two distinct elements: the figure, which stands out, has good contour, appears solid and nearby; and the ground, which is indistinct, not clearly shaped, and appears to recede into the background. Almost without exception, efforts in commercial advertisements, positioning on shelves in stores, packaging, and so on can be thought of as attempts to force the product to emerge as the figure of the consumers' attention.

us more prone to influence (Atkin & Block, 1983; Eagly, 1983). Certainly, both of these explanations may be partially correct.

Sleeper Effect

An intriguing exception to the source credibility effect has come to be called the *sleeper effect*. This refers to an increase over time in the persuasive effectiveness of communications from a noncredible source. Kelman and Hovland (1953) presented to subjects a persuasive communication that was attributed to either a distinguished judge (high credibility source) or to a man who had been arrested on a drug charge (low credibility source). The immediate results of this persuasion attempt replicated the basic source credibility effect: those subjects who had been exposed to the highly credible source were more persuaded than subjects who had been exposed to the low credibility source. However, 3 weeks later, the beliefs of the high credibility source subjects had moderated somewhat, and the beliefs of the low credibility subjects had increased. It seems almost as if the message itself might have a certain degree of persuasiveness that may define the long-term effects of the persuasion attempt once the identity of the source is forgotten. There has been a considerable amount of discussion regarding the mechanisms, and even the substantive existence, of the sleeper effect (Gillig & Greenwald, 1974; Gruder, Cook, Hennigan, Flay, Alessis, & Halamaj, 1978; Hannah & Sternthal, 1984). Although research on the sleeper effect suggests that even noncredible sources may have some persuasive effects, it is probably still the best strategy to employ a credible source (however, for an alternative point of view, see the interest box on p. 54, which contains portions of an article by Neal Rubbin of Knight-Ridder Newspapers. The article was titled "Public isn't buying words of 'celebrity schmucks' ").

Repetition

An aspect of the form of persuasive communication that has received a tremendous amount of research attention is repetition. Previously we have examined the effects of repetition on memory processes (chapter 3). In chapter 6 we examine the effects of repetition on feelings toward the product. In this context we consider the effects of repetition on two distinct aspects of cognition: evaluations of the product, and effectiveness of the persuasive communication.

Repeated exposure to commercial advertising is a fact of life. Preschoolers average about 30 hours of television viewing per week. Because approximately 22% of airtime is devoted to commercials and other promotional material:

> The world of American children is heavily populated by characters acting out scripts promoting the virtues of merchandise, the values of merchandising, and the pleasures of acquiring merchandise. American children get something like eight or nine hundred of these ten-, twenty-, and thirty-second dramas every week. It adds up to approximately a quarter of a million promotional vignettes loaded into the

Interest Box

"Consumers are getting smart," says Carol Colman of Inferential Focus, a New York consulting firm that specializes in identifying trends. "They're seeing through the phoniness of celebrity endorsers."

The beef Industry Council hired Cybill Shepherd to tell Americans she doesn't trust people who don't like hamburger. Then she told Family Circle that she avoids red meat.

People Magazine ran a photo of Pepsi spokesman Don Johnson sipping a Diet Coke.

Paris Match magazine claimed that Cher, who credits hard work and Vic Tanny for her physique, has spent $40,000 on assorted cosmetic surgery. Isiah Thomas, criticized for endorsing Japanese cars, admitted that he turned to Toyota only after American carmakers showed no interest in him.

"They barely believe celebrities," says Dave Vadehra of Video Storyboard, a New York firm that tests commercials with sample audiences. "They know celebrities are doing it because they are being paid."

Or as Southern California agent and celebrity broker Ed Adler puts it, "Some of these people would sell cancer if there was a profit in it."

[John] Houseman has become the classic example of an endorser who didn't know when to keep his mouth shut. His commercials for Smith Barney ("We make money the old fashioned way. We eaaarn it") were a smash. His spots for McDonald's bombed.

"I just couldn't imagine the guy in a McDonald's," says Steve Kopcha, chief creative officer for D'Arcy, Masius, Benton & Bowles in Bloomfield Hills.

Kopcha emphasizes that "it's crazy to go get a celebrity just because everybody else has one." In fact, "the wrong spokesman is really double trouble, because you've paid a lot of money and you could have a countervaling force there. You only use them when you have excellent reasons."

(Reprinted with permission of Knight-Ridder News Service.)

child's intimate environment before he's ready for kindergarten. By way of comparison: a child who attends religious services weekly without a single miss would hear the benediction 260 times over the same period. (Goldsen, 1978, p. 356)

One consequence of this repetition might be a change in the evaluation of the repeated stimulus. Research indicates that repetition generally leads to more favorable evaluations; this is sometimes referred to as the "mere exposure" effect. For example, Zajonc (1968) exposed people to various stimuli (e.g., men's faces, Turkish words) at varying degrees of repetition, and later had these people evaluate the stimuli on a scale from 0 to 6 (where 0 indicates dislike and 6 indicates like). The familiar, more frequently repeated stimuli were evaluated more favorably than the less familiar, less frequently repeated stimuli (cf. also Maslow, 1937; Stang, 1977).

Although this mere exposure effect is intriguing, there are three fundamental problems with this notion that may limit the generalization of this effect to consumer behavior. First, the scale values obtained in many of the studies are not consistent with the development of a positive evaluation of the repeated stimulus. For example, in Zajonc's (1968) study, stimuli with 0 previous repetitions (i.e., stimuli that the subjects had never seen before) received an average evaluation of 2.7 ("mild dislike"); on the other hand, stimuli with 25 previous repetitions received an average evaluation of 3.7 ("no evaluation"; on a scale from 0 to 6, the midpoint is 3.5). Thus, after 25 repetitions (the most frequent repetition used in much of this research), the best that can be said of the change in evaluation is that it went from mild dislike to no evaluation one way or the other. It is difficult to imagine an organization that would wish to bring about such an impotent change in cognition.

A second difficulty with trying to generalize the mere exposure effect is the likelihood that the relationship between evaluation and repeated exposure may not be a simple, linear one beyond a certain range of exposure. In everyday life, overexposure can occur. For example, eating a favorite dish over and over again may dull your appreciation for that flavor. Stang (1975) has demonstrated this phenomenon of overexposure to flavors.

Finally, the question must be raised, "Exposure to what?". Imagine someone who is repeatedly exposed to "Biggy Burger" commercials. This individual has received repeated exposure to the jingle, the name, the insignia of "Biggy Burger," and may therefore come to like the jingle, the name, and the insignia of "Biggy Burger." But what if Biggy Burgers taste like sandals? Will the repeated exposure to the commercial enhance the consumers' evaluations of the product?

Certainly, repetition of commercials can have an impact on consumer behavior. However, we should be cautious in assuming that the only, or the most important, effect is an increase in cognitive evaluations of the product.

Regarding the effectiveness of the persuasive communication, research seems to indicate that repetition of similar messages increases effectiveness, whereas repetition of identical messages may actually decrease effectiveness. For example, Johnson and Watkins (1971) found that one presentation of a message resulted in more agreement than five presentations of the same message. Belch (1982) found that increasing the repetitions of a message did not enhance attitudes or purchase intentions, and actually increased 'counter-arguing', or the internal generation of arguments against the persuasive message. On the other hand, McCullough and Ostrom (1974) observed that five presentations of similar messages resulted in more agreement than one presentation. This pattern of results is consistent with many recent ad campaigns that repeat variations on a basic theme.

This section on persuasion reveals how both the content and the form of messages conveyed in the stimulus situation can affect consumers' cognitions and preferences. Next, we turn to a consideration of two cognitively oriented theories that have been developed to explain persuasion phenomena.

COGNITIVE THEORIES OF PERSUASION

Attribution Theory

Heider (1958) is generally credited with initiating the formal development of attribution theory. Attribution theory describes the cognitive processes by which people determine the causes of behavior and events in their world. Attribution theory developed within social psychology, in studying how people attempt to understand one another's behavior. According to Heider, the ordinary person tries to discover a sufficient reason for an observed event. Once a workable explanation is found, the observer stops his or her causal search. Although attribution theory is not simply a theory of persuasion, it is able to provide many insights regarding persuasion phenomena.

Kelley (1967, 1973) proposed an elaborate extension of Heider's seminal work that specifies the type of inferences that would occur under different conditions. If more than one observation is available, covariation principles would be used to determine the cause for an event. If only one observation is available, configuration principles would be used to determine the cause for an event. These sets of principles are detailed here.

To illustrate the operation of covariation principles, suppose that you observe an actor behaving in a particular manner toward some entity. For example, you (the observer) notice that Bob (the actor) seems to enjoy (the behavior) Flurple soda (the entity). You want to determine whether this is a reflection of something about Flurple soda (the Flurple soda tastes good; an external attribution), or of something unusual about Bob (he has weird tastes; an internal attribution).

If you have access to multiple pieces of information, you may be able to utilize the covariation principles to determine the cause of this behavior. Three important dimensions of information are used to make this type of causal inference. *Consensus* refers to the response of other people toward the entity; the higher the consensus, the more likely the entity will be seen as the cause of the behavior. *Consistency* refers to the co-occurrence of the entity and the behavior across time or across different modes of interaction. The higher the consistency, the more likely the behavior will be attributed to either the actor or the entity; note that with low consistency, an observer would be unable to make an attribution to either the actor or the entity. *Distinctiveness* refers to the specificity of the occurrence of the behavior. The more that the behavior occurs only in response to the entity in question, the higher the distinctiveness, and the more likely the entity will be seen as the cause of the behavior.

Thus, if everyone else likes Flurple soda (high consensus), if Bob always likes Flurple soda, no matter whether it's day or night, hot or cold (high consistency), and if Bob likes only Flurple soda, and no other types of carbonated beverages (high distinctiveness), you would be led to infer that Flurple soda must really be good (external attribution). On the other hand, if no one other than Bob likes Flurple soda (low consensus), Bob always likes Flurple soda, no matter whether it's day or night, hot or cold (high consistency), and if Bob likes carbonated colas, champagne, Burpo-seltzer, and anything else that has bubbles in it (low distinctiveness), you would be led to infer that there is something unusual about Bob (internal attribution).

This approach can be readily applied to consumers' attempts to make sense out of the information conveyed in commercial advertisements. An organization would be best advised to structure an advertisement so as to provide information about high consensus, high consistency, and high distinctiveness. This would be likely to lead consumers to develop an external attribution (e.g., "the product must really be good"). Consider the advertisement depicted in Fig. 4.2. Note the

FIG. 4.2 An example of the application of Kelley's (1967, 1973) covariation principles in a commercial advertisement.

very direct presentation of the information regarding consensus, consistency, and distinctiveness, consistent with the pattern just suggested.

Now consider the second general facet of attribution theory, referred to as the configuration principles. For the sake of illustration, assume that you observe that Tom seems to enjoy Flurple soda. If you only have access to this single observation, you may have to rely on configuration principles in order to determine the cause for this behavior. One configuration principle involves the use of schemas, or implicit, ready-made causal formulas. For some types of events, we may have a culturally established schema that is labelled with a convenient euphemism. For example, when a person of lower status (e.g., a student) does something nice for a person of higher status (e.g., a teacher), we may infer the lower status person's kindness to have been caused by a desire to ingratiate himself or herself with the higher status person. The euphemism we use to refer to and explain such an event is "apple polishing." Of course, for many events we may not have a ready-made causal formula. Regarding Tom and his liking for Flurple soda, you may not have a schema that explains people's choices of beverages. In such events, you would have to rely on the operation of the two remaining configuration principles.

Augmentation is the configuration principle that a behavior will be more likely to be attributed to the actor when there are known costs, risks, or sacrifices associated with the behavior (e.g., Jones, Davis & Gergen, 1961). Thus, you would be more likely to infer that Tom really enjoys Flurple soda if you learned that Flurple soda was a very, very expensive beverage, or that he walked 5 miles just to get a can of Flurple.

Discounting is the configuration principle that the role of a given possible cause in producing a given behavior is discounted if other possible causes are present. One possible cause that is always present is the internal cause ("the actor performed the behavior because he really feels that way, because that's the kind of person he is"). Discounting refers to the finding that if other possible causes are also present, the behavior is less likely to be attributed internally (e.g., Jones & Harris, 1967). For example, you would be less likely to infer that Tom really enjoys Flurple soda if you learned that he drank his Flurple soda while someone held a gun to his head, or that he drank the Flurple soda after being deprived of liquids for a week.

Applied to consumers' cognitions, one would be best advised to facilitate the engagement of augmentation, and to prevent the engagement of discounting. That is, a positive claim about one's product might be more likely to be accepted when there appear to be risks or sacrifices associated with the claim, and when there appear to be no additional possible causes for the claim (beyond the stated quality of the product). This accurately describes the common varied or qualified type of advertisement (that might be seen as a particular type of two-sided message, as discussed previously). For example, the positive claim (that rum is a good drink that can be used in many ways) is more likely to be accepted when there are risks associated with the claim (admitting that there are times when drinking rum is inappropriate, such as when one is driving). Figure 4.3 presents an illustration of this type of advertisement.

Recent research has clearly demonstrated that the qualified, varied, two-sided advertising appeal tends to be quite effective (Kanungo & Johar, 1975; Mullen & Peaugh, 1985; Settle & Golden, 1974; Smith & Hunt, 1978; Swinyard, 1981). For example, Smith and Hunt (1978) presented to consumers advertisements for new television sets with a number of different product attributes (e.g., automatic color tuning, solid state, warranty length, availability of an earphone jack, and availability of a sunshield). A varied, two-sided advertisement (i.e., an advertisement that claimed superiority on most of the product attributes, but admitted that the new set lacked an earphone jack and a sunshield) was evaluated as being

FIG. 4.3 Example of the application of Kelley's (1967, 1973) configuration principles in a commercial advertisement.

more credible than a nonvaried, one-sided advertisement (i.e., an advertisement that claimed superiority on all of the product attributes).

More recently, Mullen (1984) has suggested that the importance of the disclaimed product attribute will mediate the effectiveness of the varied, two-sided appeal. For example, an advertisement describing a softdrink that tastes great but comes in the undistinctive bottle is likely to be believed, and would thereby produce a positive overall product impression. However, an advertisement describing a softdrink that comes in an attractive bottle but tastes awful might also be believed, and would thereby produce a negative overall product impression. In other words, the varied, two-sided claim seems to enhance the acceptance of the product description, but if the product description is generally unfavorable, the two-sided claim is of little value.

The Fishbein Multi-Attribute Model

The Fishbein Multi-Attribute Model (Ajzen & Fishbein, 1980; Fishbein, 1979) is a complex and powerful conceptualization of the relationships between consumers' beliefs, attitudes, intentions, and behavior. We refer to this perspective in subsequent chapters, when we examine intentions and behavior in detail. At this point, the Fishbein model provides a compelling approach to understanding how an overall evaluation of a product is derived from a consumer's beliefs.

Fishbein's general approach is represented by the following formula:

$$A_b = \varepsilon W_i B_{bi}$$

In this formula, A_b is the overall evaluation of brand b; W_i is the strength of the importance of product attribute i; and B_{bi} is the evaluative belief regarding brand b and attribute i. For example, Table 4.1 presents the evaluative beliefs and the

TABLE 4.1 Evaluation of Brand B Butter Beans by Two Consumers, as Illustrated by Fishbein's Multi-Attribute Model

	Brand B Butter Beans Are:	Evaluative Belief (B_{b_i})	Belief Strength (W_i)	$W_i B_{b_i}$
Consumer 1:	tasty	+3	3	+9
	large	+2	2	+4
	economical	−3	1	−3
			$\Sigma W_i B_{b_i} =$	+10
Consumer 2:	tasty	—	—	—
	large	+2	1	+2
	economical	−3	3	−9
			$\Sigma W_i B_{b_i} =$	−7

Where: Evaluative Belief (B_{b_i}) is measured on the following scale:

−3	−2	−1	0	1	2	3
not at all						very much

Belief Strength (W_i) is measured on the following scale:

0	1	2	3
very weak			very strong

corresponding strengths of belief for two consumers regarding brand B butter beans.

A number of important elements of Fishbein's model are illustrated in Table 4.1. Note that consumer 1 has beliefs about brand B butter beans for three product attributes, whereas consumer 2 has beliefs about brand B butter beans for two product attributes. The Fishbein model allows for differences between consumers in the array of product attributes that will be salient or relevent to the overall product evaluation. In addition, note that the beliefs that two different consumers hold about the same product may be identical (as we see here for the attribute "large"), or they may be different (as we see here for the attribute "economical"). Finally, note that the most strongly held belief for consumer 2 is "economical," which was the weakest belief for consumer 1. Similarly, the most strongly held belief for consumer 1 is "tasty," which does not even enter into consideration for consumer 2. The Fishbein model allows for differences between consumers in the strength of beliefs. Thus, although consumer 1 and consumer 2 may have difficulty in trying to come to terms with their divergent evaluations of brand B, the Fishbein model can readily explain these differences in product evaluation.

At first glance, there may be an apparent discrepancy between the Fishbein model and the two-sided, augmentation-inducing communication described previously. On the one hand, the Fishbein model suggests that the most positive overall evaluation should result from the integration of many strongly held, positive beliefs about the product. On the other hand, the two-sided, augmentation type of communication is based on the assumption that the most positive overall evaluation should result from the integration of many positive beliefs about product attributes, along with one negative belief about a product attribute.

These two perspectives can be easily reconciled. The cognitive processes assumed to be engaged by the two-sided communication may be operating at a higher level than the mechanisms proposed for the Fishbein model. The one piece of negative information included in the two-sided, augmentation communication may enter a little negative information into the Fishbein formula. However, the communicator's willingness to admit the negative piece of information may feedback to increase the strength with which consumers hold the remaining (positive) pieces of information. The resultant heavier weight given to the positive information should more than balance the little bit of negative information included in the two-sided claim. The result would be an overall increase in the evaluation of the product.

The Fishbein model can also be successfully applied to an understanding of source credibility effects. For example, consumer 1 and consumer 2 in Table 4.1 both evaluated brand B butter beans as being highly uneconomical. However, this belief was held much more strongly by consumer 2 than by consumer 1. This could reflect the fact that consumer 1 acquired this information from a stranger who happened to be standing in front of him or her in the check-out line (low credibility source). Alternatively, consumer 2 acquired this information from the local television news consumer advocate, who did a program a week before on the economics of butter beans. Beliefs acquired through exposure to a more credible source may thus come to be weighted more heavily within Fishbein's model.

CONCLUSION: A ROSE BY ANY OTHER NAME . . .

There is one subtle form of persuasion that we have not yet examined, and that has received little research attention. Partly a matter of content, and partly a matter of form, the very words used to describe products may have effects that we do not fully appreciate. Syndicated columnist Merle Ellis ("The Butcher"; 1986) discussed a variety of ways in which products can be described in accurate but misleading ways. For example, Ellis described a sign in a meat market that read, English Bangers—No Nitrites Added. Bangers are a fresh sausage product that does not require nitrites or any other preservatives. No Bangers contain nitrites, but this meat market's declaration that their Bangers have no nitrites suggests that most or all other bangers do contain nitrites (otherwise, why mention it?). Similarly, Ellis described a California poultry producer who has launched an expensive ad campaign to inform consumers that their fryers are raised without the use of "harmful hormones." Even though this may be accurate, it is misleading. According to Ellis, no one has used growth hormones in this country for the production of poultry for over 20 years, since they were outlawed. The claim that these fryers have not had harmful hormones suggests that most or all fryers have had harmful hormones (otherwise, once again, why mention it?).

Similar ambiguities can be fostered through the use of ill-defined terms like *light, natural,* and *organic.* For example, according to J. I. Rodale, editor of the popular family health-care magazine *Prevention,* organic food is any food that has been fertilized with natural organic matter (e.g., manure) rather than chemical fertilizers, and that has grown without application of pesticides (Whitney & Sizer, 1985). Technically, however, organic food is any food that has carbon atoms bonded into the molecules comprising the substance of the food. In other words, in a technical sense, any food is organic. This leads one to ask the question: does an ordinary apple taste as good as an organic apple? Probably not. Buchanan and Agatstein (1984) found that more favorable evaluations were made of products (e.g., babies' cribs, children's toys) that were described as hand-made, relative to the same products described as having been produced in a factory. Namelab is a very successful Name Development and Testing Laboratory in San Francisco, California, that specializes in advanced brand identity development. Clearly, the very words used to describe and name a product may have connotations, or subtle, implied meanings, that can dramatically affect our evaluations of the product.

5 | Learning

Learning is typically defined as a relatively permanent change in behavior as a result of practice or experience. An alternative approach is to define *learning* as the development or acquisition of an association between two stimuli, or between a stimulus and a response. In the context of consumer behavior, the result of this association is a change in the consumer's behavior toward a product. For example, the consumer might develop an association between a beverage and a pleasant musical jingle. This association between two stimuli might lead the consumer to be more likely to use the product in the future. Alternatively, the consumer might develop an association between drinking the beverage and the satisfaction of thirst. This association between a response and a subsequent stimulus might lead the consumer to be more likely to use the product in the future. Processes like emotion and motivation that are discussed in subsequent chapters will rely on many of the general principles of learning. In this chapter we examine the attributes of the stimulus situation that affect learning. Note that in this context, we treat learning as a consequent of events occurring in the stimulus situation. In this chapter we examine the two prominent perspectives in associational learning: classical conditioning and instrumental conditioning. In addition, we consider the similarities and the differences between these two perspectives. Bear in mind that our task in this chapter is to understand how consumers come to develop associations involving a particular product.

CLASSICAL CONDITIONING

One fundamental model of associational learning is the classical conditioning model. In classical conditioning, a response (the conditioned response) comes to be evoked by a previously neutral stimulus (the conditioned stimulus) that has been repeatedly paired with a stimulus (the unconditioned stimulus) that originally elicited the response (the unconditioned response). This model of learning is sometimes referred to as Pavlovian conditioning, after the Russian physiologist Ivan Pavlov (1927) who formalized and developed this model. This model is also sometimes referred to as respondent conditioning, because it is primarily concerned with beliefs that occur in response to some preceding stimulus. Fig. 5.1 illustrates this basic associational process using the typical example of Pavlov's dog.

The presentation of meat powder (the unconditioned stimulus) naturally elicits salivation (the unconditioned response) on the part of the dog. If a bell (the conditioned stimulus) is repeatedly presented immediately before the meat powder, eventually the bell will come to elicit salivation (the conditioned response). This association will become stronger as the number of pairings of the conditioned stimulus and the unconditioned stimulus increases.

Contrary to the impression sometimes conveyed in textbooks on consumer behavior (e.g., Assael, 1981), the classical conditioning model is a very powerful means of describing the effects that commercial advertisements can have on consumers (Bierley, McSweeney, & Van Nieuwkerk, 1985; McSweeney & Bierley, 1984; Nord & Peter, 1980). Classical conditioning can be used to explain the development of emotional responses toward a product (see chapter 6), as well as the development of motivational tendencies toward a product (see chapter 7). One illustration of a more general application of classical conditioning is found in a study by Gorn (1982). Subjects in this study looked at slide-projected pictures of different colored pens (the conditioned stimulus) while they listened to music (unconditioned stimulus) that they liked (unconditioned response). Eventually, the subjects developed a preference (conditioned response) for the pen that had been associated with the pleasant music.

Predictiveness of Conditioned Stimulus

One important element of classical conditioning is the extent to which the conditioned stimulus serves as a reliable predictor of the unconditioned stimulus. According to this predictiveness view, it is not sufficient for a conditioned stimulus to precede the unconditioned stimulus. In order for conditioning to occur, the conditioned stimulus must predict the unconditioned stimulus (Rescorla, 1967, 1968). At first glance, the distinction between preceding and predicting may seem rather subtle, and we should take a moment to consider this

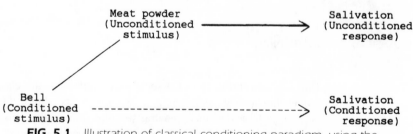

FIG. 5.1 Illustration of classical conditioning paradigm, using the example of Pavlov's dog.

important distinction. On the one hand, the conditioned stimulus must precede the unconditioned stimulus in order to predict the unconditioned stimulus. However, we can imagine circumstances in which the conditioned stimulus could precede the unconditioned stimulus without necessarily predicting it. Consider the situation where the conditioned stimulus is always followed by the unconditioned stimulus, but the unconditioned stimulus also occurs just as frequently in the absence of the conditioned stimulus. Similarly, consider the situation where the unconditioned stimulus is always preceded by the conditioned stimulus, but the conditioned stimulus also occurs just as frequently without a following unconditioned stimulus. In these situations, the conditioned stimulus is preceding, but not predicting, the unconditioned stimulus. Accordingly, these situations tend not to produce classical conditioning (Rescorla, 1968).

McSweeney and Bierley (1984) have considered some of the implications of this predictiveness view for an understanding of consumer behavior. For example, commercial advertisements that frequently present a beverage product (conditioned stimulus) but intermittently present an attractive member of the opposite sex (unconditioned stimulus) will not be likely to instill a conditioned response. In this type of situation, the product is preceding, but not predicting, the attractive member of the opposite sex. Similarly, extra exposures to the beverage product (conditioned stimulus) in a different type of advertisement that does not include the unconditioned stimulus will decrease the predictiveness of the product as a conditioned stimulus. In turn, this would decrease the likelihood of an effectively conditioned response to the product. Finally, the number of exposures to the unconditioned stimulus when it is not being predicted by the conditioned stimulus should be minimized. If a very familiar pleasant song or a very popular attractive source is used as the unconditioned stimulus, this unconditioned stimulus will frequently occur in the absence of the product (conditioned stimulus). Once again, this would decrease the predictiveness of the product, and thereby decrease the conditioning of a response to the product.

Extinction

The process by which classically conditioned associations are eliminated is referred to as *extinction*. Classically conditioned associations are extinguished by repeated presentations of the conditioned stimulus without the subsequent presentation of the unconditioned stimulus. In terms of the predictiveness view already described, extinction is accomplished by reducing the predictiveness of the conditioned stimulus. For example, inside every box of a bland-tasting breakfast cereal (conditioned stimulus), there has always been a little plastic toy (unconditioned stimulus) that young Fred has always enjoyed (unconditioned response). Eventually, young Fred may come to prefer this brand of cereal (conditioned response), reflecting a typical classically conditioned association. However, if the company stops putting the plastic toys in the cereal boxes, Fred will be continuously exposed to the cereal box (conditioned stimulus) without the toy (unconditioned stimulus). His preference for the cereal may diminish or disappear entirely, representing the extinction of a classically conditioned association.

INSTRUMENTAL CONDITIONING

The second fundamental model of associational learning is the instrumental conditioning model. In instrumental conditioning, an organism learns to make an instrumental response that leads to reinforcement. Reinforcement intuitively refers to the presentation of something pleasant or the removal of something unpleasant. More appropriate in a technical sense is the definition that reinforcement is the presentation of a stimulus that leads to an increase in the behavior that preceded the stimulus. A stimulus that has such an effect is called a *reinforcer*. For example, drinking a beverage that tastes very good will reinforce the consumption of that beverage, and lead to an increase in the likelihood that the individual will use that beverage again in the future. This model of learning is also sometimes referred to as *operant conditioning,* because it is primarily concerned with behaviors that operate on the environment.

In a direct application of instrumental conditioning to consumer behavior, Carey, Clicque, Leighton, and Milton (1976) delivered positive reinforcement to customers of a retail organization by delivering an unsolicited phone call thanking the individual for being a customer. Reportedly, sales increased by 27% relative to the same period during the previous year (a finding made more impressive by the fact that the year-to-date sales of the organization had been down 25% from the previous year).

Schedules of Reinforcement

The scheduling of reinforcement can have a big impact on the acquisition and retention of instrumentally conditioned associations. A distinction can be drawn between continuous reinforcement (i.e., reinforcing every correct response) and noncontinuous, or partial, reinforcement (i.e., providing a reinforcer only after a certain number of correct responses, or only after a correct response occurs during a certain interval of time). The partial reinforcement effect refers to the consistent finding that associations acquired under partial reinforcement are acquired more slowly, but are more resistant to extinction than associations acquired under continuous reinforcement.

Consider the following illustration of a partial reinforcement effect: If a consumer uses a particular brand of photographic flashcube that always works (continuous reinforcement), the consumer may quickly develop a strong preference for that brand. If the consumer then obtains a "bad bunch" of flash cubes that malfunction, the consumer might readily switch to another brand. Alternatively, suppose a consumer uses a brand of flashcubes that periodically malfunctioned (partial reinforcement); perhaps that was the only brand available for a considerable period of time. The consumer might not develop a strong preference for this brand very quickly, but the consumer would be more tolerant of the bad bunch of flashcubes, and might not switch brands as quickly. The partial reinforcement effect may be very relevant to consumers' reactions to these types of variations in product quality.

There are actually a number of different types of partial reinforcement schedules. Partial reinforcement schedules are defined by the regularity with which the reinforcers are delivered (fixed or variable) and by the criterion(s) by which reinforcers are delivered (interval of time or ratio of correct responses). The variable ratio schedule of partial reinforcement is especially relevant to consumer behavior. In a variable ratio schedule, the reinforcers are delivered on the average after every *n*th appropriate response. That is, for a "variable ratio .33" schedule, on the average, every third correct response would be reinforced. Sometimes, every other response might be reinforced, sometimes every fourth response might be reinforced, but on the average, every third correct response would result in reinforcement. For example, Deslauriers and Everett (1977) delivered a small reward (a token worth approximately 10¢) to passengers for riding a campus bus. Some passengers received a token for every bus ride (continuous reinforcement), while others received a token on the average for every third bus ride (variable ratio .33 partial reinforcement). This variable ratio schedule of reinforcement produced the same level of bus-riding behavior as the continuous reinforcement schedule (at one third the cost!). Similar variable ratio schedules are used in lotteries with great success.

Punishment

Punishment intuitively refers to the presentation of something unpleasant or the removal of something pleasant. More appropriate in a technical sense is the definition that *punishment* is a stimulus that leads to a decrease in the behavior that preceded the stimulus. Conceivably, organizations might try to punish consumers in some way for the use of a competitor's brand. However, organizations are usually less willing to influence consumers through the use of punishment than they are through the use of rewards. In part, this is for the simple reason that punishments may cause the recipient harm, distress, or discomfort. In addition, the consumer invariably has the freedom to escape any punishment-oriented influence tactics of an organization, and that makes punishment unlikely to be tolerated. Finally, the use of punishment often leads the recipient to view the punisher as coercive and undesirable (Tedeschi, Smith, & Brown, 1974). Hence, it seems that there is little to be gained, and much to be lost, through the strategic use of punishment in most consumer settings.

One important exception to this is the possibility of naturally occurring punishment that results from differences in product quality. If Throb pain reliever is really of substandard quality, the use of this product may actually be self-punishing. Suppose that Throb pain reliever fails to relieve pain (or, perhaps it actually causes severe headaches). Every time a consumer takes Throb, he or she will be punishing him or herself for the use of that product. Throb's competitors may take advantage of this scenario by presenting a husband and wife, both in bed with headaches. She takes Throb, and he takes the competitor's brand of pain reliever. An hour later, he is feeling great, but she still has her headache. The potentially effective portrayal of punishment of a model is discussed again later in our examination of observational or vicarious learning.

Extinction

Extinction occurs in instrumental conditioning when the individual performs the instrumental response and does not receive reinforcement. Eventually, the acquired association between the response and the reinforcer will diminish or disappear completely, and the instrumentally conditioned response will return to its preconditioning level. For example, the consumer might purchase a new brand of laundry soap and find a dishtowel or a drinking glass in the box (this type of promotion was fairly popular in the 1960s). This small, continuous reinforcement may help to maintain the consumer's preference for the new laundry soap. However, eventually the manufacturer discontinues this promotion. No more prizes are found inside the box. If the quality of the laundry soap is not a sufficient reward, the consumer's response of choosing the new brand of soap may be extinguished.

ASSOCIATIONAL LEARNING: THE INTEGRATION OF CLASSICAL CONDITIONING AND INSTRUMENTAL CONDITIONING

Just as it is important to understand the distinctions between classical conditioning and instrumental conditioning, it is also important to recognize that these two paradigms share a great deal in common (Miller, 1969). There are a number of general principles that operate in both classical conditioning and instrumental conditioning. Stimulus generalization, stimulus discrimination, and observational or vicarious learning are considered here.

Stimulus Generalization and Stimulus Discrimination

Stimulus generalization refers to a decrease in the specificity of the association involving the stimulus that precedes the response. In classical conditioning, stimulus generalization means that some previously neutral stimulus other than the original conditioned stimulus may come to elicit the conditioned response. In instrumental conditioning, stimulus generalization means that a response that was previously elicited by one stimulus may come to be elicited by another stimulus. The likelihood of stimulus generalization is increased if the second stimulus is very similar to the first stimulus. Stimulus discrimination refers to an increase in the specificity of the association involving the stimulus that precedes the response. In classical conditioning, stimulus discrimination means that only the initial conditioned stimulus is likely to elicit the conditioned response. In instrumental conditioning, stimulus discrimination means that a response that was previously elicited by a given stimulus is not elicited by any other, similar stimuli (e.g., Guttman & Kalish, 1956; Riley, 1968).

Stimulus generalization and stimulus discrimination occur as a function of the consequences of responding to similar stimuli. With reference to consumer behavior, consider the following example: A consumer has always used Snuffle brand cough drops, because the use of this brand of cough drop has always produced relief of sore throat symptoms. Suppose this consumer tried new Numbo cough drops. If new Numbo cough drops provide relief as quickly and effectively as Snuffle cough drops, stimulus generalization may occur. The result would be equal likelihood of purchasing either Snuffle cough drops or Numbo cough drops. On the other hand, if new Numbo cough drops are not as effective as Snuffle cough drops, stimulus discrimination would probably occur. The result would be a maintained high likelihood of purchasing Snuffle cough drops, and a maintained low likelihood of purchasing Numbo cough drops. This reader might use these examples as an opportunity to apply both the classical conditioning perspective and the instrumental conditioning perspective to a given consumer behavior.

Bayton (1958) discussed some applications of stimulus discrimination and stimulus generalization to consumer behavior toward products. One might want to increase stimulus generalization in a given product class in order to let one's own brand benefit from its similarity to more successful brands in the same product class. On the other hand, one might try to increase stimulus discrimination in order to benefit from the dissimilarity between one's own product and less successful brands in the product class. In addition, one might try to encourage stimulus generalization across product categories. For example, if you have a successful product in one product category and a new, or unsuccessful, brand in another product category, it might be beneficial to encourage stimulus generalization. This could enhance the likelihood that the favorable responses directed toward the successful brand in the first product category will be generalized to the new or unsuccessful brand in the second product category.

Note that this principle, sometimes referred to as *line extension,* is like a two-edged sword that can cut both ways. That is, it is possible that stimulus generalization will lead consumers to generalize their favorable responses from the established brand in the first product category to the new brand in the second product category. However, it is also possible that consumers will generalize their unfavorable responses from the new or unsuccessful brand to the established successful brand. Ries and Trout (1981) observed that some organizations attempt to increase stimulus generalization across product categories by attaching the company name to their diverse products. For example, the Colgate-Palmolive company attaches the company name to Colgate Toothpaste, Palmolive Rapid Shave, Palmolive dish detergent, and Palmolive soap. However, other organizations attempt to minimize stimulus generalization and its possible backfire by giving each brand in each product category a different brand name. For example, the Proctor & Gamble company does not attach the company name to Tide, Cheer, or Bold laundry detergents, Dawn dish detergent, or Coast deodorant soap. Some large corporations, notably General Electric and Beatrice Foods, have evidenced a recent trend of developing stimulus generalization by advertising the company name as much as advertising any specific product. Fig. 5.2 presents some examples of the potential induction of stimulus generalization both within and between product categories (see also interest box on p. 71).

FIG. 5.2 Examples of the potential induction of stimulus generalization. Within product categories, the local Hillfarm brand's package is similar to the well-known, national Philadelphia brand's package; this would be expected to induce stimulus generalization, leading consumers to react to Hillfarm cream cheese in the same way that they react to Philadelphia cream cheese. Between product categories, the introduction of Kraft's Philadelphia brand salad dressings is similar to Kraft's established Philadelphia cream cheese; this would also be expected to induce stimulus generalization, leading consumers to react to Philadelphia salad dressing in the same way that they react to Philadelphia cream cheese.

Vicarious or Observational Learning

An intriguing extension of principles of associational learning came in the 1960s with Bandura's work on social learning, or observational learning (e.g., Bandura, 1971; Bandura & Rosenthal, 1966). This work has examined the capacity of humans to learn through the observation of the antecedents and results of someone else's behavior.

Vicarious instrumental conditioning refers to the finding that when one person observes another person being instrumentally conditioned, the observer may acquire the instrumentally conditioned response. For example, Bandura, Ross, and Ross (1961) had children observe an adult model that kicked, punched, and abused a large inflatable clown named Bobo. If the adult was rewarded with a candy bar for this behavior, the child observer was more likely to punch and kick Bobo when given the opportunity. If the adult was scolded for this behavior, the child observer was less likely to abuse Bobo when given the opportunity. This acquisition of an instrumentally conditioned response occurred in spite of the fact that the observing subjects never experienced the rewards or punishments associated with the responses (cf. Liebert, Sprafkin, & Davidson, 1982). Note that this point of view assumes that many commercial advertisements are effective because they provide the consumer with valuable information about how to obtain

Interest Box

Coors *vs.* Corr's

When Robert Corr of Chicago began making natural-flavor sodas in 1978, he decided that his family name would have a familiar ring to Windy City buyers. His great-uncle Frank was a mayor of Chicago in the 1930s and founder of a football team called the Corr Flashes. But by putting the trademark Corr's on bottles and cans, the soda maker uncapped the rivalry of another proud name: Coors.

The Golden, Colo., brewer showed little concern about the sound-alike name until last year, when Corr's started showing up in grocery stores in 50 states. The beer company sued in a Denver federal court, demanding that Corr's change its name. Coors claimed that the tiny soda maker was trying to trade on the brewer's identity. As evidence, it cited one of Corr's slogans, "Made with pure Rocky Mountain water," which barely differs from the beer company's famous motto.

When the two sides met in court last week, Judge Sherman Finesilver asked them to try to work it out themselves. But the talks may resemble a family feud. Said Corr: "This is a basic principle, and I'm prepared to fight for it."

rewards. This information presumably leads to a conscious and deliberate decision to purchase the product in order to obtain those rewards.

Another type of vicarious conditioning may influence consumers in a less conscious, less deliberate manner. Vicarious classical conditioning refers to the finding that when one person observes another person being classically conditioned, the observer may acquire the classically conditioned response. For example, Bernal and Berger (1976) videotaped a subject who was being classically conditioned to blink in response to a tone. This conditioning procedure simply presents the conditioned stimulus of an auditory tone immediately before the unconditioned stimulus of a puff of air delivered to the eye (that naturally causes the eye to blink). Eventually, the auditory tone will cause the eyeblink all by itself. Vicarious classical conditioning was observed when the subjects who watched and listened to the videotape eventually came to blink in response to the auditory tone. This acquisition of the classically conditioned response occurred in spite of the fact that the observing subjects never experienced the unconditioned stimulus (i.e., they never received a puff of air to the eye) (also cf. Bandura & Rosenthal, 1966; Berger, 1962; Craig & Weinstein, 1965; Vaughn & Lanzetta, 1980; Venn & Short, 1973). This type of vicarious classical conditioning is discussed in chapter 6 when we consider the acquisition of emotional responses toward products.

Generally, then, vicarious instrumental conditioning and vicarious classical conditioning comprise mechanisms whereby watching other people's experiences with a product may influence our own subsequent reactions toward the product. In November of 1971, Bandura (1971) outlined the relevance of this generalization to consumer behavior, in testimony to the Federal Trade Commission:

> As a rule, observed rewards increase, and observed punishments decrease, imitative behavior. The principle is widely applied in advertising appeals. In positive appeals, following the recommended action results in a host of rewarding outcomes. Smoking a certain brand of cigarettes or using a particular hair lotion wins the loving admiration of voluptuous belles, enhances job performance, masculinizes one's self-concept, tranquilizes irritable nerves, invites social recognition from total strangers, and arouses affectionate reactions in spouses. (pp. 21–22)

EFFECTS OF THE OTHER INTERNAL PROCESSES ON LEARNING

Perception is likely to play a crucial role in the success or failure of various associative learning mechanisms. For example, the consumer must become aware of the conditioned stimulus in order for a classically conditioned response to develop for that conditioned stimulus. In addition, stimulus generalization and stimulus discrimination involve awareness of the new stimulus and perceptual processing of that new stimulus as equivalent to (generalization) or distinct from (discrimination) the initial stimulus.

Cognitive influence on associative learning is probably slight. Regarding classical conditioning, most of the responses typically considered in illustration of classical conditioning are involuntary, visceral, reflexive responses. Instrumental conditioning has most often been applied to more overt, operant-type behaviors that may be cognitively controlled. However, there have been numerous demonstrations of instrumental conditioning for behaviors typically thought of as involuntary, such as heart rate, blood pressure, and skin temperature (Blanchard & Young, 1973; Shapiro & Schwartz, 1972). Thus, these mechanisms of associative learning operate in a way that seems to be insulated from the effects of cognitive processes.

It seems that emotion does exert some influence on classical conditioning. Research indicates that classically conditioned responses are acquired more readily, and extinguish more slowly, under conditions of high emotional arousal (e.g., Doerfler & Kramer, 1959; Spence, 1964). This effect has also been demonstrated with vicarious classical conditioning (Bandura & Rosenthal, 1966). Thus, consumers who are emotionally aroused may be more receptive to the classical conditioning of emotional responses (see chapter 6), and to the classically conditioned acquisition of secondary motives (see chapter 7).

One implication of this is that frequent repetitions of an emotion-oriented commercial may enhance the acquisition of the emotional response as a result of: (a) the repeated association of the conditioned stimulus (product) with the unconditioned stimulus (emotion-arousing object or event); and, (b) the facilitation produced by the emotional arousal that may be lingering from the previous exposure to the commercial.

Laboratory research on the effects of motivation on learning have produced mixed results. Some studies have shown that higher levels of motivation during conditioning lead to a stronger, more extinction-resistant association (Barry, 1958; Deese & Carpenter, 1951). Other studies have shown no effect of motivation on the strength or the durability of conditioned associations (Hillman, Hunter, & Kimble, 1953; Kendler, 1945). At this point, the relationship between motivation and learning is not clearly understood (Hulse, Deese, & Egeth, 1975). From this inconclusive body of research, we cannot draw any confident inferences regarding the effects of motivation on the acquisition of conditioned associations in consumers.

CONCLUSION: 'CENTS OFF' OR 'SENSE OFF'?

Coupon-clipping has become an increasingly popular way of trying to decrease weekly grocery bills. In 1974, 65% of American households redeemed coupons ("A new look . . .," 1976). In 1980, this figure was 75% (Aycrigg, 1981). Total coupon distribution in 1982 was estimated at $119.5 billion ("Best food . . .," 1983). The cents-off deal provided by a redeemable coupon might be thought of as a small reward administered to the consumer in return for his or her selection of the brand. When considered in this light, coupons would be expected to increase the selection of the couponed brand, a la instrumental conditioning. However, this is not always the case.

Coupons have been demonstrated to induce switching to the couponed brand (e.g., Cotton & Babb, 1978; Dodson, Tybout, & Sternthal, 1978; Massy & Frank, 1965; Shoemaker & Shoaf, 1977). This basic finding is consistent with the instrumental conditioning perspective. However, the effects of retracting the coupon are not consistent with a strict instrumental conditioning perspective. If the cents-off deal provided by a coupon is a reward for brand selection, then retracting the cents-off coupon deal is, by definition, an extinction procedure. What this means is that retracting the coupon should make the frequency of brand selection return to the level obtained before the introduction of the coupon. This is not what happens. Retracting a coupon deal results in even lower selection of the (formerly couponed) brand than that obtained before the introduction of the coupon (Dodson, Tybout, & Sternthal, 1978; Doob, Carlsmith, Freedman, Landauer, & Soleng, 1969; Scott, 1976). This type of "defection" occurs for both the consumers who had switched to the brand because of the coupon, and the consumers who had been loyal to the brand before the coupon.

This may be similar to the "oversufficient justification effect" (Deci, 1971). This refers to the finding that the introduction and removal of some extrinsic reward decreases the motivation to perform a behavior. In terms of the attribution principles described in chapter 4, the administration of a cents-off coupon for the selection of a given brand may set the stage for the operation of the discounting principle. When the consumer selects a couponed brand, he or she has two plausible causes for this behavior: the intrinsic value of the product, and the cents-off deal provided by the coupon. The consumer may thereby discount the intrinsic value of the product as being the sole cause of his or her brand selection. When the coupon is retracted, one half of the justification for selecting that brand is gone. The consumer may then "defect," and switch to another brand. This is a particularly pressing problem in the restaurant industry, where the discount value of the coupons may involve $1, $2, or $3, compared to the average of 22¢ for grocery item coupons (Haugh, 1983).

One implication of this discussion is that the manufacturers should use coupons to induce consumers to try their brands. Then, the manufacturers should continue to provide coupons so as to preclude this oversufficient justification-based defection. Although this may sound like an impractical or a costly recommendation, it is actually a rather common strategy for some product categories. For things like cereal, coffee, and soaps, coupons can be continually placed within, or on, the package, and so the coupon can be maintained indefinitely. Without this type of concern for the subtlety of consumers' reactions to coupon dealing, providing cents-off deals for the consumer could, in the long run, make no sense for the manufacturer.

6 | Emotion

Emotion can be defined as a state of arousal involving conscious experience and visceral, or physiological, changes. In the context of consumer behavior, the result of the internal process of emotion is a feeling toward the product. For example, after 6 months of hearing about and using new Kona brand instant coffee, the user may come to feel really good about Kona coffee. In this chapter we try to determine how these feelings toward products develop.

The study of emotion has a long history in psychology. Theoretical conceptualizations of emotion have considered emotional experience to be a function of: interpretations of specific patterns of visceral changes (James, 1890); coinciding changes in physiological functioning and cerebral activity, resulting from changes in the thalamus (Cannon, 1929); and, cognitive interpretations of generalized arousal and situational cues (Schachter & Singer, 1962). Later in this chapter we examine the most recent theoretical approach to emotional experience, and consider its implications for consumer behavior. However, first we review some approaches to the measurement of emotional reactions. Then, we consider the various determinants of the feelings that a consumer develops for a given product. This chapter concludes with a discussion of some of the ethical questions unique to the consideration of emotions in consumer behavior. Bear in mind that our task in this chapter is to understand how consumers come to have feelings about a given product.

MEASUREMENT OF FEELING

Once again, it is instructive to begin discussion of an internal process by considering how that process is defined in terms of procedures of measurement. Measurements of feeling fall into two general categories: self-report measures and physiological measures. Self-report measures of emotion focus on the conscious experience of emotion by simply asking people to describe their emotional re-

75

sponse to a particular stimulus. For example, mothers might be asked to rate Dydie Diapers on a scale from 1 to 10 (where 1 = "Dydie Diapers make me feel awful," and 10 = "Dydie Diapers make me feel great"). Another self-report procedure would involve an adjective checklist. For example, mothers might be asked to place a check mark next to each of the adjectives that describe how Dydie Diapers make them feel. The total number of checked negative adjectives (e.g., "afraid," "guilty") is subtracted from the total number of checked positive adjectives (e.g., "thrifty," "safe," "free," "happy"), to yield an overall "positive feeling" score (e.g., 4 − 2 = 2).

These types of self-report measures sound very similar to the self-report measures of attitudes and beliefs, described in chapter 3. This is consistent with the view of attitudes as being comprised of cognitive elements and emotional elements (cf. Allport, 1935; Cartwright, 1949; Rosenberg & Hovland, 1960). These self-report measures are based on two assumptions. It is assumed that people can be accurate in their self-reports; and, it is assumed that people will be honest in their self-reports. Obviously, these two assumptions may not always be valid. Sometimes, people may not be able to describe accurately how they react to something (Nisbett & Wilson, 1977). Similarly, people may report one type of emotional reaction when in fact they are feeling a different type of emotion, in an attempt to make themselves "look good" (Baumeister, 1982; Tedeschi, Schlenker, & Bonoma, 1971).

Physiological measures of emotion focus on the visceral, or arousal, component of emotion. This approach is not based on the assumptions of accuracy and honesty of self-report. Instead, the physiological approach attempts to gauge facets of emotional response that are inherently nonverbal, uncontrolled, and "gut-level." We have already seen one example of a physiological measure of emotion: Hess' (1965) pupillary response. As indicated in chapter 2, some researchers have used pupillary response as an index of perceptual processing (Halpern, 1967; Hess, 1965; Hess & Polt, 1960). However, some researchers have used pupil dilation as an index of positive affect, or pleasure, and pupil contraction as an index of negative affect, or displeasure (Hess, 1972). More recently, researchers have come to view any changes in pupil size (dilation or contraction) as indicative of shifts in the magnitude of emotional response, without reference to the quality or direction of that emotional response. For example, Janisse (1973, 1974) has discussed research that shows that pupil dilation can occur in response to objectively pleasant stimuli (e.g., a picture of an attractive member of the opposite sex) as well as in response to objectively unpleasant stimuli (e.g., a picture of a gruesome traffic accident).

Another type of physiological measure of emotion attempts to gauge changes in arousal in terms of the degree of perspiration secreted on the surface of one's hands and fingers. Galvanic Skin Response (GSR) is a measure of the electrical conductivity of the surface of the skin. If you are sufficiently aroused, sebaceous glands in the skin of your palms and fingers will secrete perspiration. This salty perspiration is a better conductor of electricity than dry skin. Therefore, a mild, imperceptible electrical charge travels more easily across the surface of your skin when you are perspiring. The increase in electrical conductivity indicated by an increase in GSR is inferred to be a physiological representation of emotional arousal (Stern, Farr, & Ray, 1975). For example, Eckstrand and Gilliland (1948) found that the pancake-flour advertisement that elicited the greatest GSR (and, presumably, the greatest emotional response) was subsequently associated with the greatest sales.

The physiological approach to the measurement of emotion has two appealing characteristics, representing freedom from the assumptions that guided the use of self-report measures: physiological measures do not assume accuracy of self-report, nor do they assume honesty of self-report. A strong, genuine emotional reaction should elicit pupil dilation and an increase in GSR. It is generally assumed that the individual could not stop these physiological responses from occurring, nor could the individual fake these responses in the absence of a genuine emotional reaction.

However, two unique weaknesses are associated with this measurement approach. First, these physiological responses may be influenced by things other than, or in addition to, emotional experiences. For example, pupil dilation can be brought about by a decrease in illumination, as well as by exposure to a pleasant stimulus. Similarly, an increase in GSR might be brought about by drinking a strong cup of coffee, as well as by exposure to a pleasant stimulus. Therefore, one must always be careful to ensure that changes in the physiological measures are the result of the potentially emotional stimulus, and not some irrelevant environmental factor.

The second weakness of physiological measures of emotion is a lack of specificity. At best, measures like GSR and pupillary response can indicate shifts from no emotional response to some (positive or negative) emotional response. However, these measures cannot distinguish between positive emotional responses and negative emotional responses (e.g., happiness vs. sadness), let alone more subtle distinctions (e.g., happiness vs. sexual excitement). Some researchers (e.g., Lazarus, Cohen, Folkman, Kanner, & Schaefer, 1980) have been attempting to identify unique patterns of hormonal activity that may be associated with specific emotional experiences. However, at present, the best use of physiological measures of emotion might be in conjunction with self-report measures of emotion. This is certainly consistent with our initial definition of emotion in terms of both conscious experience and physiological changes.

DETERMINANTS OF EMOTIONAL RESPONSES TOWARD PRODUCTS

Repetition

One determinant of emotional response toward a product is repetition. The mere exposure effect refers to the typical finding that repetitions may lead to more favorable evaluations of the repeated stimulus. Some conceptual problems with this mere exposure effect were discussed in chapter 4. However, in addition to the effects of repetition on cognitive evaluation, it appears that increased exposure to a stimulus may enhance the emotional response toward the stimulus.

An interesting extension of this work, with an emphasis on the "feeling" results of the mere exposure effect, can be found in a recent study by Wilson (1979). This procedure utilized a dichotic listening task, where subjects wear earphones that present a different sound to each ear. In Wilson's study, six tone sequences, like brief melodies, were presented to one ear. A passage from DuMaurier's *The Birds* was presented to the other ear. Subjects were instructed to ignore any extraneous sounds, and to focus their attention on the passage from the book. Later, subjects were presented with tone sequences, some of which had been presented previously during the dichotic listening task, and some of which were new. Subjects in this procedure did not recognize the tone sequences that had been presented during the dichotic listening task. However, they did rate these previously repeated sequences as being more pleasant. Wilson's results suggest that an individual's positive feelings toward previously encountered items or events may not be dependent on the person's recognition of (memory), or beliefs regarding (cognition), the item or event. Zajonc (1980) and Obermiller (1985) have reviewed a considerable amount of research that supports this point of view. Thus, repetition of the Flurple soft drink slogan may lead the consumer to develop a good feeling toward Flurple pop, distinct from any cognitive evaluation of the quality of Flurple, or any memory of information about Flurple soft drink.

Classical Conditioning

Another determinant of emotional response toward products is past experience, and a very powerful way to characterize this influence is in terms of the classical conditioning model. This model of associative learning, presented in chapter 5, describes how a previously neutral conditioned stimulus comes to elicit a conditioned response after being repeatedly paired with an unconditioned stimulus that "naturally" elicits a similar unconditioned response.

Classical conditioning occurs continually in day-to-day exposure to product slogans and insignias along with exposure to products. For example, suppose you enjoy Biggy Burgers. One might say that, for you, a Biggy Burger is an unconditioned stimulus that naturally produces an unconditioned response of positive affect, or pleasure. Note that the Biggy Burger trademark (a pair of orange drain pipes) is present before and during each presentation of a Biggy Burger (on the doorway, on the wallpaper, on the wrappers, on the napkins). Thus, the Biggy Burger trademark may serve as a conditioned stimulus, signaling the imminent presentation of a Biggy Burger. Eventually the Biggy Burger trademark may come to elicit a positive affective response all by itself, and you may be overcome by a warm glow every time you pass by the orange drain pipes (see Fig. 6.1). This application of classical conditioning is based on the repeated demonstration of the conditionability of emotional responses (e.g., May, 1948; Miller, 1948, 1951; Watson & Raynor, 1920).

Note that stimulus discrimination and stimulus generalization may occur with this classical conditioning process, just as they were described to occur in chapter 5. Thus, through stimulus generalization you might come to experience a positive emotional response to any drain pipe you pass by; alternatively, through stimulus

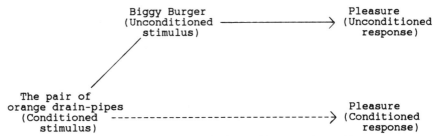

FIG. 6.1 *Illustration of the classical conditioning of a positive emotional response to a product trademark (Biggy Burger's pair of orange drain pipes).*

discrimination you might come to experience a positive emotional response only to newer Biggy Burger restaurants, whose drain pipes have not yet faded from orange to yellow.

An extremely potent context for the classical conditioning of emotional responses can be found in modern media, especially in television commercial advertisements. Some researchers (e.g., Gnepp, 1979; Goldsen, 1978) have described the manner in which television advertisements can produce classically conditioned emotional responses. For example, Goldsen (1978) described how the repeated association of a Mercury Cougar automobile (conditioned stimulus) with Catherine Deneuve (unconditioned stimulus) could eventually lead to a positive affective response (initially unconditioned response, eventually conditioned response) being elicited by the sight of the product.

This type of conditioning process accurately characterizes a tremendous number of commercial advertisements (see Fig. 6.2). For example, the communications research manager for Coca-Cola company recently revealed that successful advertisements for Coca-Cola during the previous three years had been demonstrated to establish classically conditioned emotional responses ("Coca-cola turns . . .," 1984). The classical conditioning of emotional responses to products may be very important, in light of the amount of information typically conveyed in television commercial advertisements. Recall that in chapter 4 it was reported that a relatively low percentage of television commercial advertisements contained more than a single bit of informational content. It should come as no surprise that these commercial advertisements (for which $5,147,328,600 were spent in 1980 on network television [Leading National Advertisers, 1980]) are directed toward something other than, or in addition to, cognitive persuasion.

Classical conditioning has two additional, more intricate, applications to the development of emotional responses in consumers. These applications can be considered in the context of a specific television commercial for Final Touch fabric softener described by Reed and Coalson (1977):

> In one frequently repeated commercial, a housewife's use of the product is associated with the effusive love and approval of her husband. Before embracing her in the final scene, the husband addresses their child exclaiming in a tender voice, "Billy, you've got one special Mommy!". . . . In selecting these laundry products these consumers, upon seeing "Final Touch" on the shelf, may be

FIG. 6.2 Example of a commercial advertisement that involves emotional conditioning.

induced to purchase it over a less expensive item, or over no such item, because of the "emotional glow" it evokes. (p. 745)

Reed and Coalson interpreted this commercial advertisement in terms of the simple application of classical conditioning previously described with reference to Catherine Deneuve and the Mercury Cougar automobile. However, this type of commercial is more complex than this simpler application, and appears to be operating in terms of two more elaborate processes: classical conditioning of vicarious emotional responses, and vicarious classical conditioning of emotional responses. Each of these two approaches are now considered with reference to this "Final Touch" commercial.

Classical conditioning of vicarious emotional responses represents a special case of the general classical conditioning model. When the housewife-consumer views this 60-second drama, the picture of the loving family scene creates a vicarious emotional response. That is, the housewife-consumer feels good because the family members in the commercial feel good. Certainly this type of pleasure is likely to be less intense than the pleasure that the housewife-consumer might feel if her own husband were this affectionate. Still, the housewife-consumer can experience pleasure vicariously, through the pleasure of the housewife-character in the commercial. This type of conditioning is illustrated in Fig. 6.3.

Vicarious classical conditioning of emotional responses is an alternative way to interpret this "Final Touch" commercial. Our earlier discussion of vicarious classical conditioning in chapter 5 indicated that observing someone else as he or she becomes classically conditioned may be sufficient for an individual to acquire vicariously the classically conditioned response. From this perspective, the housewife-consumer watches the housewife-character become classically conditioned to have a positive emotional response toward the product. In a sense, the housewife-consumer watches as the housewife-character serves as a subject in a classical conditioning experiment. For example, the housewife-character's use of the product (conditioned stimulus) is invariably followed by the "effusive love and approval of her husband" (unconditioned stimulus), that naturally evokes a feeling of pleasure in the housewife-character (initially unconditioned response, eventually conditioned response).

We all realize that the housewife-character is a paid actress, and that the situation

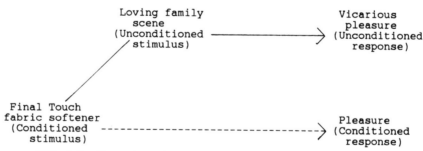

FIG. 6.3 Illustration of the classical conditioning of a vicarious emotional response, using the example of the Final Touch commercial.

is really make-believe. However, this commercial depicts a procedure that would classically condition the housewife-character to feel positively about Final Touch fabric softener if this procedure were to occur in reality as often as the commercial is telecast. As the housewife-character becomes classically conditioned to feel good about Final Touch, the housewife-consumer may also come to feel good about Final Touch. This conditioning process is depicted in Fig. 6.4.

It is important to recognize that these three variants of classical conditioning may be complementary in practice, and may simultaneously exert their effects on consumers. Classical conditioning of emotional responses, classical conditioning of vicarious emotional responses, and vicarious classical conditioning of emotional responses may all be operating as a consumer repeatedly watches a particular commercial advertisement. In addition, vicarious instrumental conditioning, or Bandura's social learning perspective (described in chapter 5), could also operate in this type of commercial advertisement. However, the classical conditioning perspective and the social learning perspective suggest different consequences of the repeated exposure to this type of commercial advertisement. The social learning perspective would hold that consumers viewing the "Final Touch" commercial would subsequently go out and purchase Final Touch in order to obtain the reinforcements that Final Touch offered to the housewife-character. On the other hand, the classical conditioning of emotional responses approach suggests a more subtle, less rational sort of influence. That is, after viewing the "Final Touch" commercial repeatedly, the consumer might not be expected to run out and buy the product in imitation of the housewife-character, but the consumer might be led to feel good about Final Touch when he or she sees it on the shelf in the supermarket.

We return to an important implication of the subtlety of this type of influence at the end of this chapter. However, the general point is that the classical conditioning model of associational learning provides a powerful means of de-

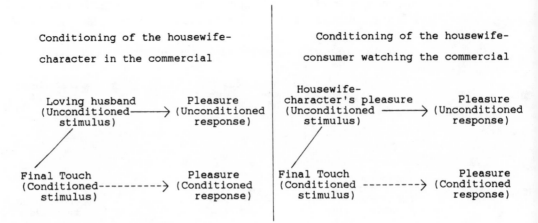

FIG. 6.4 Illustration of the vicarious classical conditioning of emotional responses, using the example of the Final Touch commercial.

scribing and explaining important aspects of consumer behavior. This statement runs contrary to the view held by the many authors who are of a more cognitive emphasis. This cognitive emphasis was illustrated by the tremendous amount of research and theory reviewed in chapters 3 and 4. For example, consider the following statement by Assael (1981):

> Principles of classical conditioning are of limited usefulness in marketing because of the required link between the conditioned stimulus and response. Such a link requires automatic response behavior. The assumption is that the Marlboro cowboy will cause a smoker to light up with no cognitive processes. Such automatic responses are unlikely (although not impossible) because advertising is not a powerful enough vehicle of communication to create the strength of association established by Pavlov. (p. 59)

The tendency to consider classical conditioning to be an interesting but laboratory-bound and inapplicable phenomenon betrays an ignorance of the subtleties of classical conditioning, or an unimaginative view of the commercial advertisement as a stimulus situation, or both. The assumption is not that the Marlboro man will cause the smoker to light up with no cognitive processes. However, it is assumed that the Marlboro man, or the Final Touch housewife, may make the consumer feel good about the product. Later, we also see how the Marlboro man or the Final Touch housewife may make the consumer desire the product (chapter 7) in terms of classical conditioning principles. Consumer psychologists (e.g., Bierley, McSweeney, & Vannieuwkerk, 1985; McSweeney & Bierley, 1984; Nord & Peter, 1980) are beginning to direct more attention toward the applications of classical conditioning to consumer behavior.

Humor

Another determinant of emotional responses toward products is humor. In chapter 4, we learned that humor might enhance the effectiveness of a persuasive appeal if it distracts the consumer from counterarguing (Osterhouse & Brock, 1970). However, the use of humor may also have an effect on the consumer's emotional response toward a product. In terms of classical conditioning, the repeated presentation of the product (conditioned stimulus) immediately before a joke, a pun, or some (unconditioned) stimulus that elicits a positive affective response (unconditioned response) may lead the product to elicit a positive affective response from the consumer (conditioned response). For example, consider the typical head cold remedy commercial advertisement: the product (conditioned stimulus) is presented in conjunction with some joke about suffering from a head cold (unconditioned stimulus), that naturally elicits from the viewer a response of laughter (unconditioned response). Eventually, the product may come to elicit the positive affective response all by itself (conditioned response).

However, as noted by Sternthal and Craig (1973), there are difficulties inherent in this approach to developing a positive emotional response toward the product. For example, humor is probably not universal; that is, something that is funny in one geographic region may not be funny in another. In addition, the repeated exposure that is necessary to establish the classically conditioned response may mitigate the humor of the joke, pun, or gag that is intended to be funny. A joke usually ceases to be funny after it is heard a hundred times (and yet, just such repeated exposure is needed to establish a classically conditioned response). Finally, the nature of the positive affective response that becomes classically conditioned may not be the "warm glow" established by other types of emotional conditioning. It is possible that consumers could come to feel a "happy silliness" when presented with the conditioned stimulus of the sight of the product. In the extreme, imagine the consumer, walking down the health care aisle in the supermarket, who giggles when he or she sees the head cold medicine that has been using a very funny advertisement campaign for the past year. This classically conditioned silliness might not be conducive to the consumer's considering the product as a serious and effective medicine. Nonetheless, humor has been used in advertising for a very long time, and will probably continue to be used. An example of the use of humor in a commercial advertisement is found in Fig. 6.5.

Fear Appeals

Another determinant of emotional response is the heavily researched impact of fear appeals. Generally speaking, a fear appeal is an attempt to arouse a negative emotional response (e.g., fear, anxiety, guilt), by showing that failure to use the product, service, or idea in question will produce disastrous consequences whereas the use of the product, service, or idea will eliminate the disastrous consequences (e.g., Harris & Jellison, 1971; Leventhal, 1970; Sternthal & Craig, 1974). An example of a fear appeal can be found in Fig. 6.6.

Recent research indicates that fear appeals will be effective only if a clear, effective recommendation that accompanies the fear arousal provides the consumer with a means of avoiding the negative consequences and reducing the negative emotional arousal. Presumably, the consumer will come to feel good about the product, and perhaps become more likely to use the product, if the product is portrayed as successfully being able to reduce the negative emotional arousal.

For example, Rogers and Mewborn (1976) examined the effects of varying levels of the frightening nature of the appeal, the probability of occurrence of the threatening event, and the effectiveness of the recommended preventative behaviors. These researchers observed that when the preventative behaviors were effective, increasing the frightening nature of the appeal and increasing the probability of occurrence of the threatening event enhanced the effectiveness of the appeal. However, when the preventative behaviors were ineffective, increasing the frightening nature of the appeal and increasing the probability of occurrence of the threatening event had no effect, or in some instances detracted from the effectiveness of the fear appeal. For example, consider the fear appeals directed toward getting drivers to increase the use of their seatbelts. If drivers are informed that wearing seatbelts can save the lives of 90% of all severe accident victims, then making the seatbelt commercial more frightening and characterizing severe traffic accidents as fairly common will lead the drivers to begin using seatbelts. On the other hand, if drivers are informed that wearing seatbelts will

FIG. 6.5 An example of the use of humor in a commercial advertisement.

save the lives of only 10% of all severe accident victims, then making the seatbelt commercial more frightening and describing severe traffic accidents as fairly common will have no effect on seatbelt use (or may even reduce seatbelt use).

Thus, fear appeals may tend to be ineffective unless clear, effective recommendations accompany the fear-arousing message. In this light, the most common

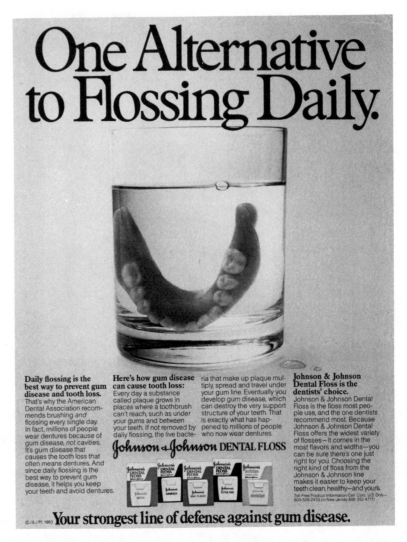

FIG. 6.6 An example of the use of a fear appeal in a commercial advertisement. Notice the provision of recommendations, and the integration of the product into these recommendations.

fear appeal might be a relatively ineffective one in practice; that most common fear appeal is the Surgeon General's warning that is printed on all cigarette products and advertisements. Many professionals believe that the warning is not frightening enough or large enough (cf. Revett, 1975; Sulzberger, 1981) to be effective. In addition, however, it should be recognized that this fear appeal is structured to simply instill a negative emotional response; there is no information or recommendation that the consumer could use to reduce the negative emotional response. It may be for this reason that some researchers (e.g., Hyland & Birrell,

1979) have found a "boomerang effect" with government health warnings; that is, the presentation of the health warning leads to an increase, rather than a decrease, in the behavior about which the individual is being warned. One simple addition to the Surgeon General's warning that might improve the effectiveness of this fear appeal would be a toll-free, "800" telephone number that could serve as a smokers' hotline. This smokers' hotline could provide smokers with the opportunity to talk to people who have quit smoking, it could disseminate information regarding regional smoking treatment organizations, and so on. The Surgeon General's warning may be a good thing, and (at some level) it might be effective. Nonetheless, it is instructive for us to consider how this particular fear appeal might be structured in an attempt to make it optimally effective (see also interest box, below).

Interest Box

(This ad was very effective in winning support for the Rat Extermination Bill.)

EFFECTS OF THE OTHER INTERNAL
PROCESSES ON EMOTION

Consider the potential effects of the other internal processes on emotion. Similar to the effect of perception on the other internal processes, perception may exert an influence on emotion. However, the extent of this effect is often unclear. Recall Wilson's (1979) study, where subjects' emotional responses to sequences of tones were observed to be a function of previous exposure, even though subjects could not recognize the sequences as having been presented before. Certainly, awareness can affect feelings, but apparently, awareness is not a prerequisite for feelings.

As suggested at the outset of our discussion of emotion, it seems likely that cognition provides an important contribution to emotional experience. A currently popular theoretical explanation for emotion is Schachter and Singer's (1962) two-factor theory of emotions. This perspective holds that emotional experience is the result of undifferentiated, nonspecific physiological arousal, and cognitive cues that are used to interpret that arousal as an emotional experience. In other words, the physiological arousal that accompanies love should be the same arousal that accompanies hate, fear, happiness, and any other emotion. The difference between each emotion is that the arousal is generally interpreted as love when we are near an attractive member of the opposite sex, as fear when we are near a rabid dog, as happiness when we are near a number of close friends, and so on. Although Schachter and Singer's (1962) initial presentation has been subjected to methodological criticism by many researchers (e.g., Marshall & Zimbardo, 1979; Maslach, 1979), the basic conceptualization seems to be a useful one, and has been retained in more recent theoretical approaches to emotion (e.g., Leventhal, 1974; Zillmann, 1978).

Let us examine the application of this two-factor theory of emotion to the development of consumers' emotional responses to products. For example, consider the beverage commercials that always depict an individual in the company of a number of cheerful and good-hearted fellows. If the consumer should ever find him or herself in such a crowd, with a can of the beverage in question in his or her hand, the consumer may develop an emotional experience as specified by the two-factor theory. That is, the consumer would be experiencing a level of arousal (in reality produced by the friendly noise, the bonfire, etc.). This arousal might be attributed to the friends (in which case, the consumer might develop a feeling of warmth and affection for these friends). Alternatively, the consumer might attribute this arousal to the can of beverage (in which case, the consumer will develop a feeling of warmth and affection toward the drink).

There are other ways in which cognition may influence emotion. For example, source credibility, discussed in chapter 4, seems to influence the effectiveness of emotion-oriented appeals. Sternthal and Craig (1974) observed that a high credibility source enhanced the effectiveness of a fear appeal, whereas a low credibility source impaired the effectiveness of a fear appeal. Recall that fear appeals are assumed to work, in part, because the recommendations that accompany the appeal provide a means of reducing the fear. In Sternthal and Craig's study, the highly credible source apparently made the recommendations more acceptable and believable, and thereby provided a more effective means of reducing the consumer's fear. Conversely, the low credibility source apparently provided a less effective means of reducing the consumer's fear. More recently, Pallak, Murroni, and Koch (1983) reported a similar finding. These researchers found that emotional product advertisements were more effective when they came from an attractive, credible source than when they came from an unattractive, noncredible source.

The impact of learning on emotion was implicit in much of our earlier discussion of emotion. Classical conditioning of emotional responses, classical conditioning of vicarious emotional responses, vicarious classical conditioning of emotional responses, humor appeals, and fear appeals may all represent instances of the effect of learning on emotion.

The membrane between emotion and motivation is probably more permeable than that between any of the other internal processes. Both are conceived as being based upon physiological mechanisms, and as being modified through classical conditioning. Indeed, the paradigm case for one is often interpretable in terms of the other. For example, fear appeals are typically considered in terms of emotion. However, fear appeals might be conceived in terms of motivation as an appeal to a need for safety, or as an appeal to a need for risk reduction. Similarly, the classical conditioning of a positive affective response toward a particular brand of junk food is typically considered in terms of emotion. However, this might be conceived in terms of motivation as the classical conditioning of a secondary motive for the particular brand of junk food. We return to the interface between emotion and motivation in chapter 7.

We have considered a number of distinct possible determinants of emotional responses toward products: repetition, classical conditioning of emotional responses, classical conditioning of vicarious emotional responses, vicarious classical conditioning of emotional responses, humor, and fear appeals, as well as the various influences of the other internal processes. One common element in all of these mechanisms should be emphasized. In each case, the issue is not whether consumers believe or accept the message (cognition); and, the issue is not whether consumers remember the product information (memory); the issue is not even whether consumers can report awareness of the product (perception). The issue that underlies the determinants of emotional response is, simply, whether the consumers feel good about the product. Considered in this light, many advertisements that seem on the surface to be childish or silly might now be viewed much more seriously. That is, many advertisements that seem to be rather unsophisticated when viewed from a rational, cognitive point of view might be seen as rather complicated and potentially powerful when considered from an emotional response perspective. The "Final Touch" commercial is a very good example of this.

CONCLUSION: A QUESTION OF ETHICS

For the first time, we begin to move away from the view of the consumer as a rational information processor who becomes aware of, develops beliefs about, and retains a memory of products in the stimulus situation. The introduction of the internal process of emotion into our model of consumer behavior alters our view of the consumer to accommodate the possibility of subtle influence of which the individual may not be aware, and over which the individual may have little control. This issue is raised in other contexts throughout the remainder of the text.

In this context, it is important to note that some scholars have begun to discuss the ethical and the legal ramifications of this issue (cf. Kozyris, 1975; Reed & Coalson, 1977). For example, consider the "Final Touch" commercial. Through the operation of some variants of classical conditioning, the repeated viewing of this commercial might produce a classically conditioned positive emotional response toward the Final Touch product. This emotional response may enhance the likelihood that the housewife-consumer will purchase Final Touch rather than some competitor's brand. However, there is an implicit promise made to the consumer in this commercial: the use of Final Touch will result in the attention and affection of the husband. Whether this is in fact the case is an empirical question, and Reed and Coalson (1977) suggest that it be put to the test. For example, we could have 100 housewives use Final Touch and another 100 housewives could be given the generic brand fabric softener. Then, we could determine whether the Final Touch housewives experienced improved marital satisfaction relative to the generic brand housewives. If not (i.e., if Final Touch does not in fact propagate love and gratitude on the part of husbands, or otherwise function as some sort of love potion), then the emotional conditioning commercials might be considered an unfair form of advertising.

Reed and Coalson suggest that the Federal Trade Commission (FTC) should become concerned with regulating this type of potentially unfair advertising. For example, just as the FTC prohibits a company from stating that its product will cure an illness when such is not the case, the FTC might begin prohibiting a company from stating that its product will encourage sexual satisfaction, make one more masculine/feminine, or promote a happier homelife when such is not the case. More attention is certain to be directed toward these issues in years to come.

7 | Motivation

Motivation refers to a state of tension within the individual that arouses, maintains, and directs behavior toward some goal. It is usually assumed that attaining the goal reduces the tension instilled by the motivation. In the context of consumer behavior, the result of motivation is a desire or need for the product. Our major concern in this chapter is to try to understand how the product becomes a goal. That is, how does a product acquire the capacity, or the appearance of the capacity, to reduce the tension instilled by the motivation?

First, we review some approaches to the measurement of needs. Then we consider two underlying currents in the research and rhetoric directed toward motivation in consumer behavior. The first approach holds that the product can be portrayed as satisfying existing motivations. This approach involves the appeal to motives. The second approach holds that the product can be portrayed in such a way as to generate the arousal and direction of behavior. Beyond simply appealing to motives, this approach involves the creation of motives. Following this, we examine the effects of other internal processes on the individual's desire for the product. Bear in mind that our task in this chapter is to understand how consumers come to want or desire a particular product.

MEASUREMENT OF NEEDS

Motivation has probably been measured less frequently than any of the other internal processes. One reason for this may be that early conceptualizations of motivation in terms of need deprivations led to operationalizations of motives in terms of procedures of manipulation rather than procedures of measurement. For example, hunger in a rat would be operationalized in terms of 6 hours of food deprivation, or maintenance of 85% normal body weight (Bolles, 1967; Spence, 1956), rather than in terms of some measurement of stomach contractions or some self-report of hunger.

91

In spite of this unique manipulation orientation toward motives, we can identify three general types of measures of needs that have relevance to consumer behavior: *focused self-report, Global Self-report,* and *Projective measures.* As implied by the term, *Focused Self-report* requires the individual to describe his or her own needs and satisfactions regarding a specific product and selected product attributes. For example, Assael (1981) illustrated focused self-report measures for consumers' needs for cola beverages that vary in sweetness and carbonation. This procedure requires consumers to describe their ideal brand in terms of sweetness and carbonation, to indicate how important sweetness and carbonation are in making a brand choice, and to evaluate the degree of satisfaction that they obtain when they use the target brand. This measurement approach can provide a fairly specific gauge of the consumer's need for a given product. However, it does not characterize any general motivational system that the product might then be portrayed as fulfilling.

The *global self-report* measurement of motivation attempts to identify broad, underlying motivations of the consumer. On the one hand, this may tell us nothing about whether the consumer is experiencing a need for the product. On the other hand, this global approach may reveal what the consumer does need, thereby identifying the need(s) to which the manufacturer may best appeal in commercial advertisements. For example, Murray (1938) developed a taxonomy of different general motivations or needs (needs for: achievement, deference, order, autonomy, exhibition, affiliation, intraception, succorance, dominance, abasement, nurturance, change, heterosexuality, and accession). Edwards (1954) developed the Edwards Personal Preference Schedule, that measures the strength of each of these motivations, resulting in a variety of different subscale scores. The Edwards Personal Preference Schedule is comprised of 210 pairs of statements, such as, "I like to talk about myself to others," and, "I like to work toward some goal that I have set for myself." For each pair of statements, the individual indicates which statement is a better characterization of him or herself. Consider an extreme illustration of the use of this global self-report measurement procedure. Suppose that the consumers of a particular model of subcompact automobile can be distinguished into two subgroups based on their responses to the Edwards Personal Preference Schedule. One subgroup is characterized by a very high need for order, while the other subgroup is characterized by a high need for dominance. The first group may be more receptive to portrayals of the subcompact car as safe, reliable, and predictable, whereas the second group may be more receptive to portrayals of the car as powerful, impressive, and exciting.

Projective measurements comprise the third general approach to the measurement of motivations. Distinct from focused and global self-report approaches, projective measurements do not assume that the individuals have conscious access to, and reliably report, their underlying motivations. Projective measurements expose the individual to some vague, incomplete, or ambiguous stimulus, and record the written or spoken response to this ambiguous stimulus. This measurement procedure assumes that important, unsatiated needs will "project" themselves into the individual's response to the ambiguous stimuli. In support of this assumption, McClelland and Atkinson (1948) had subjects deprive themselves of food before going to the psychology laboratory for an experiment. During the experiment, subjects were engaged in a visual recognition task, where subjects had to identify the thing being presented during a very brief exposure to a projected slide. A higher proportion of food-related images were "recognized" by the hungry subjects. This is particularly compelling, because all of the slides were in fact blank! This is similar to the study by Bruner and Postman (1951), discussed in chapter 2, in which words describing things that are valued or needed were more quickly recognized than words describing irrelevant things. This type of research supports the basic assumption that salient, unfulfilled needs might be revealed through the individual's responses to ambiguous stimuli.

The use of projective techniques to understand consumers' motivations is illustrated in the well-known study by Haire (1950). When instant coffee was first introduced in the late 1940s, housewives were reluctant to purchase it. In an effort to understand why, Haire developed two shopping lists and had housewives describe the type of woman most likely to have written each list. The two lists were identical except for the coffee in the list: one list included regular coffee, the other list included instant coffee. The woman who included instant coffee in her list was described as being lazy and a poor planner. From these results, Haire inferred that housewives were projecting into the vague and ambiguous stimulus of the shopping list their needs regarding coffee. Presumably, regular coffee was consistent with their needs for self-esteem and competence in their role as homemaker. Instant coffee, on the other hand, was presumably inconsistent with these needs. As a result of this study, instant coffee was (successfully) advertised in association with an efficient housewife with an approving husband. This leads into our next topic, the strategy of appealing to motives.

APPEALING TO MOTIVES

Appealing to existing motives was very popular from the mid-1950s through the early 1960s, largely through the efforts of author and marketing practitioner Ernst Dichter (1964). The paradigm case of appealing to motives involved two steps. First, the important and relevant motive had to be identified. Second, the product was presented in conjunction with the satisfaction of the relevant motive. In some cases, this seems trivially obvious, as when a soft drink might be portrayed as satisfying thirst. However, in other cases, this can be much more subtle, such as: when a product is portrayed as satisfying needs for comfort and health (Fig. 7.1a); when a tape recorder is portrayed as satisfying needs for social competence (Fig. 7.1b); when a medicine is portrayed as producing improvements in temperament (Fig. 7.1c); or, when a bicycle is portrayed as satisfying needs for affection from one's children (Fig. 7.1d).

It must be recognized that the first step in making an appeal to motives (i.e., identifying the important and relevant motive) is sometimes complicated and problematic. Psychologists have developed a variety of systems for classifying motives. For example, Murray (1938) proposed a system of basic psychological needs. This system was described previously, along with the Edwards Personal Preference Schedule, in our discussion of global self-report measurements of

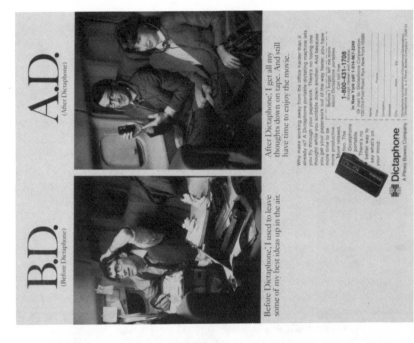

FIG. 7.1 Examples of commercial advertisements that portray a product as satisfying a particular motive.

needs. McGuire (1974, 1976) proposed a complex classification of motives based on the combinations of four psychological dimensions (cognitive–affective; stability–growth; active–passive; inner directed–externally directed), resulting in 16 different types of motives. Although these systems for classification of motives have made substantive contributions in other areas of psychological research, these broad taxonomies have received relatively little research attention within consumer psychology.

One classification of human motivation that has received noticeable attention in consumer psychology is Maslow's (1943, 1970) *hierarchy of needs*. This approach assumes that human motivations are arranged in a hierarchy from lower level needs to higher level needs. These needs, respectively, are: physiological needs, safety needs, love and affection needs, self-esteem needs, and self-actualization needs. The lower level needs are considered to be prepotent. That is, one must satisfy the lower level physiological needs and safety needs before one can begin to satisfy the higher level needs of love, self-esteem, and self-actualization.

Many commercial advertisements can be considered in terms of attempts to appeal to one (or more) of these needs. Some examples are presented in Fig. 7.2. You might recognize that there are relatively few advertisements that are based exclusively on the lower level needs. This is probably because, in our relatively comfortable and affluent society, consumers' physiological and safety needs are usually satisfied as a matter of routine, whereas the motives for love, self-esteem, and self-actualization are in constant need of gratification. In the extreme, consumers who can afford to buy designer jeans and cosmetics are not as hungry as they are in need of love and self-esteem.

Given that an important motivation can be identified, and given that the product can be portrayed as satisfying that motive, the question can be raised: is it effective? That is, does portraying the product as satisfying a particular motivation lead to an increase in the desire for the product?

Myers and Reynolds (1967) provide an anecdotal illustration of how appealing to existing motives can be effective. Reportedly, Betty Crocker cake mixes were not particularly popular when first introduced during the 1930s and 1940s, because housewives found the mixes too convenient. Presumably, for housewives of that era, baking a cake was a reflection of one's competence and a means of satisfying self-esteem needs. The "new-fangled" cake mixes that required only the addition of water might not allow the housewife to satisfy self-esteem needs, because she had so little to do with the making of the cake. The company's response to this dilemma was to change the product and packaging so that the housewife was required to add an egg to the cake mix. Apparently, this allowed the housewife to feel that she was in fact "making" the cake more-or-less from scratch, and therefore could satisfy self-esteem needs through the baking of these pre-mixed cakes. Myers and Reynolds reported that this strategy was successful, and resulted in increased sales of the cake mixes. The fact that this strategy is no longer necessary for the success of cake mixes is probably a reflection of cultural and economic changes, and the effects of these changes on the consumers of cake mixes. A substantial number of female consumers are now satisfying self-esteem needs through careers rather than, or in addition to, homemaking. Adding an egg to a cake mix may now be less of an opportunity to satisfy self-esteem needs, and simply more of an inconvenience. In fact, numerous current baking products seem to play on a need to get the job done as quickly and as painlessly as possible (e.g., "10 seconds from package to palate"). Thus, appealing to existing motives by presenting the product as a means of satisfying a particular need may be successful.

More controlled examinations of the effectiveness of appealing to motives provide further support for this approach. For example, Koponen (1960) reasoned that mail-order shoppers might be motivated by a need for change. A study was conducted that revealed that a mail-order sales promotion designed to appeal to a need for change resulted in a higher percent of customers buying, as well as a higher total return in dollars.

A more comprehensive effort to appeal to specific existing motives can be seen in the research conducted by Ackoff and Emshoff (1975). These researchers, working for the Anheuser-Busch Brewery Company, attempted to identify the motivations behind alcoholic beverage consumption, and to examine the effectiveness of portraying the use of the product in conjunction with the satisfaction of such motivations. After an extensive program of research (based in part on Carl Jung's theory of personality), Ackoff and Emshoff identified four general motivations for the consumption of alcoholic beverages. The *Oceanic* drinker tends to drink in order to become more extroverted and gregarious. The *Indulgent* drinker tends to drink in order to become more withdrawn and introverted. The *Reparative* drinker tends to drink in order to ease the transition from work to non-work, and to reward himself or herself for the many sacrifices made on behalf of others. Finally, the *Social* drinker tends to use alcoholic beverages as a social lubricant, and as an activity associated with the friendliness and acceptance of others.

After identifying these relevant motivations, Ackoff and Emshoff solicited regular beer drinkers to participate in an effort by Anheuser-Busch to bring one of four new beers out on the market. All of these consumers first took a personality test that could be used to categorize them as being directed by one of the four motivations described above. Then, each consumer viewed four television commercials, each commercial consisting of three segments. In the first segment, a character, who was clearly one of the four types, was shown in a situation that was typical for that type (e.g., the Oceanic might be seen leaping off a fishing boat with his buddies). In the second segment, the character was shown drinking one of the four brands of beer. In the third segment, the character was shown again, now with his or her personality having been transformed in the manner specified by the underlying motivation (e.g., the Oceanic drinker was now boisterous, rowdy, and "havin' fun"). After viewing the four commercials, the consumers were allowed to taste each of the four brands of beer. In actuality, the four brands were all the same beer, with different black and white labels of the brand names (Bix, Zim, Waz, and Biv beers).

At the end of this procedure, the consumers were asked to express their preferences among the four brands, and to select a case of one of the brands to take home with them. Ackoff and Emshoff reported that these consumers tended to express strong preferences for the brand portrayed as satisfying their individual motivations for alcohol consumption. As these authors describe their results: "all

a. Physiological

b. Safety

FIG. 7.2 Examples of commercial advertisements appealing to a motive in Maslow's (1943, 1970) hierarchy of needs.

c. Love

d. Esteem

e. Self-Actualization

99

the subjects believed that the brands were different and that they could tell the difference between them. Most felt that at least one of the four brands was not fit for human consumption." (Ackoff & Emshoff, 1975, p. 12). Thus, not only did these motivational appeals generate preferences on the part of the consumers; these appeals generated dramatically perceived differences where none really existed (see also interest box, below).

CREATING MOTIVES

The discussion heretofore revealed how appeals to existing motives might be successful. A second possible operation of the internal process of motivation involves the creation of motives. In this light, a product may come to be accepted simply because it was associated with a desirable object or event (King, 1981; Moschis & Moore, 1981).

The distinction between primary motives and secondary motives becomes important here. Primary motives (e.g., hunger) are based on an organism's physiochemical processes, and are considered to be largely unlearned. On the other hand, secondary motives (e.g., greed) are generally thought to be acquired through classical conditioning, in much the same way that emotional responses were seen to be classically conditioned in chapter 6. In the discussion that follows, consider the similarity between the mechanisms believed to determine the acquisition of motivations and the mechanisms believed to determine the acquisition of emotional responses (it is interesting to note that the words "emotion" and "motivation" both stem from the Latin "movere," "to move").

Interest Box

Soft Suds

Taking the kick out of beer

Like most beer ads, the TV commercial for Texas Select foams over with machismo. The blurb, aired in Houston and Dallas, portrays a group of poker-playing buddies whooping it up while holding aloft glasses filled with an amber beverage. Then comes the kick or, rather, the lack of one. Texas Select is virtually alcohol free. Claims the card-party host: "The guys couldn't tell the difference."

Texas Select is one of at least six new brews that look and taste much like regular beer but have little or no intoxicating effect. With these lighter-than-Lite beverages, U.S. brewers are making their boldest move since the introduction of low-calorie beer in the mid-1970s. Brewers hope the new brands will put fizz back into sales, which have gone flat following strong growth in the 1970s.

Next week the biggest U.S. brewer, Anheuser-Busch, will roll out a brand called L.A., for light alcohol, in ten test markets from California to Rhode Island. Detroit-based Stroh, the third-largest

The new brands look and taste much like regular brew but have little or no intoxicating effect

brewer, this week will announce a low-alcohol brand called Schaefer L.A. The customers thirstiest for the new brands are expected to be males over 25 who have begun to worry about their health. Industry watchers say Anheuser-Busch will spend up to $30 million on its ad campaign featuring such modern life-style exemplars as a businessman bicycling to his job and a fitness buff working out in a health spa.

Last August Cincinnati's Hudepohl launched reduced-alcohol Pace beer partly as an answer to Ohio's strict drunk-driving laws. A six-pack of Pace, with less than 2% alcohol, produces the effect of only three cans of regular beer, which

contains about 4%. In beer-loving Australia, where lawmakers cracked down on drunk driving in 1976, low-alcohol brew has captured 10% of the market.

The new beverages generally mimic all the trappings of premium beer, including the price tag of $3 or more per six-pack. Moussy, a nonalcoholic Swiss-made product, is bottled like a prestige import beer, complete with foil wrapper. White Rock Products, which distributes Moussy (pronounced *moose*-y) in the U.S., expects to sell 650,000 cases this year. The company is now running a special advertising campaign in the Midwest aimed at churchgoers who have given up alcohol for Lent. ∎

(*Time*, 1984, April 2, p. 76. Copyright © Time Inc., reprinted by permission.)

To illustrate the acquisition of a secondary motive, consider a study by Cowles (1937). In Cowles' study, chimpanzees performed a task in order to obtain plastic poker chips (conditioned stimulus), that could be exchanged in a "chimp-o-mat" for raisins (unconditioned stimulus), that in turn produced a positive affective response (initially unconditioned response, eventually conditioned response). As per the classical conditioning of emotional responses described in chapter 6, eventually the poker chips came to be valued in and of themselves. Reportedly, the chimpanzees began greedily hoarding their chips, evidencing the value that the chips had acquired for the chimpanzees.

These types of acquired associations can sometimes be very long-lived. To explain this phenomenon, Allport (1937, 1961) developed the concept of *functional autonomy*. This refers to the fact that an object or event that was initially instrumental to some other end acquires a value that outlives its instrumentality. Thus, the chimpanzees began with a primary motive (hunger) that could be satisfied by obtaining a specific goal (raisins). The chimpanzees ended with an additional, secondary motive (greed) that could be satisfied by obtaining a different specific goal (poker chips). Note that this suggests an additional dimension to the discussion of classically conditioned emotional responses presented in chapter 6. That is, consider the effects of repeated association of the fabric softener and the loving family scene. Not only might the housewife-consumer come to feel positive affect toward the product; she may also eventually develop a motive (i.e., a state of tension that arouses, maintains, and directs behavior) that can only be satisfied by obtaining the (previously value-less) laundry product.

One reasonable illustration of the creation of motives is found in the influence of television programming and commercials on consumers' dietary habits. Kaufman (1980) analyzed the content of prime-time television programs and commercial advertisements. Close to 80% of all references made to food were to non-nutritious foodstuffs. Television characters rarely ate a balanced meal; they snacked, ate "on the go," and used food to satisfy social and emotional needs (rather than hunger). These patterns of food choice and eating behavior are usually associated in real life with obesity (Nisbett & Gurwitz, 1970; Schachter & Rodin, 1974). In order to determine if these patterns of food choice and eating behavior were producing on television the consequences that they produce in reality, Kaufman analyzed the body types of television characters. What Kaufman found was intriguing: 38% of the television characters were classified as thin, 42% were classified as average, 15% were classified as overweight, and only 5% were classified as obese. Thus, television seems to be presenting to viewers a world-view where eating in a way that is guaranteed to make one fat is associated with staying slim and trim.

The situation depicted in prime-time television by Kaufman's research sets the stage for the development of a motivation that can only be satisfied (at least temporarily), by obtaining foods with low nutritional value. One approach to the creation of a motive for foods with low nutritional value is based upon the classical conditioning of vicarious emotional responses. Consider what happens when food of low nutritional value (conditioned stimulus) is repeatedly paired with the television character's exposure to "the good life" (i.e., average or thin body types, being witty, sophisticated, successful, etc.) (unconditioned stimulus), that naturally elicits a vicarious positive emotional response (initially uncondi-tioned response, eventually conditioned response). Eventually, food of low nutri-tional value may come to evoke a pleasant emotional response all by itself. Through functional autonomy, this association may develop into an acquired secondary motive that can only be satisfied by obtaining junk food.

Another approach to the creation of a motive is based on the vicarious classical conditioning of emotional responses. Consider what happens when the consumer observes the television character being classically conditioned in the following way: food of low nutritional value (conditioned stimulus) is repeatedly associated for the television character with the satisfaction of the television character's social and emotional needs (i.e., with warm and friendly social contexts) (unconditioned stimulus) that results in a positive affective response (initially unconditioned response, eventually conditioned response). Eventually, the television character will become conditioned to have a positive emotional response to junk food, and the observing consumer might vicariously acquire this classically conditioned emotional response. Again, through functional autonomy, this association may develop into an acquired secondary motive that can only be satisfied by obtaining junk food.

This foregoing extension of basic conditioning principles is intriguing, espe-cially in light of evidence regarding the unhealthy dietary habits of American consumers (e.g., Sorenson, Wyse, Wittwer, & Hansan, 1976). Consistent with this is Gorn and Goldberg's (1982) demonstration that snack food choices (candy vs. fruit) could be easily influenced. During a 2-week summer camp, children who watched candy commercials were more likely to choose candy snacks than children who watched fruit commercials. Cravings for junk food may, in part, be a reflection of this type of creation of motives. A similar process is illustrated in the observation that the American coffee break is largely attributed to an advertising campaign launched by the Joint Coffee Trade Publicity Committee in the early 1920s (see Fig. 7.3).

A second plausible illustration of the development of motives among consum-ers involves what has come to be called the "Pain–Pill–Pleasure" model (Shimp & Dyer, 1979). The case can be made that a great deal of advertising promotes the notion that any physical or emotional discomfort can be mitigated by taking the appropriate pill. For example, many commercial advertisements for over-the-counter (OTC) drugs begin with the portrayal of a character who is suffering from cold symptoms and/or emotional dysfunction. Sometime in the middle of the commercial, the character takes the pill. At then end of the 60-second commercial, the cold symptoms have abated, and the emotional dysfunctions have been alleviated. This type of advertisement might be expected to lead to an increase in OTC drug consumption, perhaps as well as an increase in illicit/illegal drug consumption. At this point, the reader can see how the OTC drug advertisement might influence consumers in the same way as the fabric softener advertisements and the junk food advertisements, discussed previously.

There has been very little research on the Pain–Pill–Pleasure model, and the research that has been conducted has produced mixed results. For example, some studies have found a relationship between television advertising exposure and illicit drug use (e.g., Brodlie, 1972), whereas other studies have found no such

When the clock swings 'round to four—

COFFEE

Right at the peak of the day's duties it pays to pause for a chummy, cheery cup of Coffee.

It is a stimulus to effort in the office or in the home—it coaxes cheerful spirits and clear-thinking for the rest of the day.

As regularly as the clock swings 'round to four, drink an appetizing, reviving cup of Coffee. Not very far from wherever you are, there is a coffee house, soda fountain, restaurant or hotel which makes a feature of Afternoon Coffee.

This advertisement is part of an educational campaign conducted by the leading COFFEE merchants of the United States in cooperation with the planters of the State of Sao Paulo, Brazil, which produces more than half of all the COFFEE used in the United States of America.

This is the sign of The Coffee Club. Look for it in dealers' windows. It will help you find good coffee.

JOINT COFFEE TRADE PUBLICITY COMMITTEE, 74 Wall Street, New York

COFFEE — -the universal drink

This advertisement will appear during the week ending October 8th.

FIG. 7.3 Advertisement that was part of the campaign launched by the Joint Coffee Trade Publicity Committee in the early 1920s.

relationship (e.g., Atkin, 1978b). Nonetheless, within certain limits, the Pain–Pill–Pleasure model might characterize the acquisition of a secondary motivation for drug use, with potentially dire social consequences.

At this point, we have come full circle. That is, once a motivation has been created and becomes functionally autonomous of the situation that generated it, there is a new motivation to which the sponsor can appeal. Clearly, this is not a simple "(1) create a motive, (2) appeal to that motive" sequence of events. It would seem more likely that the media are simultaneously a factor contributing to the development of secondary motives, and a vehicle for appealing to existing motives.

EFFECTS OF THE OTHER INTERNAL PROCESSES ON MOTIVATION

Consider the potential effects of the other internal processes on motivation. Similar to the effect of perception on the other internal processes, perception may be affecting motivation, although the extent of this effect is often unclear. Recall Wilson's (1979) demonstration of the acquisition of emotional responses without conscious awareness. Over time, through the development of functional autonomy, secondary motives may be acquired without conscious awareness. Certainly, awareness can affect desire, but apparently awareness is not a prerequisite for desire.

One view of the effect of cognition on motivation that has received a great deal of attention is *cognitive dissonance theory*. Festinger (1957) formulated cognitive dissonance theory in terms of the motivating effect of contradictory relations between cognitive elements. Dissonance refers to an unpleasant state of tension that results from inconsistency between cognitive elements. Presumably, the individual is motivated to reduce this dissonance by resolving the inconsistency. This might be accomplished by: decreasing the importance of the cognitions; adding new cognitions that alter the relationship between existing cognitions; modifying behavior linked with one of the dissonant cognitive elements; distorting one or both of the cognitive elements; and so on.

The most common applications of dissonance concepts to consumer behavior have involved the phenomenon called *post-decisional dissonance*. Any nontrivial decision is supposed to produce dissonance, because one has automatically given up the positive aspects of the rejected alternative and accepted all of the negative aspects of the selected alternative. This dissonance might be reduced by changing one's evaluations of the alternatives after the decision has been made. That is, by derogating the rejected alternative, and by praising the selected alternative, the two alternatives will become spread apart in favor of the selected alternative, and there will be no more inconsistency. For example, Brehm (1956) had females rate eight gifts in terms of attractiveness. These females then chose one gift from two alternatives that were either rated similarly to begin with (high dissonance), or dissimilarly to begin with (low dissonance). After having made their choice, the subjects were asked to evaluate the gifts once again. Brehm found that the value of the chosen alternative was enhanced, and the value of the rejected alternative was diminished. Moreover, the effect was exaggerated in the case of highly similar alternatives (high dissonance). This type of result has been replicated in the evaluation of swim suits (Mittelstaedt, 1969), the estimation of the chance of race horses winning (Knox & Inkster, 1968), and the evaluation of college courses scheduled during preregistration (Rosenfeld, Giacalone, & Tedeschi, 1981), to name just a few examples.

In spite of the high replicability of this type of effect, we should be cautious of over-applying this social psychological theory to the context of consumer behavior. Many researchers in this area are becoming dissatisfied with cognitive dissonance as the sole explanation for post-decisional dissonance phenomena. The point is not whether the post-decisional dissonance type of derogation/enhancement occurs; it seems readily apparent that these effects do occur. The question, however, is whether cognitive dissonance is the underlying mechanism for such effects. Tedeschi, Schlenker, and Bonoma (1971) have proposed that subjects in this type of research are engaged in efforts to "manage the impressions" that the experimenter may be forming about them. This type of impression management is important, because the impressions that others form about us will determine such things as how they treat us, the rewards they deliver to us, and the opportunities they provide for us in the future. Consider the application of this line of reasoning to the post-decisional dissonance effect. By enhancing the reported value of the chosen alternative, and by diminishing the reported value of the rejected alternative, the consumer can create the impression that he is rational and has sound judgement. The alternative would be to continue to report that the two alternatives were highly similar, suggesting that the consumer really had little or no good reason for making the decision that was made.

Recent research is coming to support this impression management reinterpretation of cognitive dissonance effects (e.g., Goethals, Reckman, & Rothman, 1973; Rosenfeld, Giacalone, & Tedeschi, 1983). Although this issue is far from resolved, it seems to suggest that the effect of cognition on motivation is a complex one.

The impact of learning on motivation was described previously. The acquisition of secondary motives through classical conditioning provides an illustration of this type of effect.

As noted earlier, it may be more useful to consider the interface between motivation and emotion as a matter of emphasis as much as a matter of substantive difference. The typical example of the acquisition of emotional responses is often interpretable as a typical example of the acquisition of a secondary motive, and vice versa. Similarly, the typical example of a fear appeal is often interpretable as a typical example of an appeal to some existing motive, and vice versa.

CONCLUSION: A TRANSITION

Almost everything that has been described up to this point in the text has been concerned with the internal processes. How do we become aware of (perception), develop beliefs about (cognition), remember (memory), acquire associations regarding (learning), develop feelings toward (emotion), and acquire desires for (motivation) the product. We have been able to consider each of these internal processes separately in turn. Nonetheless, it becomes increasingly apparent that the internal processes influence one another, occur simultaneously, and have multiple and diverse determinants.

At this point we have a clear, albeit complicated, picture of what happens inside the consumer in response to the stimulus situation. The next question is: What does the consumer do as a result of all of these interrelated and simultaneous internal responses? An understanding of the transition from the consumers' internal responses to the consumers' overt behavior is the goal of chapter 8.

8 | Intention and Behavior

Intention can be defined as a plan to perform some specific behavior. *Behavior,* simply, refers to an act or a response. Within the context of consumer behavior, intention refers to the plan to acquire or use the product, and behavior refers to the actual acquisition or use of the product. In this chapter, we begin our consideration of intention and behavior by examining the relationships between the internal processes, intention and behavior. Next, we examine Fishbein and Ajzen's Theory of Reasoned Action, and consider its applications to the intentions and behaviors of consumers. At the end of this chapter, we consider the practice of psychographics, or the use of individual differences in the internal processes to predict intentions and behavior. Bear in mind that our task in this chapter is to understand how consumers develop plans to use a product, and how such plans lead to the actual use of the product.

INTENTION AND BEHAVIOR AS CONSEQUENTS
OF THE INTERNAL PROCESSES

Some of the research already cited in this book has used intention as the dependent variable in experimental procedures manipulating some aspect of the stimulus situation. For example, Kanungo and Johar (1975; cited under Attribution Theory in chapter 4) found that qualified, varied advertisements resulted in higher believability, although they also resulted in equivalent or lower intention to buy.

Intention has acquired value in consumer psychology almost exclusively in terms of its status as an intervening variable. That is, intention is presumed to provide a link between the internal processes' reaction to the stimulus situation, and the actual acquisition or use of the product. Thus, intention has been treated as a dependent variable (i.e., a consequent of the internal processes), as well as an independent variable (i.e., an antecedent of behavior). Regarding the consideration of intention as a consequent of the internal processes, it is generally assumed that favorable results of the internal processes (i.e., awareness of the product, favorable beliefs about the product, remembering the product and its attributes, acquiring strong associations with the product and with the use of the product, positive feelings toward the product, and/or desire for the product) will result in intentions to buy the product.

Some of the research previously mentioned has focused on behavior as the dependent variable in experimental procedures manipulating some aspect of the stimulus situation. For example, Russo, Krieser, and Miyashita (1975; cited under Price in chapter 3) observed the purchase of cheaper brands as a result of new list-type displays of unit price information.

Regarding the effects of the internal processes, it is generally assumed that favorable results of the internal processes will lead to the actual acquisition or use of the product. On the whole, this assumption seems to be consistent with the evidence. For example, Reibstein, Lovelock, and Dobson (1980) examined the relationships between beliefs (cognition), affect (emotion), and use (behavior) regarding public transportation services. It was observed that beliefs regarding the convenience and availability of bus service were associated with positive affect regarding bus service, that in turn was associated with actual use of the bus service. Stang (1977) examined the influence of recall of Presidents of the United States (memory), evaluations of the Presidents (cognition), and sales of Presidential decanters (behavior). It was reported that sales were moderately related to evaluations, and highly related to recall.

The difficulties with this type of research are twofold. First, very often the intervening variable of intention is not included in the conceptualization or the measurement procedures of this research. Regardless of whether the researcher believes that the consumers' behavior is guided by intentions or not, intention has received sufficient treatment in the past to warrant its examination in studies examining the relationships between the internal processes and behavior. Second, and perhaps more telling, there is seldom a comprehensive approach taken to the vast interrelationships between the various internal processes, intentions, and behavior. That is, a particular study may indicate the relation between recall and sales, the relation between affect and sales, or the relation between the result of one other internal process and sales. However, without similar indications of the relations between evaluation and sales, and awareness and sales, and desire and sales, we fail to get a complete picture of the events leading up to the purchase of the product. We return to this issue shortly.

BEHAVIOR AS A CONSEQUENT OF INTENTION

The relation between intention and behavior is similar to the relation between attitudes and behavior (cf. Fishbein & Ajzen, 1972, for discussion). As a result of this similarity, some light may be shed upon the relationship between intention and behavior by examining the research on the relation between attitudes and behavior. For example, it has been found that increasing the specificity of the attitude question increases the accuracy of attitudes as predictors of behavior.

(e.g., Heberlein & Black, 1976). Thus, increased predictive accuracy of stated intentions might be achieved by increasing the specificity of the intention measurement. For example, someone who states, "I will try a new brand of butter beans in the future" may be less likely to perform that behavior than someone who states, "I will buy a can of new brand X1 butter beans tomorrow at Miller's supermarket."

However, the intention–behavior issue is larger than the attitude–behavior issue. Attitudes are typically conceived as being comprised of cognitive, affective, and conative components (i.e., cognition, emotion, and motivation). Intentions, on the other hand, are conceived as being a result of such components, plus perception, plus learning, plus their interactions. Thus, it is informative but not sufficient to make reference to the research examining the attitude–behavior relationship.

What is the evidence regarding the relationship between intention and behavior? Generally, intention seems to predict behavior fairly accurately, although the relationship is by no means a perfect one. Banks (1950) and Katona (1960) both observed that purchase rates were about 60% for consumers reporting an intention to purchase, and about 30% for consumers reporting an intention to not purchase. More recently, Taylor, Houlahan, and Gabrael (1975) observed that 35% of those consumers indicating an intention to buy a new product actually did buy the new product, and that 0% of those consumers indicating no intention to buy a new product actually did buy the new product. Morrison (1979) has proposed a general framework for analyzing purchase intention data. The consumers' stated intentions are transformed into estimated purchase probabilities. Statistically sophisticated approaches like Morrison's may provide viable means of predicting behavior from intentions.

AN INTEGRATION: THE THEORY OF REASONED ACTION

Fishbein and Ajzen (1975; Ajzen & Fishbein, 1980) have provided a very elegant integration of the relationships between attitudes, intentions, and behaviors. Fishbein and Ajzen's *Theory of Reasoned Action* is presented in Fig. 8.1. According to this theory, behavior results from intention, and intention results from two independent influences: overall evaluation of brand b, and subjective norms. According to Fishbein's Multiattribute Model (discussed in chapter 4), the overall evaluation of brand b is defined as a weighted sum of the beliefs about a particular brand (where each belief is weighted by the strength or importance of the beliefs). Subjective norms are defined as the weighted sum of normative beliefs about a particular brand (where each normative belief is weighted by the individual's motivation to comply with important others' expectations regarding that brand).

We should recognize a number of implications of this theory. First, the attitudinal elements (A_b) are assumed to be independent of the normative elements (SN_b). Second, the attitudinal effects on behavior and the normative effects on behavior are assumed to be indirect. That is, attitudes and norms influence

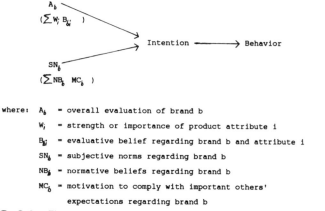

where:
A_b = overall evaluation of brand b

W_i = strength or importance of product attribute i

B_{bi} = evaluative belief regarding brand b and attribute i

SN_b = subjective norms regarding brand b

NB_b = normative beliefs regarding brand b

MC_b = motivation to comply with important others' expectations regarding brand b

FIG. 8.1 Fishbein and Ajzen's (1975, 1980) theory of reasoned action.

behavior exclusively through their effects on behavioral intentions. Finally, the normative beliefs component is assumed to be a simple, one-dimensional construct.

These assumptions have not been accepted uncritically. The first assumption of the independence of attitudinal and normative elements is inconsistent with research from other contexts. For example, normative information has been demonstrated to influence attitudes in social psychological research on conformity (Asch, 1955; Mullen, 1983; Nemeth, 1985). Conversely, individual attitudes influence the acceptance and the use of normative influence (Mullen et al., 1985; Ross, Greene, & House, 1977). The second assumption of exclusively indirect effects of attitudes and norms on behavior has been confirmed in some studies (e.g., Bagozzi, 1981), but disconfirmed in others (e.g., Bentler & Speckart, 1981). The third assumption of the one-dimensionality of normative beliefs has been criticized by researchers who have demonstrated the existence of independent, distinct sources of normative influence (e.g., Ryan & Bonfield, 1980; Warshaw, 1980).

However, despite these criticisms, the evidence has generally been supportive of this integrative approach to consumer behavior. The theory of reasoned action has been successfully applied to such diverse phenomena as purchase of clothing items (Miniard & Cohen, 1981), dating behavior (Bentler & Speckart, 1981), and coupon usage (Shimp & Kavas, 1984). Intentions to use the product generally result from positive overall evaluation of the product in conjunction with subjective norms supporting the use of the product; in turn, actual use of the product generally results from the stated intention to use the product. Note that this theory of reasoned action includes many of the elements of our General Model of Consumer Behavior, originally present in Fig. 1.1. Correspondences can be drawn between this theory's A_b and the General Model's cognition, between MC_b and motivation, and between NB_b and the social context. Such correspondences should not be surprising, because the General Model of Fig. 1.1 was developed after this important work, with an eye toward incorporating the viable aspects of Fishbein and Ajzen's Theory of Reasoned Action.

PSYCHOGRAPHICS

Psychographics is defined as quantitative research intended to differentiate and aggregate consumers in terms of psychological dimensions. The term *psychographics* is attributed to marketing researcher Emanuel Demby (1974). Psychographics is often contrasted with market segmentation, or demographics, where consumers are differentiated and aggregated in terms of sociological, socioeconomic variables (cf. Engel, Fiorillo, & Cayley, 1982). One can think of psychographic research with regard to its use of the various internal processes as psychological dimensions along which consumers can be differentiated and segmented.

The practical implication of this approach is that an organization may be able to construct and deliver specific appeals that would be most effective for particular subgroups of consumers. The validity and usefulness of psychographic techniques has received critical evaluation (e.g., Wells, 1975), and this is a relatively active area of ongoing research. We now consider some examples of the psychographic use of each of the internal processes.

Becherer and Richard (1978) developed a psychographic approach to perception using the dimension of self-monitoring (Snyder, 1979). High self-monitors are sensitive to self-presentation concerns, and they attend to and perceive social cues; low self-monitors are less sensitive to self-presentation concerns, and they attend to and perceive internal standards. Although self-monitoring might be viewed as basically an interpersonal style, it also identifies distinct differences in perceptual style. Becherer and Richard reasoned that low self-monitors would be more likely to follow their own brand preferences, whereas high self-monitors would be more likely to be influenced by situational variables. These researchers found evidence to support this reasoning, indicating that these particular perceptual styles may determine whether or not the consumer will attend to and perceive information about the appropriateness of the product.

In another psychographic approach to the internal process of perception, Kelman and Cohler (1959) distinguished between two perceptual styles, *Sharpeners* and *Levelers*. Sharpeners are prone to accentuate differences between stimuli, whereas Levelers are prone to minimize differences between stimuli. Kelman and Cohler found that Sharpeners actively seek out new information, and tend to notice differences between messages and product characteristics. Alternatively, Levelers were found to seek a greater degree of perceptual simplicity, and they avoid ambiguous and complex information. Similar to Becherer and Richard's (1978) research, this suggests that consumers may differ in the extent to which they attend to and perceive product information.

One example of the psychographic approach to cognition was anticipated in chapter 3. Johnson (1971) was previously cited as applying market space concepts to the Chicago beer market. In the context of this type of application of market space concepts, recall that different subgroups of consumers might have different ideal products. The identification of these differences in the structure of beliefs represents a clear illustration of the psychographic approach to cognitions, the practical implications of which were discussed in chapter 3.

Vinson and Scott (1977) provided an example of a psychographic approach to learning. These researchers reasoned that importance of product attributes and overall preference for product type are values that are learned socially and culturally. Therefore, one would expect consumers exposed to different social and cultural learning histories to acquire different learned values. Vinson and Scott compared students from a liberal west-coast university with students from a conservative southern university, and found that the two groups differed dramatically in terms of their acquired values regarding automobiles. For example, the liberal west-coast students thought that pollution emission, workmanship, and engineering were important product attributes, and preferred compact cars. Alternatively, the conservative southern students thought that smooth ride, size, and prestige were important product attributes, and preferred standard-size cars. Note that this particular study is also relevant to cognition, motivation, and cultural context.

Emotion is the internal process that has probably received the least attention from the psychographic point of view. One intriguing possibility would be to distinguish and aggregate subgroups of consumers defined in terms of the primary determinant of their emotional experience. Research suggests that some people's emotional experiences may be primarily determined by external, situational cues, whereas other people's emotional experiences may be primarily determined by internal, self-produced cues (e.g., Duncan & Laird, 1980). This may set the stage for a psychographic approach to emotion. We discuss this possibility further in chapter 9.

Motivation is the internal process that has probably received the most attention from the psychographic point of view. For example, Grubb and Hupp (1968) observed that owners of Volkswagen Beetles and Pontiac GTOs reported differences in self-descriptions that are consistent with motivational stereotypes about automobile preferences. For example, the Volkswagen drivers tended to describe themselves as thrifty, whereas the GTO drivers tended to describe themselves as adventurous. Similarly, Mittelstaedt, Grossbart, Curtis, and Devere (1976) compared high sensation seekers (people with the need to seek out excitement and stimulation) with low sensation seekers (people with the need to avoid excitement and stimulation). It was found that high sensation seekers tended to try more new products, and to reject fewer new products without trial, relative to low sensation seekers. An alternative illustration of the psychographic approach to motivation was found in Ackoff and Emshoff's (1975) typology of motivations for the consumption of alcoholic beverages (cited in chapter 7). Recall that these researchers observed that an appeal made to a specific motive was more effective for the subgroup of consumers characterized as being directed by that specific motive.

CONCLUSION: ACTIONS SPEAK LOUDER THAN WORDS

In so many ways, consumer behavior is really the point of this book. On every page, we are trying to understand why consumers will or will not use a particular product, good, or service. Questionnaire responses are often useful and informative, but the action taken by the consumer is usually the "bottom line." Therefore, the measurement of consumer behavior comprises a crucial step in the enterprise of consumer psychology.

Actual sales figures often are used as an index of consumer behavior. For example, Kotzan and Evanson (1969) observed fluctuations in sales, derived from store inventory records, that varied as a function of the amount of shelf spacing devoted to the product. Similarly, Starch (1961) observed fluctuations in sales that varied as a function of the number of pages of advertising found per year in a given magazine. Blattberg (1980) has described the development of computer scan purchase diaries. This refers to an automatic recording of an individual's buying behavior as the UPC symbols are processed by a computerized check-out register. The consumer presents a coded card at the check-out, and the purchased goods are recorded in the individual's personal, automated diary. These computer scan purchase diaries keep a precise and completely detailed listing of the products and brands purchased by a given consumer on a daily basis.

In conjunction with the development of this high-tech measurement of consumer behavior, another high-tech device has come on the scene. Scanner cable television channels refer to the delivery of commercials to consumers on a house-by-house basis, using otherwise unused channels on a cable television system. Issac Asimov (1980) speculated that by the year 2000, 20% of all American households would have a specific television channel individually assigned to them, just as most households today have individual telephone numbers.

These technological innovations set the stage for the tailoring and presentation of commercial messages to the most particular subgroups of consumers. For example, sometime in the not-too-distant future, both you and your next door neighbor will be watching the Movie of the Week in the comfort of your own homes. Computer scan purchase diaries, purchased from the local supermarket by any large company, indicate that you are a regular consumer of Loca-cola, whereas your neighbor is a regular consumer of milk. Flurple Soft Drink Company beams a scanner cable commercial to your house during the first commercial break that presents Flurple in association with the fun and excitement typically associated with cola beverages. However, at the same time, your neighbor is watching a commercial that extols the sugar-free, caffeine-free, cholesterol-free, and "natural" ingredients in Flurple.

Such applications have the ring of a distant, future Orwellian 1984. However, like the actual year 1984, these applications have already arrived. Adtel Marketing Services and Information Resources, Inc., both of Chicago, have implemented preliminary versions of these high-tech behavior measurement and advertisement targeting in Pittsfield, Massachusetts; Marion, Indiana; Eau Claire, Wisconsin; Midland, Texas; Portland, Maine; Evansville, Indiana; and Orlando, Florida (Poindexter, 1983; see also interest box, opposite).

Although this technology is still in development, these preliminary applications raise a number of fascinating practical and ethical questions. How many different versions of a commercial for a given brand can be sent out across a community during one 60-second commercial break? How can we track the effectiveness of this highly refined targeting procedure? Are the ethical considerations for this highly refined targeting procedure any different from those involved in the nation-

Interest Box

Another high-tech innovation that has already arrived is the VideoCart (Johnston, 1988). The VideoCart (developed by Information Resources, Inc.) is a shopping cart with a liquid crystal display mounted on its handle. The displays will show grocery ads along with other useful information about the store and the world at large. Ads created can be transmitted nationally by satellite to each store, which can then use its own computer to transmit the information to each VideoCart. The technology that would allow the VideoCart to display the ads appropriate for different locations in the store is emerging. Also foreseeable is the focusing of the grocery cart ads to the particular likes of the shopper as has been predicted earlier for television ads. Regardless, the VideoCart enables advertisers to bombard the consumer at a point very close to the actual behavior part of the process.

wide presentation of a single version of a commercial for a given brand? Who should, or should not, be allowed access to these computer scan purchase diaries? The old saying has it that one picture is worth a thousand words. However, if the pictures that come flickering across the television screen do have any significant effects on our actions, then the people who implement these new technologies will be banking on the assumption that actions speak louder than words.

9 | Behavioral Feedback and Product Life Cycle

The view of consumer behavior presented up to this point is one of complex interactions. However, this view of consumer behavior has also been one of unidirectional and atemporal or timeless influence. This view has been unidirectional in the sense that the sequence of events that we have been considering progresses from stimulus situation to internal processes to intention to behavior. Also, this view has been atemporal or timeless in the sense that this sequence of events progresses with no reference to variations that might occur depending on the length of time that the product has been around. However, human behavior is more dynamic than this unidirectional, atemporal perspective suggests. Not only is behavior influenced by the internal processes; the internal processes are also influenced by behavior. Similarly, consumers may engage in these processes one way for new products (e.g., videodiscs), and another way for established products (e.g., phonograph records).

The emphasis of this chapter is upon these dynamic elements of consumer behavior. Here we examine the effects that behavior may have on the internal processes. When behavior influences the internal processes that produced the behavior, we refer to this as behavioral feedback. We also examine variations that may occur in the general model of consumer behavior depending on how long the product has been around. The concept of the product life cycle is used to understand these changes. Bear in mind that our task in this chapter is to understand how the effects of behavioral feedback and the product life cycle influence the various principles and mechanisms we have reviewed up to this point in our discussions of consumer behavior.

FEEDBACK: BEHAVIOR AS AN ANTECEDENT OF THE INTERNAL PROCESSES

The effects that behavior may have on perception often bear considerable overlap to the effects that behavior may have on cognition and memory. If consumers use a product, they will have greater opportunity to be exposed to the product

114

and information about the product, possibly resulting in increased awareness of the product (perception), and increased retention of information about the product (cognition and memory).

For example, Howard (1977) described an interesting examination of the effects of redeemable coupons. A sample of consumers who had received the redeemable coupon were asked whether they had received the coupon, and whether they had used the product. Awareness of the coupon (perception), and recall of the receipt of the coupon (cognition and memory) were apparently affected by the behavior of the consumers toward the product. For example, only 10% of those who did not try the product recalled having received the coupon; 45% of those who tried the product once but did not repeat the purchase recalled having received the coupon; and, 55% of those who tried the product and later repeated the purchase recalled having received the coupon. Thus, behavior may influence perception and memory insofar as the use of the product may provide the consumer with additional opportunities to be exposed to additional aspects of the product. These additional exposures to the product are likely to result in additional engagements of the processes of perception and cognition and memory.

In the discussion of behavior as an antecedent of cognition and persuasion, emotion, and motivation, we rely on a distinct theoretical perspective. This perspective is self-perception theory (Bem, 1965, 1972), and should be described here briefly. Self-perception theory can be thought of as a portion of the general set of propositions referred to as attribution theory (discussed in chapter 4). This particular application of attribution theory is based on two propositions. First, individuals come to know their own internal states (beliefs, feelings, desires) partially by inferring from observations of their own overt behavior, and/or the circumstances in which the behavior occurs. Second, to the extent that internal cues are weak, ambiguous, and uninterpretable, the individual is functionally in the same position as an outside observer who must rely on those external cues to infer internal states. Thus, a consumer may come to infer his or her beliefs, feelings, or desires regarding a product as a result of his or her behavior toward the product and/or the circumstances in which the behavior occurs. In this context, we now consider the effects that behavior can have on cognition, emotion, and motivation.

One effect that behavior may have on cognition involves the price–quality relationship. Recall that one of the explanations proposed in chapter 3 for the price–quality relationship is that the effort (money) expended to obtain the product leads to higher satisfaction. Two perspectives discussed previously can provide alternative justifications for this explanation. On the one hand, cognitive dissonance theory (Festinger, 1957) would interpret this type of effect as an example of *insufficient justification*. When an individual performs a neutral or negative behavior and receives a neutral or negative outcome, this is assumed to create dissonance that can only be reduced by enhancing the cognitive evaluation of the outcome. For example, if I spend a lot of money on a case of Loca-Cola, and then find out that it tastes awful, cognitive dissonance theory holds that I should experience discomfort that can only be reduced by enhancing my evaluation of Loca-Cola. The result is an improved evaluation of the product, produced by an effort to reduce cognitive dissonance.

On the other hand, impression management theory (Tedeschi, 1981; Tedeschi, Schlenker, & Bonoma, 1971) would interpret this effect as evidence for the simple assumption that people do not want to appear irrational or unwise. Therefore, when an individual performs a neutral or negative behavior and receives some neutral or negative outcome, the individual becomes concerned with how other people will evaluate this poor judgment. For example, if I spend a lot of money on a case of Loca-Cola, and I later find out that it tastes awful, I become concerned with how other people will evaluate this poor judgment, and so I describe the product in positive terms. The result is a positive public statement (although not necessarily an enhanced cognitive evaluation). In other words, cognitive dissonance theory would interpret the price–quality relationship as a reflection of an attempt to reduce dissonance, whereas impression management theory would interpret the price–quality relationship as a reflection of an attempt to avoid appearing foolish.

Self-perception theory provides a third possibility. According to self-perception theory, the consumer might not have a clear, apparent evaluation of the product just purchased, and so may have to infer the quality of the product from some observable behavior. The amount of money expended provides an easily observable behavior. For example, when asked to evaluate the quality of the brand of butter beans just purchased (which is indistinguishable in taste from five other brands), the consumer might infer from the high purchase price that the chosen brand really must taste pretty good. Note that this self-perception approach serves to integrate two of the proposed explanations for the price–quality relationship. That is, the expended effort (the purchase price paid) may simultaneously lead to satisfaction with the chosen alternative, and provide a concrete index of quality of the product.

Another example of the effect of behavior on cognitions can be found in a study by Dholakia and Sternthal (1977). These researchers presented to subjects a persuasive message that was from either a high credibility source or a low credibility source, and had subjects express their attitudes either before or after being asked to sign a petition in favor of the issue being proposed in the persuasive message. When attitudes were measured before behavior, the typical source credibility effect was observed, with the more credible source eliciting higher persuasion. However, when attitudes were measured after the request to sign the petition, the subject's own behavior of compliance/noncompliance appeared to serve as a cue for determining his or her attitudes. In some cases, this appeared to undermine the typical source credibility effect.

For example, consider the subject who complied to the request after hearing the message from a highly credible source. The configuration attribution principle of discounting seemed to occur for this type of subject. That is, there were two plausible causes for his or her having signed the petition: (a) (the plausible cause that is always present) he or she truly believed in the issue at hand; or, (b) he or she was swayed by the highly credible source. The presence of the second plausible cause makes the first one less likely, and these subjects expressed relatively weaker attitudes. On the other hand, consider the subjects who did not comply to the request after hearing the message from a highly credible source. The configuration attribution principle of augmentation seemed to occur for this type of subject. That is, the behavior of not complying to the request occurred in the face of an environmental constraint that should have led to compliance (i.e., the high credibility of the source of the persuasive message). This suggests that the subjects' attitudes regarding the issue at hand must be rather strongly opposed to the position advocated in the message, and these subjects expressed relatively strong, oppositional attitudes.

The results of these types of applications suggest that behavior can affect cognitions, as specified in terms of self-perception theory.

As mentioned in chapter 6, recent theoretical considerations of emotion propose that emotions are the result of arousal and cognitions relevant to that arousal (e.g., Leventhal, 1974; Schachter & Singer, 1962). As per self-perception theory, the individual may attempt to infer his or her emotional experience from observations regarding overt behavior and/or the situation in which the behavior occurs. On the one hand, research has indicated that reliance on situational cues can affect emotional experience (e.g., Cantor, Zillmann, & Bryant, 1975; Valins, 1966). For example, Cantor et al. (1975) led subjects to "misattribute" exercise-induced arousal to an erotic film, resulting in enhanced reports of sexual arousal as a result of the film. On the other hand, research has indicated that reliance on behavioral cues can also effect emotional experience (e.g., Laird, 1974; Leventhal, 1974). For example, Laird (1974) had subjects control and relax facial muscles so that they smiled or frowned (under the pretext that the experimenter was studying the effect of the activity of facial muscles under various perception conditions). The subjects who were surreptitiously led to smile reported more positive emotional experiences than the subjects led to frown.

Consider the following extension of this research to the emotional responses of consumers. Assume that one wishes the consumer to experience positive emotions in conjunction with exposure to the product, so that some form of association between the product and the positive emotion might develop. There are two ways in which this can occur. First, as we have seen repeatedly, the product might be presented in a context providing situational cues suggestive of positive emotional experiences (e.g., the loving family scene). Second, the product might be presented in a way that would elicit self-produced, behavioral cues from the consumer that would lead to an inference of a positive emotional experience. For example, consider the catchy little commercial theme songs that television viewers may find themselves humming during the day. These theme songs typically have two things in common: they have happy phrases, melodies, and tempos, and they mention the product name. One consequence of this is that, on his or her own time in addition to the time during commercial exposure, the consumer will provide self-produced behavioral cues that would lead to the conjunction of a positive emotional experience and the product name.

Alternatively, the consumer is sometimes induced to smile through product-irrelevant means. This may be one previously unconsidered way in which humor influences consumers. That is, the consumer may come to "misattribute" the positive emotional response from the joke to the product. The induction of a smile on the part of the consumer can be even more direct, as when a well-known comedian in a recent soft drink advertisement tells the consumers that they are smiling.

Some current research is beginning to examine individual differences in the types of cues typically used by the individual for inference of emotional experiences. For example, Duncan and Laird (1980) have observed that some people are more influenced by situational cues, whereas other people are more influenced by self-produced behavioral cues. This provides a unique perspective on the psychographic approach to emotions. That is, consumers who are more responsive to situational cues in inferring their emotional experiences may be more affected by the commercials employing a loving family scene, whereas consumers who are more responsive to behavioral cues may be more affected by the commercials that employ humor (and lead the consumer to smile in the presence of the product).

We have already considered one way in which behavior can influence motivation in our discussion of oversufficient justification and coupons (in the conclusion of chapter 5). When the consumer purchases a desired brand using a redeemable coupon, there are two plausible causes for this behavior: (a) (the plausible cause that is always present) the consumer truly desires this brand; and, (b) the consumer selected this brand because of the savings obtained by using the coupon. The attribution principle of discounting apparently leads to a decrease in desire for the given brand once the coupons are retracted.

Little evidence has accumulated regarding the direct effects of behavior on intentions. However, behavior is assumed to influence intentions indirectly, via behavior's influence on the internal processes (that in turn influence intention). For example, the Dholakia and Sternthal (1977) study cited earlier included a measure of "hypothetical support" in their measure of attitudes. This measure of support might have actually gauged some rudimentary form of intention. In light of their findings, it may be that plans to use a product may be influenced by the cognitive attribution principles, suggesting an indirect link from behavior to cognition to intention. The influence of behavior on intention is examined in more detail later. In chapter 12 (Sales Interactions), we consider some sales techniques that begin by eliciting some behavior from the consumer and end with the consumer's plan to purchase the product.

THE PRODUCT LIFE CYCLE

The general model of consumer behavior, initially presented in Fig. 1.1, has allowed us to summarize and integrate a great deal of theory and research regarding consumer behavior. However, one thing that the general model does not directly address is the possibility of variations in the model over time. For example, although the same general principles are likely to be involved, it would be reasonable to expect that consumers would behave somewhat differently regarding a relatively established product category (e.g., televisions) than they would regarding a relatively recent product category (e.g., home computers).

Howard (1977) has presented a rather elaborate theoretical perspective on consumer behavior. Although similar in many ways to other current approaches (the present general model of Fig. 1.1 included), Howard's orientation is unique in its explicit incorporation of the possibility of changes occurring over time. Our consideration of the psychology of consumer behavior has much to gain from an examination of Howard's point of view.

Howard described the concept of a product life cycle as a general tendency for a product category to grow slowly at first, then to rise rapidly, then to level off, and finally to begin to decline. This is equivalent to Robertson's (1970) discussion of the generalized cumulative diffusion pattern. A central theme of Howard's orientation is that consumers pass through three stages of learning how to buy, largely depending on where the product is in the product life cycle. This product life cycle, and the three stages of learning how to buy, are represented in Fig. 9.1. Note that the product life cycle might be characterized as product-specific and brand-generic. That is, the pattern depicted in Fig. 9.1 characterizes a trend within a particular product category that may eventually include dozens of particular brands.

The Three Stages of Learning How To Buy

The earliest stage of learning how to buy is called *extensive problem solving* (EPS). During this period, the consumer is confronted with an entirely new product category. Much information is required about this heretofore unknown object, and decisions are made relatively slowly. Never having seen a brand that is even similar, the consumer must construct a new market space.

The next stage of learning how to buy is called *limited problem solving* (LPS). During this period, the consumer is confronted with a new brand in a known product class. The criteria for evaluating brands have already been established. That is, the dimensions that are used to define the market space for this product category have already been identified. During this phase, the consumer does require information about the new brand's valuation on these criteria, or the

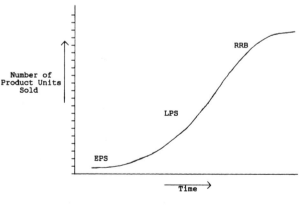

EPS = Extensive Problem Solving

LPS = Limited Problem Solving

RRB = Routinized Response Behavior

FIG. 9.1   Howard's (1977) product life cycle and the three stages of learning how to buy.

location of the new brand in the established market space. A moderate amount of information is required about this new brand and decisions are made in a moderate amount of time.

The final stage of learning how to buy is called *routinized response behavior* (RRB). During this period, the consumer is confronted with a choice between familiar brands. The criteria for evaluating brands, and the evaluation of available brands on these criteria, have already been determined (or, the market space for this product category has already been constructed, and all available brands are located within this market space). During this phase, the consumer requires little information and comes to a decision rather quickly. If prices are stable, if products are of consistent quality, and if suppliers consistently make the products available, then the consumers' behavior becomes habitual, automatic, and "brand loyal." Note that some authors (e.g., Assael, 1981; Jacoby, 1971) distinguish between brand loyalty and habitual buying (the former is argued to involve less rational deliberation than the latter).

These generalizations deserve some qualifications. As Howard noted, it is not assumed that all consumers will reach a given stage of learning how to buy at the same time. For example, Mittelstaedt et al.'s (1976) high sensation seekers and Robertson's (1970) innovators and early adopters probably enter and pass through this sequence earlier and faster than their respective counterparts. Nonetheless, this sequencing seems to be a compelling description of what happens with frequently purchased products.

This leads to another probable limitation on this perspective. As Howard recognized, important but infrequently purchased products ("consumer durables," such as cars or washing machines) probably do not fit this pattern for a number of reasons. Choice criteria, or market space dimensions, may be forgotten in the interval between these important purchases. Technological changes that occur between purchases may result in new product design and new product features, requiring the acquisition of new product information. Finally, the consumer's cognitions, emotions, motivations, and so on, may have changed in the interval between purchases; this might require the construction of a new market space that would be appropriate to these new beliefs, feelings, desires, and so on.

In spite of these limitations, it is valuable to consider the variations that occur over time in the basic principles of consumer behavior. This approach provides a context for understanding otherwise anomalous aspects of consumer behavior. For example, consider the extensive emphasis on cognitive processes found in current research (mentioned in chapter 3). Most of this research could be characterized from Howard's point of view as examinations of different aspects of LPS or EPS. This makes a great deal of sense when you realize that most empirical studies use new brand names or fictitious products in order to control for past experience (Scott, 1976). However, because most products eventually move out of EPS and LPS and into RRB, such cognitive, information-processing, problem-solving principles might be of limited applicability when talking about consumers' behavior regarding product categories that have been around for a while.

Almost by definition, EPS involves more perception, cognition, and learning, while RRB involves more memory, emotion, and motivation. Howard (1977) has interpreted and discussed a great deal of empirical research in these terms (for a similar treatment, cf. Newman & Werbel, 1973). This orientation allows our theoretical constructs to be as responsive to temporal, historical changes as is the behavior we are trying to explain.

CONCLUSION: FASHIONS

An intriguing extension of these ideas can be found in the consumer phenomenon variously referred to as fashions, fads, or crazes. One approach to this phenomenon is found in Sproles' (1974) theory of fashion behavior. Sproles has proposed that a fashion object: (a) is subject to change, obsolescence, and eventual replacement by newer objects; (b) has a value that is based on qualities other than functional utility; and, (c) is characterized by conspicuous newness and novelty. The list of examples of fashions, or fads, is virtually endless. In recent American culture, the hoola hoop, the miniskirt, the maxi-skirt, the Nehru jacket, the Frisbee, the polyester leisure suit, Rubik's cube, Pac Man, and Cabbage Patch Kids all exemplify outstanding (if quickly forgotten) fashions or fads (see also interest box on p. 122).

Feinberg, Mataro, and Burroughs (1983) have proposed that people use fashions, and in particular clothing fashions, to define and communicate their social identity to others. These researchers studied the social meanings of designer jeans and complete clothing outfits. It was found that people were able to make inferences about the personalities of individuals who wear specific types of clothing, and that these inferences may generally be accurate. In a sense, the way in which we participate in a fashion may be a means of impression management and self-presentation.

It may be that fashions represent an important exception to the EPS-LPS-RRB transitions described by Howard (1977). Fashions, almost by definition, do not last long enough for RRB (and possibly even LPS) to develop. This would suggest that consumers are likely to be in an EPS stage when considering the purchase of a fashion object. At the same time, the nonutilitarian, pleasure-orientation of many fashion products seems to indicate a heavy influence of emotion and motivation, rather than cognitive, rational choices. This would suggest that consumers are likely to be in a RRB stage when considering the purchase of a fashion object. Although fashion has been a topic of interest for a very long time (cf. Veblen, 1899), fashions, fads, and crazes are probably among the most intriguing and least understood phenomena of consumer behavior.

Interest Box

Hall of Shame

Gee, your hair smells like yogurt

Not every new product can be a knock-out, like light beer or TV dinners. Of the more than 5,000 items that annually appear on supermarket shelves, as many as 80% are commercial duds. Last week marketing specialists who attended the World New Products Conference in Toronto tried to learn some lessons from an exhibit of about 900 less-than-successful items.

Many failed efforts are simply misunderstood by consumers. When Heublein put its Wine and Dine dinners on sale in the mid-1970s (price: $1.35), buyers thought they were getting a macaroni dinner along with some wine to sip. The wine was actually a salty liquid intended for use in cooking the noodles. Trading on its success with infants, Gerber tried to market such grownup fare as beef burgundy and Mediterranean vegetables. The company's mistake was to put the food in containers that looked like baby-food jars. Gerber compounded its problem by labeling the product SINGLES. Later research showed that adults generally dislike being pegged as singles who eat alone, even if they do.

Other products have sunk for a variety of unexpected reasons. In 1980 Campbell received a tepid response to its new instant soup. The product was a single serving of highly concentrated soup to which the consumer added boiling water.

Not fast enough   **Baby-food image**

As it happened, this was scarcely more instant than Campbell's regular soup, to which a consumer simply adds water or milk and then boils. General Foods stirred a short-lived sensation with Pop Rocks, a carbonated candy that crackled and popped when eaten. The candy was so effervescent that the company had to disprove rumors that children who swallowed the granules too fast would get a stomachful of carbonation. But the candy was nothing that youngsters could sink their teeth into, and the fad eventually lost its fizz.

A classic mistake was a shampoo test-marketed by Clairol called A Touch of Yogurt. As Robert McMath, chairman of Marketing Intelligence Service, a New York consulting group, points out, "People weren't interested in putting yogurt on their hair, despite the fact that it may be good for it. Maybe they should have called it A Touch of Glamour, with Yogurt." ■

(*Time*, 1984 October 22, p. 78. Copyright © Time Inc., reprinted by permission.)

10 | The Social Context

The social context refers to the totality of social stimulation that is influencing the individual. This can include the real, imagined, or implied presence of others (e.g., Baron & Byrne, 1987). The social context may be composed of friends, family members, and sales personnel (although discussion of sales personnel is postponed until chapter 12). The social context may also be populated by more indirect, symbolic others, including prominent figures, cultural heroes, and cartoon characters.

The general model of consumer behavior presented in Fig. 1.1 portrays the stimulus situation, the internal processes, intention, behavior, and all of their interactions as being immersed in this social context. The effect of the social context on all of the previously discussed facets of consumer behavior is examined in this chapter. To begin, we consider the effects of the social context on perception, cognition, learning, emotion, motivation, intention, and behavior. Next, we consider a few individual differences that have relevance to social influences. Although these individual differences could just as easily have been considered in the treatment of psychographics in chapter 8, we pay close attention in this chapter to individual differences that seem to moderate the effects of the social context on the consumer. Finally, we consider the effects of two distinct sources of social influence: opinion leaders and family members. Bear in mind that our task in this chapter is to understand how the social context influences consumer behavior.

EFFECTS OF THE SOCIAL CONTEXT

Perception

The classic illustration of the effect of the social context on perception is found in the study by Sherif (1935). This study took advantage of a perceptual phenomenon known as the autokinetic effect, that is the tendency for a motionless point of light in an otherwise dark room to appear to move. Sherif had subjects report on the extent of this (apparent) movement either alone or in groups. Subjects performing this task in groups tended to converge toward some commonly perceived range of movement that was unique to each group. These group-generated perceptions would endure beyond the presence of the group. That is, subjects tested individually afterwards maintained these group-established perceptions. This indicated that the social context actually affected perception, and not just some superficial behavioral compliance.

Similarly, Foster, Pratt, and Schwortz (1955) had subjects report on the (apparent) differences in taste between identical samples of pineapple juice. Once the first group member identified a particular sample as sweeter, other subjects in the group tended to agree that it was the sweeter sample. Generalizing beyond these specific studies, this suggests that the social context may influence whether the consumer becomes aware of the product, or whether the consumer becomes aware of attributes of the product (attributes that may, or may not, in fact exist).

Cognition and Persuasion

The discussion of cognition and persuasion in chapter 4 revealed a number of ways in which the social context can influence the consumer's beliefs. For example, source credibility effects refer to a more or less one-directional social influence, from the source of the persuasive communication to the consumer. Another way in which the social context may affect beliefs can be found in George R. Goethals' (1976) attribution theory analysis of social influence phenomena. Goethals' work involves an integration of attribution theory with social comparison theory (e.g., Festinger, 1954; Suls & Miller, 1977), that describes how people seek to evaluate their abilities, thoughts, and so on by comparing them with those of other people. Goethals reasoned that people may seek different sorts of comparisons, depending on whether they wish to evaluate a belief or a value. A value is a preference or a liking/disliking for the object of concern. A belief is a potentially verifiable assertion about the true nature of the object of concern. To illustrate this distinction, suppose you are interested in determining whether your positive evaluation of the new film "Rocky XIII" is appropriate. If you try to determine whether your enjoyment of the film is appropriate, you are dealing with a value. If you try to determine whether your appreciation of the technical competence of the film is appropriate, you are dealing with a belief.

Suppose you are concerned with evaluating your values about the film. If you learn that Sally (who is similar to you in terms of interests and background) liked the film, you would be led to infer that your enjoyment of the film was reasonable and justified. If, on the other hand, you learn that Sally did not like the film, that might make you stop and reevaluate your liking for the film. In this instance, learning what Fred thinks of the new film would really be irrelevant if Fred is very dissimilar to you in interests and background.

On the other hand, suppose you were interested in evaluating your beliefs regarding the film. The attribution configuration principles of augmentation and discounting will determine the meaning of agreement or disagreement by a similar or dissimilar other regarding a belief. Suppose that Sally agrees with your belief that the film was technically competent. Discounting leads to the inference that she might agree because you are correct, or because her similarity to you makes her subject to the same biases that led you to your (possibly incorrect) belief. So, agreement from someone similar to you regarding a belief is at best ambiguous. However, suppose that Sally disagrees with your belief that the film was technically competent. Augmentation leads to the inference that her similarity to you should make her likely to agree with you, and therefore her disagreement is probably not a result of biases generated by your (and her) background and interests. So, disagreement from someone similar to you regarding a belief provides fairly persuasive evidence that you are wrong.

Suppose that Fred agrees with your belief that the film was technically competent. Augmentation leads to the inference that his dissimilarity to you should make him likely to disagree with you, and therefore his agreement is probably not a result of biases generated by your background and interests. So, agreement by someone dissimilar to you regarding belief provides fairly compelling evidence that you are right. However, suppose that Fred disagrees with your belief that the film was technically competent. Discounting leads to the inference that he might disagree because you are incorrect, or because his dissimilarity to you makes him subject to biases that lead to his (possibly incorrect) belief. So, disagreement from someone dissimilar to you regarding a belief is at best ambiguous.

Goethals has reported research that supports this line of reasoning (e.g., Goethals & Ebling, 1975; Goethals & Nelson, 1973; Reckman & Goethals, 1973). This work is consistent with recent research in consumer psychology, examining the influence of peer groups on consumers (e.g., Capella, Schnake, & Garner, 1981; Moschis, 1976; Witt, 1969; Witt & Bruce, 1970).

The implications of this type of effect of the social context for an understanding of consumer behavior are fairly straightforward. If a consumer is interested in evaluating his or her beliefs about a product, he or she may be likely to seek out both similar and dissimilar others for social comparison. If a consumer is interested in evaluating his or her values about a product, he or she may be likely to seek out similar others for social comparison. It is interesting to note that Moschis (1976) reported that females tend to select cosmetics in accord with those selected by friends. This may reflect a reliance on similar others to determine the "preferability" of a product (as compared to the objective quality of the product, that would best be evaluated by comparison with both similar and dissimilar others).

It is likely that consumers will be more concerned with evaluating beliefs, and comparing with both similar and dissimilar others, during EPS (Extensive Problem Solving, discussed in chapter 9), whereas consumers will be more concerned with evaluating values, and comparing to similar others, during LPS (Limited Problem Solving). For example, we might seek out the guidance of both our friends and the experts when we plan to purchase a home computer or a new-fangled widget, but we may simply compare with our friends when we consider buying sunglasses or a brand of cereal.

Learning

As outlined in previous chapters, the social context impacts on learning in at least two ways. First, observational learning represents a type of vicarious instrumental conditioning. Second, some variants of classical conditioning involved vicarious learning, such as vicarious classical conditioning of emotional responses and classical conditioning of vicarious emotional responses. In each case, the individual indirectly acquires an association by observing some model who is directly acquiring the association.

Of course, the consumer's learning might be affected by deliberate educational efforts. Such deliberate efforts might take the form of a family discussion of television commercials, or consideration of good buying practices in a home economics class. However, Ward's (1974) discussion of consumer socialization suggests that purposive, systematic training of consumer knowledge and skills was rare. The social context probably has its biggest influence on learning in the more subtle ways mentioned in this subsection.

Emotion and Motivation

Discussions of emotion and motivation in previous chapters have dealt with the effect of the social context in great detail. The classical conditioning of emotional responses and the acquisition of secondary motives often rely on some social event or interaction. These previously considered processes can be extended by noting that the type of social stimuli portrayed in conjunction with the product in a television commercial may also be associated with the product at the dinner table, in the locker room, or at the office. Just as one can acquire an association vicariously by watching the product in some social context on television, one may also acquire an association vicariously by watching a friend, relative, or co-worker enjoying the product (emotion) or satisfying a need for the product (motivation).

There is the possibility that being in the presence of others may in and of itself facilitate the acquisition of emotional responses and/or secondary motives. Some researchers (e.g., Cottrell, 1972; Geen & Bushman, 1987; Sanders & Baron, 1975; Zajonc, 1965) have suggested that the presence of other people can increase the individual's level of physiological arousal. As noted in our discussions of emotion in chapter 6, research reveals that classically conditioned responses are acquired more quickly, and extinguish more slowly, under conditions of arousal. This suggests that the classically conditioned emotional response and the acquired secondary motive may be more likely to be established if the individual repeatedly watches the appropriate commercial with a group of people, rather than alone. If this line of inference is accurate, it suggests that (all other things held constant) emotional-conditioning commercial advertisements would be most effective if presented when and where consumers congregate (e.g., in train stations; during prime-time family television shows).

Finally, we have already discussed another way in which the social context can affect emotional responses. In chapter 6 we considered Schachter and Singer's

(1962) two-factor theory of emotional experience. Recall that this two-factor theory holds that emotional experience is a result of interpreting physiological arousal in terms of cues that are consistent with some emotional experience. For example, physiological arousal in the presence of an attractive member of the opposite sex is interpreted as "love." Sometimes, other people can provide cues that help us to interpret physiological arousal in terms of a reaction to a product. Suppose your friend gets you to try new Loca-cola, that happens to be loaded with physiologically arousing caffeine. If your friend begins praising this new beverage as the caffeine begins coursing through your veins, you may use this praise to interpret your caffeine-produced arousal as "enjoyment" or "pleasure." Products like coffee, soft drinks, and chocolates, that contain physiological stimulants, are prime candidates for misattributing caffeine-produced arousal to the quality of the product. The current vogue for caffeine-free soft drinks may have the unintended long-term consequence of reducing this type of misattribution of arousal and its associated effects on product evaluation.

Intention

In chapter 8, intentions were portrayed as representing the combined and interactive effects of the internal processes. Therefore, the previous discussion of the effects of the social context on perception, cognition, emotion, and so on, implies an indirect influence of the social context on intention. In addition, a study by Capretta, Moore, and Rossiter (1973) directly addressed the effect of the social context on intentions. In this study, certain food items were observed to have feminine connotations (e.g., cottage cheese, peaches), and other food items were observed to have masculine connotations (e.g., steak, onions). Capretta et al. reported that adolescent boys were reluctant to agree to try foods that had feminine connotations, especially when in the presence of other boys. This suggests that in addition to (or perhaps in spite of) the effects of the internal processes, the social context may effect the individual's intentions.

Behavior

Presumably, the social context exerts its effects on behavior more or less indirectly, through its effects on the internal processes and intention. However, a number of interesting studies that examine the effects of the social context have only measured some type of behavior, and not any internal processes. Without operationalizing any type of internal processes, the researcher is left to speculate about the mechanisms underlying the change in behavior. Nonetheless, these studies do shed some light on the pervasive influence of social contexts.

For example, Duncker (1938) had children select from six types of food; the children performed this choice behavior either alone or in pairs. It was found that approximately 25% of the choices were the same when the children made their choices independently, whereas approximately 81% of the choices were the same when the children made their choices in pairs. Marinho (1942) conducted a follow-up study, and found that children's choices were influenced by the choice of the first child, and that these "socially influenced" choices persisted even when the first child was no longer present (especially for children of initially indefinite preferences regarding the food selection). These types of influences may be operating when we go shopping with other people. For example, Granbois (1968) observed that individual shoppers visit more stores, and make more unplanned purchases, when shopping with others than when shopping alone.

Bourne (1956) examined the interaction between consumers' beliefs about the effect of product use on health and friends' product use. Not surprisingly, consumers were found to be more likely to use products they believed to have a good effect on health, and less likely to use products they believed to have a bad effect on health. However, this influence of the consumers' beliefs was moderated by the friends' product use. That is, products having a good effect on health were less likely to be used if friends did not use them than if friends did use them. Similarly, products having a bad effect on health were more likely to be used if friends did use them than if friends did not use them. Thus, the adolescent who knows that smoking cigarettes may be hazardous to his or her health may begin smoking anyway if a number of his or her friends smoke.

Generally, research evidence indicates that the social context can have a wide range of effects on consumer behavior (e.g., Newman & Staelin, 1973; Robertson, 1971; Ward, 1974). Other people can affect the consumer's awareness, beliefs, associations, feelings, desires, intentions, and behaviors. We can now consider several unique phenomena that serve to further illustrate the influence of the social context.

INDIVIDUAL DIFFERENCES RELEVANT TO THE SOCIAL CONTEXT

There are a number of psychological dimensions that can influence social contexts, or interact with the effects of social contexts. These psychological dimensions are generally conceived as personality types, and may reflect fundamental consistencies in the operation of the individual's perception, cognition, learning and memory, emotion, and motivation processes. The use of these dimensions to distinguish and aggregate consumers into subgroups constitutes further examples of the psychographic approach discussed in chapter 8. However, because of their special significance for social contexts, a few examples of individual differences are considered here.

Compliant-Aggressive-Detached Personality Types

The personality psychologist Karen Horney (1945) proposed a tripartite model of interpersonal personality styles. Accordingly, people can be classified as either compliant (moves toward people), aggressive (moves against people), or detached (moves away from people). Cohen (1967) developed a measurement instrument that could be used to identify an individual's interpersonal personality style, and then examined patterns of product use that covaried with this measurement instrument. It was reported that compliant consumers were more likely than the other types of consumers to use mouthwash and deodorant bath soap; aggressive consumers were more likely to use mechanical (rather than electrical) razors; and detached consumers were more likely to use tea.

This psychological dimension seems to characterize the stance taken by the individual toward his or her social context. In that light, these product usage patterns may facilitate the individual's approach to his or her social context. For example, it is reasonable for compliant consumers to use mouthwash and deodorant bath soap, because such product usage will (presumably) facilitate their efforts to move toward people. These personality styles are not assumed to override all effects of perception, cognition, learning, and so on. However, these personality styles may be considered as determinants of the social context that might moderate the influence of perception, cognition, learning, and so on.

Social Character

Riesman (1950) described a difference between inner-directed individuals who use internal standards to guide their behavior, and other-directed individuals who rely on other people for direction and guidance. Mizerski and Settle (1979) reported on some differences between inner- and other-directed consumers. For example, inner-directed consumers were less influenced by advertisements than were other-directed individuals. Also, when consumers wanted additional information about a product, the other-directed consumers preferred social information, such as information regarding available styles, whereas inner-directed consumers preferred objective information, like information regarding product construction. These findings are similar to those reported by Becherer and Richard (1978), cited previously in our discussion of psychographics. Becherer and Richard found that the behavior of high self-monitors (comparable to Mizerski and Settle's other-directed consumers) was more influenced by environmental cues than that of low self-monitors (comparable to inner-directed consumers). Thus, the extent to which the individual relies on the social context for information and for guidance will determine his or her responses toward products.

Authoritarianism/Dogmatism

Authoritarianism refers to a willingness to accept and identify with socially established sources of authority (Adorno, Frenkel-Brunswik, Levinson, & Sanford, 1950). Dogmatism refers to a tendency to experience discomfort in the face of ambiguity and uncertainty, and a willingness to accept prestigious persuasive communications (Rokeach, 1968). A considerable amount of research supports the generalization that authoritarian/dogmatic individuals may be more likely to yield to influence than their egalitarian/nondogmatic counterparts (e.g., Crutchfield, 1955; Hartley, 1968; Vidulich & Kaiman, 1961).

Applied to consumer behavior, this suggests that authoritarian/dogmatic consumers might be more likely to consume products defined as "appropriate" by advertisement, reference group norms, and so on. In one examination of this individual difference dimension, Blake, Perloff, and Heslin (1970) observed that highly dogmatic consumers were more likely to prefer recent products than established products, and that recent products were preferred more by high dogmatism consumers than by low dogmatism consumers. Perhaps accepting the commercial advertisement declaration of the appropriateness of a given product, the dogmatic consumer may begin the EPS-LPS-RRB sequence (see chapter 9) earlier than other consumers.

Research examining the influence of these social context-related individual differences has revealed the range of influence that social context can exercise on the consumer. The consumer's general approach toward social contexts (e.g., compliant, aggressive, and detached personality types), reliance on social contexts for information (social character), and readiness to accept definitions of appropriateness from social contexts (authoritarianism/dogmatism) can all influence consumer behavior. These individual differences may be important because they represent consistent differences between individuals regarding the responsiveness of the internal processes. In addition, this individual difference research literature highlights differences in the strength of influence of social contexts on different consumers.

OPINION LEADERS

In order for us to understand what an opinion leader is, and what effects an opinion leader has, consider a basic distinction between models of interpersonal communication (cf. Katz, 1957). A one-step flow model of communication (Fig. 10.1a) holds that the manufacturer directs his or her message to each consumer as an individual. The assumption here is that the message will reverberate through each consumer's internal processes and hopefully result in some purchase behavior. There is no interaction or exchange between consumers seen to occur within this model.

A two-step flow model of communication (Fig. 10.1b) holds that the manufac-

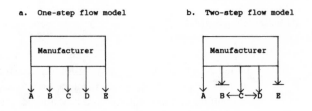

FIG. 10.1   Illustration of one-step flow model of communication and two-step flow model of communication (after Katz, 1957).

turer directs his or her message to each consumer as an individual. However, the message is received and processed by some consumers (e.g., consumers A, C, and D in Fig. 10.1b), but not all of the consumers (e.g., consumers B and E). Some of the consumers who do receive and process the message may pass the information along orally to other consumers (e.g., consumer C passing the message to consumers B and D).

This oral transmission of information between consumers has come to be called *word-of-mouth* (WOM). This WOM itself becomes an element of the stimulus situation for consumers who are recipients of this oral message (e.g., consumers B and D). WOM provides functionally new information to those consumers who had not previously processed the message (e.g., consumer B). WOM may also provide a repetition for consumers who had previously processed the message (e.g., consumer D). Cox (1961) referred to this type of multiple exposure to persuasive appeals as *complementary reinforcement*. In this context, the opinion leader can be defined as the individual who engages in this type of oral transmission of product information (e.g., consumer C). This conceptualization of opinion leader is consistent with the maxim that, "the best salesperson is a happy customer." Arndt (1968) has noted that consumers may not always be passive recipients of information from the opinion leaders; very often, consumers might actively seek out information from the opinion leader.

Certainly, it would be in the best interest of the manufacturer to capitalize on the existence of opinion leaders. This could be accomplished by locating the opinion leaders and directing special communications to them (sometimes called a "rifle" approach), to supplement the broad advertising campaign directed toward all consumers (sometimes called a "shotgun" approach). As Robertson (1971) noted, this may not be an easy task, but it may be effective in the long run. Alternatively, if the opinion leaders can be identified, providing free samples of the product to them may predispose them to influence other consumers on behalf of the manufacturer (see also interest box on p. 132, which contains copy from an advertisement informing the manufacturing organization about services that will direct product information toward opinion leaders and certain members of the family).

There are two distinct approaches to the identification of opinion leaders. One approach involves the attempt to discover underlying characteristics that distinguish opinion leaders from other consumers. For example, Reynolds and Darden (1971) found that opinion leaders were more likely to be self-confident in their evaluations of products, and more likely to be socially active. Tigert and Arnold (1970) observed that opinion leaders were more involved in clubs and community affairs, more price conscious, and more style conscious than other consumers. Engel, Kollat, and Blackwell (1969) and Summers (1970) found that opinion leaders were more likely to read magazines dealing with their product area of interest (e.g., automotive magazines, fashion magazines) (also cf. Rogers & Shoemaker, 1971). This suggests that one might develop a scale measuring social activity, price/style consciousness, subscriptions to magazines, and so on, in an effort to identify opinion leaders. Some authors (e.g., Assael, 1981) propose that such measurement efforts may not be successful, because opinion leaders may tend to be leaders in specific limited topic areas. Childers (1986) has successfully developed a measurement of opinion leadership that incorporates

Interest Box

TARGET/AID SEPARATES THE MEN FROM THE BOYS

Even the men 18–24 from the boys 18–24. Not to mention the boys from the girls, the old money from the new money, the Mercedes set from the tractor set from the Mercedes *and* tractor set. . . . In fact, TARGET/AID helps to define audiences to a degree never possible before. TARGET/AID uses ClusterPlus, a powerful marketing segmentation tool developed by Donnelley Marketing Information Services and Simmons Market Research Bureau, to profile a market or an audience by lifestyle characteristics. That gives you a big advantage over just age and sex demographics, because lifestyles are much better indicators of the products and services consumers are likely to buy.

TARGET/AID can bring a whole new perspective to broadcast advertising. Now you can determine more than just the specific demographics of a broadcast audience; you can see what kind of *consumers* those numbers represent.

TARGET/AID lets you sharpen and refine your sales and marketing approach. You can differentiate stations, programming and formats from others with seemingly identical audience ratings. Even markets with similar rankings can be totally different when you examine the lifestyles of their populations. TARGET/AID is the tool that allows you to pinpoint those audience differences and use them to your advantage.

That means agencies can make better media recommendations and you can spend your advertising dollars more effectively.

So whether your audience drives a tractor, or a Mercedes or both, TARGET/AID can help you identify your targets and deliver them more efficiently. Because TARGET/AID defines audiences like never before.

TARGET/AID—The Ratings and Lifestyle Connection

(© 1983 Arbitron Ratings.)

---

this dimension of product specificity. Opinion leadership for a given product category is represented by talking to neighbors a lot about the product category, convincing other people about one's own ideas (rather than listening to their ideas), and giving other people a lot of information about the product category.

An alternative approach to identifying opinion leaders is through the use of sociograms and network analysis. These are sociological methods that graphically represent the patterns of interaction and influence among members of a group. For example, Menzel and Katz (1955) were able to identify opinion leaders among the medical doctors in a New England community by asking the doctors to indicate the other doctors with whom they interacted most frequently. The doctors receiving the highest number of these "sociometric choices" are inferred to function as opinion leaders for the group. Coleman, Katz, and Menzel (1966) considered evidence that suggests that such physicians do have more influence, and might function as opinion leaders.

Given that opinion leaders can be identified, the question remains as to whether the use of opinion leaders is effective. Drawing an example once again from the medical profession, it seems that opinion leaders were sought and used to promote the sale of thalidomide (a drug prescribed to reduce morning sickness in pregnant women in the late 1950s, and that caused severe birth defects). In covering the senate subcommittee proceedings that investigated this drug, one newspaper reviewed the materials that were given by the manufacturer to its salesmen, in order to promote the use of the drug among doctors: "Over and over the salesmen were urged to hand-pick influential doctors—to get them to use the drug. They, in turn, theoretically, would influence their colleagues" (McCartney, 1963, p. 1). The intense (although brief and tragic) popularity of this prescription drug may attest, in part, to the potential effectiveness of using opinion leaders as unpaid salespersons.

Whyte (1954) observed the proliferation of air conditioners in a suburban Philadelphian housing development (note that this was at a time when air conditioners were a relatively recent innovation). It was observed that the adoption of air conditioners proceeded in clusters of adjacent homes on one side of a street, while across that street no air conditioners might be found. In light of the fact that social traffic occurred up and down the streets, rather than across the streets, Whyte attributed this pattern of adoption to the "web of word-of-mouth." Presumably, an innovator/opinion leader would make an early purchase of this new product, and start a chain reaction of purchasing among interacting neighbors (i.e., neighbors residing on the same side of the street).

More recent empirical studies have supported the basic notion that this type of social influence can be effective. For example, Arndt (1967) found that consumers who received positive WOM were more likely to purchase a new food product than those receiving negative WOM. Similarly, the most important reason for selecting a particular medical doctor is recommendation by a friend or a relative (Blackwell, Engel, & Talarzyk, 1977).

FAMILY MEMBER INTERACTIONS

Davis (1976) has discussed recent research on decision making within the family. Various types of decision making strategies have been examined. Davis and Rigaux (1974) have proposed a two-dimensional representation of husband and wife decision making, presented in Fig. 10.2. This model identifies different categories of products in terms of how husbands and wives tend to make their decisions. The two dimensions comprising this representation are: (a) relative influence of the spouses (such that the husband can make the decision, the wife can make the decision, or the decision can be made jointly by husband and wife); and (b) extent of role integration (or, the percentage of families that report that the decision is made jointly). This results in four general categories of decisions.

Wife dominant decisions involve product categories wherein the wife is more likely to make the decision in most families. Examples might be kitchenware or food. *Husband dominant* decisions involve product categories wherein the husband is more likely to make the decision in most families. An example might be insurance. *Autonomic* decisions involve product categories wherein either the wife or the husband is more likely to make the independent decision, although the one to make the decision will vary with the individuals involved. Examples might be appliances or alcoholic beverages. Finally, *syncratic* decisions involve

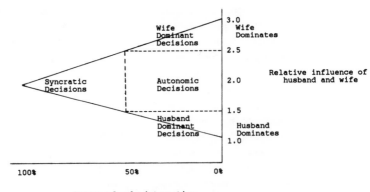

FIG. 10.2 *Two-dimensional representation of husband and wife decision making (after Davis & Rigaux, 1974).*

product categories wherein the husband and the wife are likely to make the decision jointly. Examples might be housing or vacation plans.

Although these examples may sound "sexist," it is important to remember one thing: these categories do not refer to what researchers say should happen. These categories describe what typically does happen. It should not be inferred from this set of examples that there is supposed to be something innately masculine about buying insurance, or that there is something innately feminine about buying kitchenware. Cunningham and Green (1974) have observed similar patterns of decision making. Burns and Granbois (1977) found that conflict between husband–wife consumers was reduced if the couple had previously delegated the purchase decision to one or the other, if one of them was more involved with the consequences of the decision, and if one of the members of the couple was more empathic (i.e., sensitive to the needs of others).

Within a given culture, at a given time, these types of decision making categories are probably useful in distinguishing the product categories where some, little, or no interaction will occur between husband and wife consumers as the decision is made. If a product can be identified as falling into one of these four types of decisions, the manufacturers might be able to tailor their commercial advertisements to fit the wife, or the husband, or both the wife and husband. The manufacturer might also be able to select the best media outlet (e.g., television commercials during soap operas, television commercials during football games, or television commercials during the evening news).

A considerable amount of research has been directed toward interactions between parents and children in the context of consumer behavior. Some of this work has considered the extent to which children, as developing consumers, are influenced by their parents. For example, Parsons, Bales, and Shils (1953) and Riesman and Roseborough (1955) suggested that children are most influenced by their parents when it comes to rational aspects of buying behavior, whereas children are most influenced by their friends when it comes to expressive or affective aspects of buying behavior. In terms of processes we have considered previously, it may be that parents have more influence on the cognitive processes that guide children's behavior as consumers, whereas the peer group has more influence on the emotional processes (and possibly the motivational processes) that guide children's behavior as consumers. It is interesting to consider Moschis and Moore's (1979) results in light of this inference. These researchers examined the decision making patterns of teenaged consumers. Parents were generally the preferred source of product and buying information. However, this was most especially the case for products where price and performance were critical attributes (e.g., wrist watches and pocket calculators). For products where social acceptance was a critical attribute (e.g., sunglasses), preference for peers as an information source increased substantially. This might reflect differential influence of specific aspects of the social context on specific internal processes.

Some of the work examining parent–child interactions has considered the extent to which parents as consumers are influenced by their children (e.g., Berey & Pollay, 1968; Heslop & Ryans, 1980; Kanti, Rao, & Sheikh, 1978). One recent study (Atkin, 1978a) observed parents interacting with children during the purchase of breakfast cereals. The results of the observation of 516 such episodes are presented in Fig. 10.3. Note the two most common scenarios: (a) the child demands a particular brand of cereal, and the parent yields (30%); and, (b) the parent invites selection of the brand, the child selects, and the parent agrees with

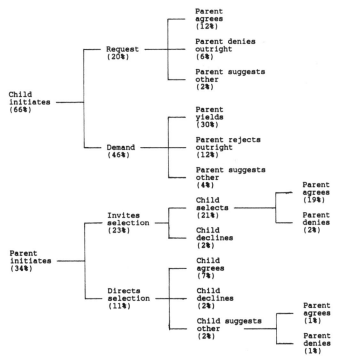

FIG. 10.3 Results of 516 parent-child interactions regarding brand selection of breakfast cereal (after Atkin, 1978a).

the selection (19%). Regardless of whether the parent or the child initiates the selection, the child seems to be directing the brand selection for this particular product. However, one might consider whether the Atkin (1978a) data reflect the child's demanding a particular brand, or the child's anticipating (perhaps in a peremptory manner) the brand that has always been purchased in the past. Ward and Wackman (1972) noted that 87% of those mothers interviewed yielded to their child's request for a particular brand of breakfast cereal. Other product areas where children seem to exert influence over their parents are games, toys, and snack foods.

In response to concerns of the Children's Advertising Review Unit of the Council of Better Business Bureaus, and the Federal Trade Commission, a considerable amount of recent research has been directed toward examining the effects of commercial advertisements on children. For example, some research indicates that younger children may have trouble distinguishing between program and commercial (e.g., Butter, Popovich, Stockhouse, & Garner, 1981; Robertson & Rossiter, 1974; Rossiter, 1979). Children seem to prefer commercials using physical action, humor, good music, or cartoons, involving products they already own, and seen as informational rather than persuasive (e.g., Robertson & Rossiter, 1974; Rust & Watkins, 1975; Ward, 1972). Commercial advertisements do seem to influence children's preferences and purchase decisions (e.g., Frideres, 1973; Goldberg & Gorn, 1978; Gorn & Goldberg, 1980; Rossiter 1979), although it is not known to what extent these influences are more or less extreme than they are among adults.

CONCLUSION: WHO ARE YOU GOING TO LISTEN TO: THE TELEVISION OR YOUR MOTHER?

Both the National Association of Broadcaster's Code (1976) and the Children's Review Unit of the Council of Better Business (1977) prohibit advertisers from urging children to ask their parents to buy something. However, it should come as no surprise that advertisements are a primary source of product information for child consumers. For example, positive correlations have been repeatedly observed between the amount of television advertising seen and purchase requests for Christmas presents (Robertson & Rossiter, 1976), food products (Clancy-Hepburn, 1974), toys and cereals (Atkin, 1975a), and over-the-counter drugs (Robertson, Rossiter, & Gleason, 1979). Kanti, Rao, and Sheikh (1978) reported that information from the mother did have some effect on the child's evaluation of moderately attractive toys, but that the mother had no influence on the child's evaluation of toys that had been portrayed as highly attractive on television commercials.

How frequently do parents yield to childrens' requests to purchase a particular product? Our earlier discussion of parent–child interactions suggested relatively high yielding to child requests for cereal. However, parents have been observed to yield to requests for snack food 63% of the time, for toys and games 54% of the time, for toothpaste 39%, for shampoo 16%, for pet food 7% (Ward & Wackman, 1972), and for Christmas gifts 43% (Robertson & Rossiter, 1976). Thus, the extent to which a parent yields to a child's purchase request depends on the product category, and possibly on the extent of the child's direct involvement with the product.

Atkin (1975b) has suggested that children's exposure to advertisements has no direct effect on parent–child conflict. However, there may be an indirect effect of advertisements on conflict, through the effect of advertisements on frequency of purchase requests. As a child watches more television advertisements, he or she is likely to make more purchase requests. Within most middle-class homes, the more purchase requests a child makes, the more purchase requests will have to be denied (because there is only a limited amount of money available). Atkin observed that 50% of the children in his sample argued with their mother sometimes or a lot after being denied a toy they had requested, and 60% became angry sometimes or a lot. Similar observations have been reported by Goldberg and Gorn (1978). Because it is the parents that inevitably control the family purse strings, it is usually the mother that wins out over the television. However, this would seem to be less and less satisfactory to the children as they are exposed to more and more commercial advertisements.

11 | The Cultural Context

The *cultural context* can be defined as the totality of the customs, arts, sciences, religions, politics, and economics that distinguishes one society from another, and that influences the individual consumer's behavior. *Subculture* is usually defined as a category of people who share a sense of identification that is distinguishable from that of the culture as a whole. This shared sense of identification may result from a shared set of values, from a common history, or from similarity in sociodemographic attributes. Social class is perhaps the type of subculture that is most often used by consumer psychologists. The attribute that distinguishes between levels of social class is the relative level of social benefits (e.g., influence power, prestige, income).

There are three basic methods for gauging social class. The *reputational* method asks people to classify or rank other individuals with whom they are familiar. For example, Warner and Lunt (1941) used this approach, and established six general social classes. The *subjective* method asks people to classify or rank themselves. For example, Morris and Jeffries (1970) asked people to place themselves in one of Warner and Lunt's (1941) six social classes. Finally, the *objective* method classifies people according to their standing on various objective criteria (e.g., occupation, educational level, residence, income, etc). For example, Hollingshead and Redlich (1958) established five major social classes by summing together weighted measures of occupation (weight = 9), residence (weight = 6), and income (weight = 5). These methods produce similar, although not at all identical, results. For example, Table 11.1 presents the percent of the population falling into each social class in the three illustrative studies just cited.

The constructs of culture, subculture, and social class can be considered one at a time in examining their effects on consumers. However, these three levels of cultural context are examined collectively in this chapter. Bear in mind that our task in this chapter is to understand how the cultural context influences consumer behavior.

TABLE 11.1   Comparison of Applications of Three Approaches to Social Class

Social Class	Reputational (Warner & Lunt, 1941)		Subjective (Morris & Jeffries, 1970)		Objective (Hollingshead & Redlich, 1958)	
High	upper upper	1.4%	upper upper	3.0%	I	3.4%
	lower upper	1.6%	lower upper	22.0%	II	9.0%
	upper middle	10.2%	upper middle	50.0%	III	21.4%
	lower middle	28.1%	lower middle	5.0%	IV	48.5%
	upper lower	32.6%	upper lower	16.0%	V	17.7%
Low	lower lower	25.2%	lower lower	2.0%		

Note: percentages indicate the number of people in the sample classified in each social class.

EFFECT OF THE CULTURAL CONTEXT ON CONSUMERS

Perception

One way of considering the effect of cultural context on perception is to consider variations in the stimulus situation across different cultures. Although the presence of stimuli does not necessarily guarantee their perception (as noted in chapter 2), perception of such stimuli is likely to become less frequent if the stimuli are themselves less frequent. Consider, for example, the cultural variability in the availability of televisions and newspapers, two important sources of consumer information (cf. Moschis & Moore, 1979). Table 11.2 reveals that the United States has the highest relative number of televisions (571 per 1,000 population,

TABLE 11.2.   Number of Television Sets and Newspapers Per 1,000 Population (circa 1977; from Heron House, 1978).

Country	Number of television sets per 1,000 population	Number of newspapers per 1,000 population
United States	571	293
Canada	366	235
United Kingdom	315	443
Austria	297	308
Belgium	252	247
Denmark	308	355
France	235	220
West Germany	305	289
Ireland	178	236
Italy	213	526
Japan	233	526
Norway	256	391
Spain	179	96

or approximately one television for every two people). On the other hand, the United States has a moderate relative number of newspapers (293 per 1,000 population, or approximately one newspaper for every three people). Compare these figures with those for Japan, where there is approximately one television for every four people, and one newspaper for every two people. These figures may indicate cultural differences in primary modes of exposure to product relevant information. In countries or cultures where televisions are more prevalent than newspapers, manufacturers may be better able to attract consumers' attention (with loud noise, motion, and color) as compared to countries or cultures where newspapers are more prevalent than televisions.

With reference to social class, the general findings can be summarized as follows: upper class consumers have tended to buy more newspapers, to read more of the newspaper they buy, and to watch less television; middle-class consumers have preferred to purchase the morning paper, and watch television to some extent; and, lower class consumers have preferred to purchase the afternoon paper, and watch television regularly (Levy, 1966; Levy & Glick, 1962). Again, this may represent an indirect influence of the cultural context on perception through the influence of cultural context on mode of exposure to product relevant information.

However, these are relatively indirect approaches to the effects of culture on perception. A more direct examination of this type of influence was described in chapter 2 (Perception). Adams (1920) observed that the left side of the page received more attention than the right side of the page among English-speaking subjects. Yamanake (1962) observed that the right side of the page received more attention than the left side of the page among Japanese-speaking subjects. This difference is entirely reasonable, considering where writing in each language begins on a printed page (left for English, right for Japanese). This subtle cultural difference could direct the consumers' attention toward or away from product-relevant elements of the stimulus situation. One approach to the effects of cultural context on cognition is embodied in the anthropologist and linguist Benjamin Whorf's (1956) linguistic relativity hypothesis: differences in linguistic habits may cause differences in nonlinguistic behavior, such as thought. Evidence regarding the linguistic relativity hypothesis (e.g., Berlin & Kay, 1969; Rosch, 1975) suggests that Whorf may have overstated the influence that language has on thought. Nevertheless, thought (cognition) and language (culture) are intricately interrelated.

For example, some interesting difficulties have arisen in the translation of product slogans from one culture to another. For example, the Pepsi-Cola slogan of a few years back, "Come alive with Pepsi," was translated into other languages as "Come out of the grave with Pepsi," and "Pepsi brings your ancestors back from the grave." Needless to say, the "spirit" of the original slogan was lost in the translation. Similar problems have been described in a book by Ricks, Arpan, and Fu (1975), entitled *International Business Blunders*. A technique designed to reduce these difficulties is called *back-translation*. This procedure requires that a number of language experts independently translate different versions of the slogan from the original language to the new language, and back again to the original, in the hopes of catching these semantic quirks (see also interest box, opposite).

Interest Box

AP Laserphoto

Photograph is taken from a television screen of a Pepsi-Cola commercial being aired for the first time on Soviet TV by a U.S. company. Slogan besides the Pepsi logo reads: "The new generation chooses Pepsi".

U.S.-made TV ads shown comrades

State-run Soviet network runs first paid commercials

By Andrew Katell
The Associated Press

MOSCOW — Madison Avenue is speaking to the socialist masses with Soviet TV showing commercials that featured bottles of Pepsi-Cola popping their tops to the riffs of rock music.

Sony TV sets and Visa credit cards are also flashing across the screens to millions of viewers during the late-evening in a five-part series on life in the United States.

They were the first paid commercials on staid, state-run Soviet TV, and they came in advance of President Reagan's visit to Moscow later this month.

Each company had one brief advertisement on the hour-long program, which premiered Tuesday night featuring commentator Vladimir Posner interviewing a panel of Americans in Seattle about life in the United States.

The ads broke clumsily without explanation into the show, titled "Posner in America."

Pepsi's ad showed a group of young people looking for a way to open several bottles of Pepsi, a drink that has been available in the Soviet Union for almost 30 years. When no bottle opener appeared, a red-headed guitarist pops them open with a long riff from his guitar and the screen proclaimed in Russian: "The new generation chooses Pepsi."

Sony and Visa got their chance around midnight Moscow time, about five minutes before the program ended.

Visa showed athletes preparing for the Summer Olympics in Seoul, South Korea, and told viewers its credit card was good in any country in the world. Sony promoted the quality of its electronics products.

But Sony electronics products and Visa cards aren't available to the average Soviet consumer.

"I expect we might get some angry letters from people saying, 'Why are you advertising Sony TVs when we can't buy any,'" Posner had said earlier this month at a news conference announcing his series.

The colorful, fast-paced commercials contrast sharply with most programming on Soviet television. Two of Pepsi's commercials to be shown during the week feature pop star Michael Jackson, who is well-known to Soviet youth from music videos shown occasionally on TV here and recordings that circulate unofficially.

One commercial has Jackson dancing and singing his hit song "Bad." Another ends with a shot of U.S. and Soviet flags accompanied by Pepsi labels in Russian and English.

Posner said the commercials aren't being shown on Soviet TV for consumer sales — at least not right away.

In the West, commercials try to get consumers to buy one company's product over a competitor's, but in the Soviet Union, there's no need to stimulate demand because consumer goods are in short supply, Posner said.

Officials refused to disclose how much money the advertisers were paying for air time, but reports in the United States said the Soviet broadcast agency Gostelradio received $10,000 for each 30-second ad.

Soviet TV already features infrequent homemade commercials that advertise shoes, shortwave radios and personal stereos, but the products they pitch aren't always available.

Western commercials have been seen previously on Soviet television during "space bridges" — international satellite television programs involving discussions between Americans and Soviets — but the advertisers did not pay Soviet television for that air time.

Posner said his program's audience was expected to be about 120 million people.

(Reprinted with permission of the Associated Press.)

Cognition, Memory, and Persuasion

More generally, cultural context has been demonstrated to affect individuals' beliefs about common objects. For example, Dennis (1957) observed differences between American and Lebanese children in their responses to the question, "What is a (blank) for," where the blank was replaced by things like a cat, hands, trees, sand, and so on. If different cultures hold different beliefs about the function of a particular product, then one would expect consumers immersed in those two different cultural contexts to hold different beliefs about the nature of the product. For example, urban, temperate-climate Americans might consider a good beverage to be one that makes you "feel alive," whereas rural, desert-dwelling Arabs might consider a good beverage to be one that quenches your thirst.

Another example of the effect of the cultural context on cognition lies in the observation that social class seems to determine the development of the assumed relationship between price and quality (discussed in chapter 3, Cognition). Fry and Siller (1970) observed that lower class consumers are more likely than higher class consumers to rely on price as an index of product quality. This may be because higher class consumers feel that they can evaluate a product independent of the banal consideration of how much it costs. Alternatively, this may be because money is much more salient to the lower class consumer due to its scarcity. In either case, this represents another influence of the cultural context on consumers' cognitions.

Learning

Culture is generally considered to involve learned, rather than innate, distinctions. Therefore, in a sense, all of the effects of the cultural context might be seen as occurring as a result of learning. In addition, it should be noted that the cultural differences in exposure to televisions and newspapers (discussed previously) might determine the likelihood of the consumer being subjected to observational learning procedures (chapter 5), as well as the classical conditioning of emotional responses (chapter 6), and the acquisition of secondary motives (chapter 7). In order for these learning processes to occur, the consumer must be exposed to the observational learning stimuli (such as product, model, vicarious reinforcement, and so on). Obviously, this exposure becomes more likely within cultures that have more television sets.

Emotion

Ekman and Friesen (1971) have demonstrated considerable cross-cultural consistency in the facial expressions corresponding to general classes of emotions (such as happy, sad, afraid, angry, surprised, and disgusted), as well as in the types of situations reported to arouse those general classes of emotion. Cross-cultural consistency has also been observed by Prost (1974) for the emotional posturing of the trunk and limbs. Consistent with Darwin's (1872) initial presentation, this research seems to suggest that culture might have little impact on the experience and expression of emotional states.

However, more focused observations have revealed a number of illustrations of the effect of the cultural context on emotion. For example, Zborowski (1969) compared reactions of various subculture groups to pain. Some subculture groups (e.g., Irish patients) were nonexpressive and nonvocal, while other subculture groups (e.g., Italian patients and Jewish patients) were quite expressive and vocal. The British physician P. E. Brown observed unanesthetized tonsillectomies in China carried out on a line of smiling 5-year-olds, at the rate of less than 1 minute per patient (cf. Chaves & Barber, 1973).

In spite of the cross-cultural consistencies observed by Ekman and Friesen, and Prost, for general categories of emotions, research suggests that different cultures may differ dramatically in their manifestations of these emotions. It remains for future research to determine whether these cultural differences extend to differences in responses to fear appeals, the use of humor, or the classical conditioning of emotional responses. For example, public service announcements for some health issues may be most effective in some parts of the world when presented as a classic fear appeal accompanied by clear, effective recommendations. However, fear about personal health may not be so easily evoked in other parts of the world, where a different strategy may be more effective.

Motivation

Teevan and Smith (1967) discussed the effects of cultural context on the development, operation, and manifestation of motivations. Recall the distinction between primary motives, that are unlearned, based directly on physiological needs, and secondary motives, that are learned, and presumably based indirectly on physiological needs through classical conditioning. Regarding primary motives, consider the cultural differences that have been observed for the motivations of hunger and sex. The Balinese are reported to dislike eating in public, and to conceal their eating behavior as much as possible (Teevan & Smith, 1967). This parallels how most Americans feel about sex. On the other hand, the Trobriand Islanders are reported to encourage sexual play among children, and to promote sexual experimentation among adolescents (Malinowski, 1953; Teevan & Smith, 1967). This parallels how most Americans feel about hunger. Although culture probably has little effect on the genesis of primary motives, it seems to affect the operation and manifestations of these motives.

One implication of this cultural influence on primary motives is that appeals to motives may be more or less effective, depending on the cultural response to the motive addressed in the appeal. Speculation suggests that an appeal to motive "X" will be relatively effective in a culture that is repressive, or deprived, regarding motive "X" (because that motive is in a continual state of prepotent need). Similarly, an appeal to motive "X" will be relatively ineffective in a culture that is permissive, or affluent, regarding motive "X" (because that motive is in a continual state of satiation). For example, an advertisement for Loca-cola based on an appeal to thirst may be more effective among consumers in Phoenix, Arizona than among consumers in Seattle, Washington.

Regarding secondary motives, similar cultural differences have been observed. For example, the Zuni of New Mexico reportedly evidenced little or none of the acquired needs for status and power, whereas the Dobu of northwest Melanesia have been characterized as fiercely competitive regarding status and power (Benedict, 1934; Teevan & Smith, 1967). Again, one implication of this is that appeals to a given motive may be more or less successful, depending on the cultural context.

Another implication has to do with the acquisition of secondary motives. The extent to which a new motive can be generated among consumers may depend on how the culture is characterized regarding the underlying primary motive upon which the secondary motive will be based. For example, it might be unsuccessful to try to generate a secondary motive for a laundry product by associating the product with a loving family setting, connubial affection, and so on, if these "unconditioned stimuli" were genuinely present and satisfying in real life. Increasing rates of divorce, child abuse, and spouse abuse may prime the commercial viewing audience for the sentimental "Final Touch" commercial. It is a sad comment on modern middle-class American society that laundry product advertisements may be effective because loving family settings and connubial affection are becoming increasingly difficult to develop and maintain.

Intention

Hall (1960) has discussed cultural differences in something that may be analogous to stated intentions. Hall compared the cultural stance taken toward business contracts by Greeks, Americans, and Arabs. The Greeks were described as viewing the signed contract as one "way-station" among many in the process of negotiation, a process that will cease only when the job is done. Americans were described as considering the negotiations to conclude as soon as the contract is signed. Arabs were described as viewing a person's word as just as binding, if not more binding, than a signed document. If we accept the analogy between a consumer's intention and a business person's contract, this suggests that stated intentions may be more or less pliable and flexible in different cultures. Stated intentions to buy may be a better predictor of consumer behavior in Arab countries and a poorer predictor of consumer behavior in Greece, as a result of this cultural influence.

Behavior

Presumably through the intervening variables described in the previous subsection, the cultural context has been found to influence consumer behavior (cf. Dichter, 1962; Hall, 1960). Table 11.3 depicts the extent to which a selection of products are purchased in a number of nations. It can be seen that there are considerable differences between these nations. Bear in mind that the nations represented in this table (and in Table 11.2) are mostly Western, industrialized nations, and thereby share a great deal in common regarding culture. Other

TABLE 11.3 *Use of Various Products in Different Countries (circa 1977; from Heron House, 1978).*

Country	Percent of households buying soap	Percent of households buying toothpaste	Percent of women using lipstick	Percent of men shaving with an electric razor	Percent of population smoking cigarettes
United States	97	95	71	25	37
Canada	98	96	90	40	41
United Kingdom	99	90	74	28	37
Austria	83	85	57	62	37
Belgium	91	81	61	60	32
Denmark	100	80	43	60	42
France	91	86	68	46	43
West Germany	84	83	69	59	43
Ireland	72	53	na	28	37
Italy	98	94	48	26	32
Japan	na	na	na	49	44
Norway	100	75	40	60	42
Spain	94	87	55	52	37

nations/cultures would differ from these to the extent that they might purchase some of these products infrequently, if at all.

Social Context

With reference to social class, Graham (1956) examined the relation between social class and adoption of new products. Graham found that innovations seem to be accepted to the extent that the innovations are compatible with the cultural attributes and lifestyle of the social classes. For example, television was more quickly accepted by the lower classes, while the card game Canasta was more quickly accepted by the higher classes. Some of the product categories in which social class has been found to mediate consumer behavior are credit cards (e.g., Plummer, 1971), clothing (e.g., Rich & Jain, 1968), and leisure activities (e.g., Bishop & Ikeda, 1970).

Since the issue was raised in an article by Wasson in 1969, researchers have been debating whether these effects are due to social class or income (e.g., Myers & Mount, 1973). Recently, Schaninger (1981) compared the relative effectiveness of social class and income, as well as their combination, in predicting consumer behavior over a wide range of consumption areas. Schaninger's results can be summarized as follows: Social class is superior to income for products that do not involve a high dollar expenditure, but that do reflect underlying lifestyle or value differences (e.g., wines, evening television exposure). Income is superior to social class for products that do require substantial expenditures, but that no longer serve as symbols of status (e.g., major kitchen and laundry appliances). Finally, the combination of social class and income is superior for products that serve as social class symbols (or status symbols within social class), and require either moderate or substantial expenditure (e.g., clothing, automobiles, television sets). Schaninger's integration helps to clarify our understanding of the influence of the cultural context on consumer behavior. Income exerts an influence when the product of concern is expensive, and social class exerts an influence when the product of concern can be seen as a reflection of the consumer's social class. This provides a useful approach to the operationalization of "subculture" for particular product categories.

It is necessary to recognize that the social context is immersed within, and influenced by, a cultural context. Consider Murdock's (1949) distinction between the types of families that arise in modern, industrial societies. The family of orientation is the family into which one is born, where one serves as a child. The family of procreation is the family created by marriage, where one serves as spouse and parent. This pair of family types is contrasted with the traditional extended family, where grandparents, parents and children live together. Myers and Reynolds (1967) discussed some of the effects of this type of culture-determined family structure on consumer behavior. For example, the elderly may tend to be left alone more than they would have with extended families, creating a separate and identifiable segment of the consumer population. The marriage creates a new household, usually requiring a complete complement of new towels, toasters, and television sets. The elders may be displaced from positions of expert authority, leaving the newly wed couple to rely on alternate sources for purchase information (such as peers, salespersons, or mass media). These types of effects would not be expected in other cultures, where the traditional extended family is still relatively intact.

Similarly, Hsu (1970) has proposed that cultural contexts can influence the critical relationships between family members in such a way as to influence the "national character," or the dominant personality types found in a given culture (Benedict, 1934). For example, Kohn (1963) compared middle class and working class parent–child interactions. Middle-class parents expected children to be happy, cooperative, and curious, and middle-class parents attempted to control their children through the development of self-direction, and through punishment based on the intent of the act. Alternatively, working-class parents expected children to be neat, obedient, and respectful, and working-class parents attempted to control their children through external proscriptions, and through punishment based on the consequences of the act. Similar social class differences have been observed for husband–wife consumer interactions (e.g., Komarovsky, 1961).

Thus, the cultural context appears to influence the social context, which is itself a determinant of consumer behavior. Recall Atkin's (1978a) study, cited in chapter 10, examining the parent–child interactions that occurred during the purchase of breakfast cereals. The influence of cultural context on social context (and thereby on behavior) might be seen in social class differences in child rearing practices, that influence the interactions between parents and children of a given social class, that in turn influence the interactive decision to purchase some brand of cereal.

CONCLUSION: PSYCHOLOGICAL GEOGRAPHY

Manufacturers must often take into account differences among regions of the United States in the use of certain products. Snow skis are seldom sold in Florida, and surfboards are seldom sold in Colorado. Obvious regional differences in geographic and climatic variables can account for some of these product consumption differences. However, other regional product consumption differences are not so easily explained. For example, iced tea and homemade biscuits are more common in the Southeast than anywhere else. Brandy consumption is more common in part of the Midwest than anywhere else. General Foods flavors its Maxwell House coffee differently, depending on the region of the country: people in the West prefer, and are provided with, a stronger tasting coffee (Kotler, 1983). Wells and Reynolds (1979) attempted to explain these types of regional differences in consumption in terms of regional differences in lifestyles and values. This approach, labelled by Wells and Reynolds as *psychological geography,* involves the identification of geographically defined subcultures. Lesser and Hughes (1986) argued that if strong and consistent regional differences in lifestyles, values, and other psychographic dimensions can be demonstrated, then national advertising campaigns might better be abandoned in favor of region specific campaigns.

The specification of the psychological geography of the United States can be accomplished in a variety of different ways. Figure 11.1 illustrates three different attempts to define specific regions of the United States. Wells and Reynolds' (1979) approach is presented in Fig. 11.1a. Note that Wells and Reynolds' approach is not exhaustive, in the sense that several (in fact, more than half) of the states are not included in this scheme. This is because these researchers were trying to typify differences among regions, rather than characterize the country in its entirety.

The Bureau of Census division of the country is presented in Fig. 11.1b. This perspective, used by the Bureau of Census (see Kahle, 1986) to report regional birth rates, unemployment, and so forth, is highly similar to the more selective categorization provided by Wells and Reynolds. Note, however, that the Bureau of Census system is exhaustive in the sense that it encompasses all 48 of the continental United States.

In 1981, Joel Garreau published a book entitled, *The Nine Nations of North America*. Travelling across the continent like a cultural anthropologist, Garreau studied cultural differences among regions. The nine regions (or "nations," as Garreau calls them) derived from this ambitious enterprise are presented in Fig. 11.1c. Note that this perspective is not only exhaustive of the 48 continental United States, but it also includes Canada, Mexico, Alaska, the Caribbean, and everything else on the North American continent. Garreau's regions presumably follow cultural boundaries rather than political boundaries.

Just how useful are these approaches for identifying regional subcultures? Wells and Reynolds found significant variation among 1,491 male consumers in

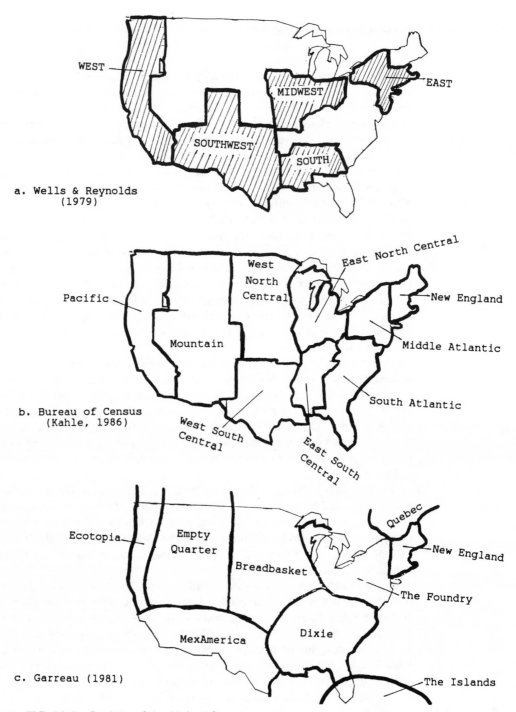

FIG. 11.1 Regions of the United States.

the various regions on a number of different dimensions. Generally, the South was characterized as very traditional, the West was characterized as relatively liberal and concerned with "natural" things, and the East was characterized as cosmopolitan and innovative. However, expected characterizations of the Southwest as innovative and recreation-oriented, and the Midwest as conservative and inhibited, were not confirmed.

In a more comprehensive effort, Kahle (1986) measured the most important value for each of 2,235 consumers from across the United States (where the value choices were: sense of belonging, fun and excitement, warm relationships with others, self-fulfillment, being respected, sense of accomplishment, security, and self-respect). Generally, both Garreau's (1981) nine nations and the Bureau of Census's nine regions revealed significant differences among regions and the two perspectives produced similar results. For example, consider comparisons between regions for the value of self-respect. The Bureau of Census's Mountain region had the highest rating for this value, as did Garreau's (roughly correspond-ing) Empty Quarter. The Bureau of Census's West North Central region had the lowest rating for this value, as did Garreau's (roughly corresponding) Breadbas-ket. The Bureau of Census's regions generally revealed more distinct differences between regions than Garreau's nine nations.

This research confirms the existence of significant, useful regional differences in values and in consumption patterns. This highlights and justifies the practical recommendation that manufacturers may wish to tailor the introduction and advertisement of new products for specific regions. However, this view must be tempered by an appreciation for the limits of psychological geography. In addition to the significant differences discussed here, there is also a considerable amount of consistency across the "nine nations of North America." For example, Wells and Reynolds (1979) reported that (regardless of region) consumers said that they were concerned with dependability and price, that they were not spendthrifts, and that large companies took advantage of the energy crisis to increase their profits. More recently, Lesser and Hughes (1986) have demonstrated a consider-able amount of consistency across geographic regions of the country on a variety of psychographic dimensions.

Although regional differences can be identified, some authors propose that regional differences in this country are steadily decreasing (Engel et al., 1982; Zelinsky, 1973). Interregional migration required by changing economic condi-tions, and homogenized mass media, may contribute to the steady "McDonaldiza-tion" of American subcultures. At any rate, targeting commercial advertisements to particular psychographic segments of consumers may be just as, if not more, effective than targeting commercial advertisements to particular geographic seg-ments of consumers.

12 | Sales Interactions

In this chapter we devote our attention to the sales interaction; that is, to the interaction between the sales person and the consumer. The salesperson can be thought of as a dynamic, adaptable, and important element of the stimulus situation that is at the same time a part of the social context. Although we have discussed sales interactions in chapter 10 as part of the social context, sales interactions seem sufficiently unique to deserve separate consideration. In addition, if the investment of time and effort is any indication, this particular type of interaction is also uniquely important to organizations. For example, Weitz (1981) noted that expenditure for the training of a single industrial salesperson was over $15,000, and that billions of dollars are spent annually in training sales personnel. Kotler (1976) estimated that organizations spend half again as much on personal selling as is spent on advertising.

Many of the principles and phenomena discussed in foregoing chapters may be influenced by the salesperson. For example, the salesperson may embody a source of some credibility (e.g., Busch & Wilson, 1976) (chapter 4). Similarly, the salesperson may use an emotional appeal (e.g., Newton, 1967) (chapter 6). Granted that the salesperson probably affects consumer behavior via his or her influence on the internal processes and intention (as outlined previously), most research in this area has scrutinized only some form of consumer behavior (e.g., whether or not the consumer purchased the product after interacting with the salesperson). Therefore, this chapter reviews three areas of extensive research on the effect of the salesperson on consumer behavior. These three areas of research address the characteristics of effective salespersons, the effects of similarity between the salesperson and the consumer, and a variety of influence techniques. Bear in mind that our task in this chapter is to understand how a salesperson can influence the consumer.

CHARACTERISTICS OF EFFECTIVE SALESPERSONS

An early approach to the study of sales interactions was to simply describe the individuals working as salespersons (e.g., Husband, 1953). Rogers (1959) compared the beliefs of sales managers, salespersons, and a psychologist regarding the characteristics of salespersons. Rogers observed that salespersons could be described as success-oriented, social, dominant, and confident. Kirchner and Dunnette (1959) characterized the salesperson as outgoing, bluff, hardy, and aggressive.

Following these efforts to characterize salespersons, research efforts became directed toward identifying attributes that distinguished successful salespersons from unsuccessful salespersons. For example, Pruden and Peterson (1971) reported that the salesperson's belief of having power over the consumer was associated with increased sales performance. Pace (1972) found that a high level of communication skills distinguished the successful salesperson from the unsuccessful salesperson. Bagozzi (1978) found a positive relationship between self-esteem and sales performance. Similar to the discussion of source credibility effects in chapter 3, Busch and Wilson (1976) and Woodside and Davenport (1974) observed that high expertise salespersons were more effective than low expertise salespersons.

Although this research appeared promising at first, interest in the characteristics of successful salespersons has recently begun to diminish. This may be due in large part to a general inconsistency in the results obtained in using this approach. Sometimes a given characteristic of salespersons predicts successful sales, and sometimes it does not. Weitz (1981) reviewed a number of previous studies that illustrated the contradictory results regarding the relations between various characteristics and sales effectiveness. For example, in some studies (e.g., Greenberg & Mayer, 1964) empathy was related to sales effectiveness, whereas in other studies (e.g., Lamont & Lundstrom, 1977), it was not. This suggests that the effectiveness of a salesperson's performance may be due to things other than/in addition to the characteristics of the salesperson's personality. A more recent perspective incorporates the personality of the salesperson and the personality of the consumer.

SIMILARITY BETWEEN SALESPERSON AND CONSUMER

A seminal article by F. B. Evans (1963) initiated the second area of research on sales interactions. Evans proposed the hypothesis that, "The sale is a product of the particular dyadic interaction of a given salesman and prospect, rather than a result of the individual qualities of either alone" (Evans, 1963, p. 76). This point of view suggests that both the characteristics of the salesperson and the characteristics of the consumer exert an influence on the outcome of the sales interaction.

This concern for the characteristics of both the salesperson and the consumer has generally taken the form of examinations of the effects of similarity between the salesperson and the consumer. For example, Evans (1963) presented some evidence that indicated that insurance salespersons were more likely to make a sale to those prospects with whom they had the most in common (e.g., age, smoking habits, religious affiliation, political party). Similarly, Riordan, Oliver, and Donnelly (1977) found that similarity between insurance agents and consumers enhanced the effectiveness of the sales attempt. Brock (1965) demonstrated that a paint salesperson who used an amount of paint similar to that used by the consumer was more likely to convince the consumer to change to a higher priced paint than the salesperson who used twenty times the amount of paint used by the consumer.

Incorporating the "characteristics of the salesperson" approach with the "similarity between salesperson and consumer" approach, Woodside and Davenport (1974), Busch and Wilson (1976), and Bambic (1978) compared the effectiveness of expertise of the salesperson and the similarity between the salesperson and the consumer. These studies reported that both salesperson expertise and salesperson–consumer similarity enhanced the effectiveness of the sales attempt; in all three studies, expertise seemed to exert more influence than similarity.

One implication of this pattern of results relates to its similarity to Goethals' (1976; cited in chapter 10) treatment of the social comparison of values and beliefs. Recall that Goethals' work suggests that consumers will be most interested in information from similar others when trying to evaluate their *values* regarding a product, and that consumers will be most interested in information from dissimilar others (e.g., experts) as well as similar others when trying to evaluate their *beliefs* regarding a product. The integration of the results of Woodside and Davenport (1974), Busch and Wilson (1976), and Bambic (1978) with Goethals' work suggests that consumers in a sales interaction may be more involved in evaluating their beliefs than in evaluating their values. The effectiveness of salesperson expertise indicates reliance on a dissimilar other, that is more likely for beliefs than for values. However, the finding that salesperson–consumer similarity can enhance the success of the sales interaction may indicate that consumers are still concerned with evaluating values to some extent.

The relative effectiveness of salesperson expertise and salesperson–consumer similarity may vary as a function of the nature of the product, characteristics of the consumer, or characteristics of the purchasing environment. Some recent research efforts have begun to examine these interactive dimensions of the sales interaction. For example, Rao and Misra (1976) have found that different types of consumers are more receptive to different sales styles (e.g., low need consumers were more receptive to product-centered presentations, whereas high need consumers were more receptive to company-centered presentations). Similarly, Weitz (1978, 1981) has developed an elaborate "contingency framework" for studying sales effectiveness. Weitz's work represents a contingency framework in the sense that a successful sales interaction will be contingent on, or will depend on, a number of mediating variables such as the style and characteristics of the salesperson, the characteristics of the consumer, and the nature of the sales interaction situation. According to Weitz, the successful salesperson is able to form an accurate impression of the consumer and his or her needs, to formulate and deliver an appropriate strategic message, and to evaluate and adjust the influence attempt throughout each stage of the interaction. This approach highlights the complexity of interactions between salespersons and consumers.

INFLUENCE TECHNIQUES

In a uniquely comprehensive descriptive study, Willett and Pennington (1966; cf. also Pennington, 1968) observed a number of regularities in sales interactions. For example, the average sales interaction was approximately 23 minutes long, with the salesperson being responsible for approximately two-thirds of the behavior in each interaction. Further, the salesperson's reference to delivery and style of the product appeared to enhance sales effectiveness, whereas the salesperson's reference to price or negative aspects of a competitor's product appeared to impair sales effectiveness. This type of research is extremely valuable, in that it helps develop a "topography" of sales interactions as they tend to occur in the real world. Unfortunately, this type of research effort is relatively rare (however, cf. Olshavsky, 1973, for another valuable exception).

A more common research paradigm has been to identify influence techniques (derived from sales folklore or from basic research in social psychology), and consider their applications to, and implications for, sales interactions. A number of these influence techniques are considered in the following subsection.

Engagement of Augmentation

An extremely general influence technique involves Kelley's (1967, 1973) attribution theory configuration principle of augmentation (discussed in chapter 4). The salesperson may attempt to lead the consumer to engage the process of augmentation, in the hopes of leading the consumer to form a particular type of inference. This engagement of augmentation could be accomplished by the salesperson making some generally positive claim about his or her product in a way that involves some possible risk, cost, or sacrifice. For example, the salesperson might expound on the superiority of his or her other product, and then admit (with a flush of self-disclosure) that his or her product is more expensive than a competitor (similar to the price–quality relationship, discussed in chapter 3). If the salesperson is willing to admit that the product is more expensive, he or she must be truthful, and therefore the claimed superiority of the product is more believable.

This should be considered a general influence technique for the following reason: during the application of any other influence technique, the consumer will be trying to infer the true quality of the product based on (among other things) the salesperson's behavior. Thus, regardless of what other techniques may be applied, the consumer may always be susceptible to the artificial initiation of augmentation.

Reactance Reduction

Another general influence technique is the reduction of psychological reactance. *Psychological reactance* (Brehm, 1966) refers to an attempt to restore or maintain freedom that the individual feels is lost or threatened. Regarding influence techniques, any sales interaction can be seen as an attempt on the part of the salesperson to control the behavior of the consumer. This is in some ways a threat to the consumer's freedom, and psychological reactance might be evidenced in the consumer's selection of a competitor's brand (simply as an assertion of the consumer's freedom and power of decision). Therefore, reactance reduction tactics have been developed that attempt to convince the consumer that they are not being subjected to an influence technique. For example, during implementation of a sampling technique (a more specific influence technique described later), a reaction reduction tactic might be to tell the consumer that they are under no obligation to purchase the product. Recent research has demonstrated these tactics to be effective (e.g., Clee & Wicklund, 1980; Yalch & Bryce, 1981).

Reactance reduction should be considered a general influence technique for the following reason: during the application of any other influence technique, the consumer may interpret the sales interaction as a threat to his or her decisional freedom. In the example suggested in the previous paragraph, reactance reduction was shown to fit in with the implementation of a more specific influence tactic (i.e., sampling). Thus, regardless of what other techniques may be applied, the consumer may always be susceptible to the reduction of reactance. The remaining influence techniques are more specific in focus.

Foot-in-the-Door

The foot-in-the-door effect refers to the phenomenon of obtaining compliance on a critical request by first obtaining compliance to an initial, smaller request (Freedman & Fraser, 1966). For example, the salesperson who wants you to buy a car may begin by asking you to test-drive the car: similarly, the door-to-door cutlery salesperson who wants you to buy an 8-piece carving service may begin by asking you to cut a thick piece of leather with one of the knives. In each case, compliance to the critical request (e.g., buying the car, buying the carving service) will be enhanced as a result of obtaining compliance to the initial, smaller request. This influence technique has been empirically extended to the context of consumer behavior (e.g., Reingen & Kernan, 1977). Achieving compliance to the initial request might be thought of as the salesperson's metaphorically getting his or her "foot in the door."

One explanation for this effect is in terms of self-perception theory (described in chapter 9). Once the consumer has complied to the initial, smaller request, he or she may come to see himself or herself as the type of person who "does that sort of thing." After having test-driven the car, he or she may infer from that behavior that he or she is the kind of person who drives that particular type of car; after having tried that cutlery, the consumer may infer from that behavior that he or she is the type of person who uses that particular knife. When the critical request is finally presented, the consumer may be predisposed toward complying to that request.

Goldman and Creason (1981) have proposed an interesting extension of the foot-in-the-door technique, that these researchers called the two-feet-in-the-door technique. In this procedure, the individual receives two initial, smaller requests before being presented with the critical request. Goldman and Creason found this alternative to be more effective than the foot-in-the-door technique (cf. Schwartz, 1970).

Door-in-the-Face

The Door-in-the-face effect refers to the phenomenon of obtaining compliance on a critical request by first obtaining noncompliance to an initial larger request (Cialdini et al., 1975). For example, the salesperson who wants you to buy a subcompact car may begin by asking you to buy a Cadillac; similarly, the door-to-door cutlery salesperson who wants you to buy the 8-piece carving service may ask you to buy the 98-piece flatware and carving service. In each case, compliance to the critical request (i.e., buying the subcompact car, buying the 8-piece carving service) will be enhanced as a result of obtaining noncompliance to the initial, larger request. This influence technique has been empirically extended to the context of consumer behavior (e.g., Mowen & Cialdini, 1980). Achieving noncompliance to the initial request might be thought of as the salesperson's metaphorically having the "door (slammed) in his face."

Two complementary explanations for this effect can be considered. On the one hand, this technique may make salient the norm of equity (Adams, 1965). Equity describes a state of affairs where each individual's outcomes are proportional to his or her inputs. Inequity, where outcomes are not proportional to inputs, is apparently discomforting, and people generally attempt to reduce inequity. For example, the president of a company may make a higher salary (outcome) than the company janitor, but this is generally considered to be proportional to the training, experience, skills, and expertise (inputs) that each individual brings to the company. During the door-in-the-face procedure, the consumer's noncompliance to the first request is followed by the salesperson's concession to a more reasonable request. This creates an inequitable relation. The salesperson has modified his desired outcomes, although the consumer has not done so, and the consumer can resolve this inequity by making a concession and accepting the salesperson's new proposal.

On the other hand, the door-in-the-face technique may make salient the norm of reciprocity (Gouldner, 1960). Reciprocity refers to the tendency to do to others what they have done to you. If someone is nice, it is normative for you to be nice in return. Thus, when the salesperson makes a concession and moderates his request, it is normative for the consumer to make a concession and accept that request.

There may appear to be a discrepancy between the door-in-the-face technique and the foot-in-the-door technique described previously. The door-in-the-face technique suggests that compliance to the critical request is facilitated by first obtaining noncompliance, whereas the foot-in-the-door technique suggests that compliance to the critical request is facilitated by first obtaining compliance. However, this discrepancy is only an apparent one, because the foot-in-the-door effect will be most likely to occur except under certain conditions in which the door-in-the-face effect will occur. In order for the door-in-the-face effect to occur, the concession from the large request to the moderate request must be made immediately after noncompliance to the large request, and by the same salesperson who solicited that initial noncompliance (e.g., DeJong, 1979). These seem to be the conditions under which the norms of equity and reciprocity become salient. For example, if you refuse a large request from Salesperson 1 today, you would be under no normative obligation to comply to a more moderate request from Salesperson 2 next week. Indeed, this type of situation has been demonstrated to produce a decrease in compliance to the moderate request, in line with the self-perception explanation (Snyder & Cunningham, 1975).

It may occur to the reader that a two-doors-in-the-face technique might be found to be an effective alternative to the door-in-the-face technique (just as Goldman & Creason's, 1981, two-feet-in-the-door technique was found to be an effective alternative to the foot-in-the-door approach). That is, the salesperson might engage in multiple concessions, leading to the critical request. Social psychological research on bargaining (cf. Rubin & Brown, 1975; Tedeschi, Schlenker, & Bonoma, 1973) suggests that such an approach would probably not be effective. For example, Komorita and Brenner (1968) observed that regular, consistent concessions led to the impression of a weak bargainer from whom further concessions could be expected (cf. also, Pruitt & Drews, 1969). Thus, this proposed two-doors-in-the-face technique would probably be less effective than the simple door-in-the-face.

"Even a Penny Helps"

Research indicates that making the request appear to be trivial can increase compliance to the request. This has been referred to as the "even a penny helps" effect, as a result of the use of this phrase to emphasize the triviality of a request for money in a study by Cialdini and Schroeder (1976). This approach has been found to increase the proportion of people complying to the request, as well as the overall amount of money solicited.

This technique may be successful because it enhances the individual's subjective probability of being able to successfully perform the behavior embodied in the request (Carver & Scheier, 1981). That is, "even a penny helps" may convey to the consumer that it will be easy to comply. This technique can be seen in operation when a salesperson portrays an $8,000 car loan as "$50 down and $50 a month" (without specifying that, with interest, it will take 63 years to pay off the loan).

Low-Balling

Low-balling describes the technique where two individuals arrive at an agreement, at some specified level of cost for each individual, and then one of the individuals increases the cost to be incurred by the other. For example, after the consumer has agreed to purchase a car for $8,000, the salesperson begins to add on $100 for tax, $75 for handling, $200 for tires, and so on. This approach is surprisingly effective (Burger & Petty, 1981; Cialdini, Cacioppo, Bassett, & Miller, 1978). These additional costs presented after agreement has been reached might be thought of as a metaphorical "low ball" that the salesperson throws the consumer.

One explanation for the effectiveness of low-balling is in terms of self-perception theory. When the consumer agrees to purchase the product under the original terms, that behavior might be used by the consumer to infer his or her sincere interest in the product. This inferred sincere interest in the product may enable the consumer to endure the increased cost. An alternative explanation is in terms of impression management theory. If the consumer were to withdraw from the deal after the "slight" change in the terms of agreement, he or she might foster the rather undesirable impression of being an irresponsible consumer who was unaware of these necessary charges, and who could be discouraged in such an important decision by a slight change in the amount of money he or she would have to spend.

Sampling

Practically anyone who has ever visited a modern shopping mall or supermarket has been exposed to the sales technique of sampling. In all of its varieties, sampling involves the salesperson's giving a small amount of the product to the consumer, and then providing the consumer with the opportunity to purchase the product. A common illustration of sampling can be found in many shopping mall specialty food shops. The salesperson offers passersby a sample of the chocolate/cheese/sausage that is on sale that week, and then the salesperson asks the chewing consumer how much of the product they would like to buy. Research has demonstrated sampling to be relatively effective (e.g., Yalch & Bryce 1981).

There are a number of different possible explanations for the effectiveness of sampling. Self-perception theory would hold that the behavior of accepting the sample would be used by the consumer to infer that he or she must in fact like this product and would thereby be inclined to purchase some of it. The norm of equity would be made salient by sampling, in which the consumer's outcome (enjoyment of the free goodie) has been made proportionately large, with no corresponding increase in their input. The way to resolve this inequity would be for the consumer to purchase some of the product (thereby bringing the consumer's input back into proportion with his or her outcome). Similarly, the norm of reciprocity would be made salient by sampling, in that the salesperson has done something nice for the consumer (providing the free goodie), and now the consumer is obligated to do something nice for the salesperson (purchasing some of the product).

Considering all of these influence techniques collectively, there is very little evidence to indicate which techniques are most effective, or (perhaps the more reasonable question) which techniques are more effective under what conditions. A few studies have examined two of the techniques at the same time. For example, Reingen (1978) used the door-in-the-face technique, the "even a penny helps" technique, and both techniques in combination. Considered separately, the two techniques were found to be significantly and equivalently effective. The combination of the two techniques (achieving noncompliance to an initial large request, and then presenting the moderate request along with "even a penny will help") was also found to be effective, although not significantly more or less effective than either approach alone. Yalch and Bryce (1981) observed that the use of a reactance reduction technique almost doubled the effectiveness of a sampling procedure.

However, these few studies examining more than one of the influence techniques are rare exceptions. Most valuable would be a research effort that: (a) compared the relative effectiveness of augmentation engagement, reactance reduction, foot-in-the-door, door-in-the-face, "even a penny helps", low-balling, and sampling, all within the same consumer population, using the same product and salespersons; (b) examined various combinations of techniques to determine if there are any potent interactions that occur when these techniques are used in concert; and (c) examined sequential effects for combinations of two or more techniques. For example, extending from the Yalch and Bryce study (1981), is reactance reduction followed by sampling more effective than sampling followed by reactance reduction? Finally, the interaction between influence techniques and characteristics of the salesperson/salesperson–consumer similarity has yet to be examined. For example, the door-in-the-face technique may be more effective when the salesperson is similar to the consumer, whereas the foot-in-the-door technique may be more effective when the salesperson is high in expertise. Empirical examination of these possibilities will further our understanding of the dynamics of sales interactions.

CONCLUSION: "THE SALES EDGE"

Human Edge Software Corporation of Palo Alto, California, has developed a computer program called The Sales Edge. This program requires the salesperson to evaluate himself or herself by agreeing or disagreeing with 80 personal statements (e.g., "I worry about selling more than most"), and to evaluate the consumer by agreeing or disagreeing with 50 personal adjectives (e.g., "argumentative," "intellectual"). On the basis of this information, The Sales Edge outputs a 10-page, detailed sales strategy report, listing what to expect from the consumer, how to succeed, preparation, specific opening strategies, and specific closing strategies. This computer program, that lists for $250, represents a high-tech implementation of the contingency approach to sales interactions, described previously.

Note that this approach is not limited to stereotypical door-to-door sales.

Rogers (1984) reported that the *London Financial Times* experimented with the Sales Edge to see how Margaret Thatcher might be recommended to "sell" Ronald Reagan on her policy for NATO spending. The Sales Edge produced the recommendations that "Your tendency to place emphasis on details may bore R.R.," and "R.R. is inclined to seek the limelight, to perform for others. Appeal to R.R. with flattery" (Rogers, 1984, p. 52). However, there may very well be limits to the applicability of this program. Future research will have to establish whether The Sales Edge can provide a student with a sure-fire teacher–student specific appeal that will get the teacher to accept a late term paper!

13 | Applications to Nonprofit Settings

In the previous chapters, most of the discussion and examples have revolved around commodity-type products. Consumers have been scrutinized as they drank cans of soda pop, ate Biggy Burgers, and bought used automobiles. This is legitimate insofar as the most common applications of the foregoing concepts and principles are found in private sector (i.e., profit-oriented) settings. Certainly, the lion's share of research and theory has developed with regard to private sector, commodity-type products. However, the introduction in chapter 1 suggested that the product that is used by consumers could be a school's educational product, a religious group's spiritual product, or something other than some physical object. In this chapter, we consider the application of the concepts and principles presented in previous chapters to these nonprofit settings. It is hoped that widening our focus of application at the end of this text will provide worthwhile and stimulating closure to this material.

Nonprofit settings is the term most often used to identify these types of application (e.g., Gaedeke, 1977; Kotler, 1975; Lovelock & Weinberg, 1978). Other terms that have been used to identify these nontraditional, noncommodity areas of application are *ecological settings* (e.g., Henion, 1976), *nonbusiness settings* (e.g., Lovelock, 1977), and *social settings* (e.g., Green, 1980). The areas of application to nonprofit settings that are considered hereafter are religion, criminal justice, energy conservation, and political campaigns. Although these situations may or may not be thought of as profit oriented, and they may or may not appear to embody all of the trappings of a genuine business, they share in common the attribute of offering to consumers some service or idea rather than some physical commodity. Other possible applications are briefly considered at the end of the chapter. Bear in mind that our task in this chapter is to understand how the psychology of consumer behavior can be applied to nonprofit settings.

Application of the principles of consumer behavior to nonprofit settings is similar in many ways to such application in the private sector. In many ways, consumers would be expected to behave toward a politician in a manner analogous to how they behave toward a can of butter beans. That is, the stimulus situation would influence the internal processes, intention and behavior within a social context and a cultural context, as delineated in previous chapters. Of course, there are also some obvious differences between nonprofit setting applications and their private sector counterparts. As Green (1980) observed, the product of nonprofit organizations (e.g., religious faith; highway safety) may often be more emotionally involving than a can of butter beans. Novelli (1980) discussed some of the practical differences between nonprofit setting applications and private sector applications. For example, given that the product in a nonprofit setting may be more emotionally involving, it may be more difficult to obtain accurate indices of consumers' beliefs. In other words, people may be more honest when telling you their preferred brand of butter beans than they are when telling you about their church attendance or their highway driving speed. Another implication of this greater emotional involvement is that nonprofit settings may be especially potent contexts for applications of the various principles of emotional responses, presented in chapter 6. For example, fear appeals may be more effective for influencing church attendance and highway driving speed than for influencing selection of soft drinks or butter beans.

Certainly, the principles presented in previous chapters have been implicitly, unintentionally applied to nonprofit settings for centuries. However, some sources (e.g., "Advertising increasing . . .," 1980) trace the development of intentional applications to nonprofit settings to the formation of the War Advertising Council. This council, created in 1941 after the attack on Pearl Harbor, placed the resources of the advertising industry at the disposal of the United States government. In an attempt to assist the war effort, the War Advertising Council developed a number of public service campaigns, such as promoting the development of "victory gardens," the prevention of forest fires, and the purchase of War Bonds. After the war, the War Advertising Council became the Advertising Council, that continues to contribute resources to nonprofit promotional campaigns (cf. Fig. 13.1). Another critical event in the emergence of intentional nonprofit applications was a paper by Philip Kotler and Sidney Levy (1969), that explicated how marketing techniques developed in the private sector could find useful application in various nonprofit settings. Fifteen years later, such applications have become almost commonplace; some examples are considered hereafter.

RELIGION

Numerous "trade" journals for religious organizations (e.g., "Advertising your . . .," 1977; "Religious media's . . .," 1978) have discussed the possibilities of considering religion as a nonprofit area of application for principles of consumer behavior. Dunlap and Rountree (1981) have presented a number of analogies between attributes of private sector consumer behavior and attributes of religious organization consumer behavior. For example, in the context of religious groups, the product is "the (re)discovery of the individual's identity as it relates to God." Similarly, the pricing associated with this product is the time and effort required by volunteer duties, as well as monetary tithes and donations offered to the

I SHOULD'VE VOTED.

You know that's what you're going to say if your candidate doesn't win.

Bill Cosby says: "Help us, help vets."

American Red Cross

FIG. 13.1 Illustration of the efforts of the Advertising Council.

church. The "spreading of the gospel" is comprised of persuasive appeals that become elements of the congregation members'/consumers' stimulus situation (cf. Fig. 13.2). Finally, these elements of consumer behavior are seen to operate within a social and cultural context.

Ries and Trout (1981) describe the application of market space principles to the problem of declining attendance in Catholic churches. The Vatican II Council (1962–1965) produced a number of changes in the Catholic church: many rules and regulations were eliminated; the liturgy became vernacularized (i.e., translated into the spoken language of the congregation members). Ries and Trout proposed that these changes moved the Church away from the position it had always occupied as "teacher of the law," without redefining the church in any way. Thus, in terms of the belief structures of the consumers of the Catholic

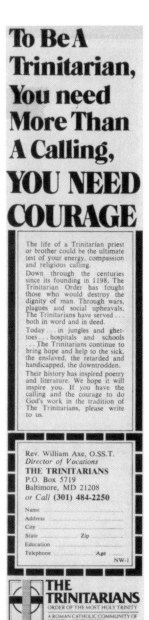

FIG. 13.2 *Illustration of information directed toward consumers in the context of religious groups.*

church's spiritual product, the church ceased to be what it had always been without becoming something else in return. According to Ries and Trout, Vatican II did not displace the church from one point to another in the consumers' market space. Rather, Vatican II simply removed the church from its old position in the market space, and did not place it in a new position. The results of this "unpositioning" were a decrease in church attendance, a decrease in the number of incoming priests, brothers, and nuns, and a decline in the church's influence over human affairs. Ries and Trout suggested the development of a new position for the Catholic church, consistent with the reforms of Vatican II, as "Teacher of the Word." The goal of this newly positioned product/organization would be "keeping Christ alive in the minds of each new generation and relating His word to the problems of their time" (Ries & Trout, 1981, p. 204). Even though this suggestion was not implemented by the administration of the Catholic church, it illustrates the application of principles of consumer behavior to the nonprofit setting of a religious organization.

Blackwell, Engel, and Talarzyk (1977) described an attempt to assess the needs of members of the Presbyterian Church of Brazil. It was found that, relative to other evangelical denominations in Brazil, Presbyterians expressed less need for change in learning to study the Bible, and more need for change in learning to love others. Identification of these areas of relative need provided the leaders of the Presbyterian church with specific motives that needed to be addressed in order to maintain (and possibly increase) attendance and participation among congregation members.

Perhaps the most explicit illustration of an approach to religion in terms of consumer behavior can be found in the efforts of Robert Schuller, the well-known religious television minister. Schuller's Garden Grove Community Church in California started in a drive-in theatre; Schuller (1974) has described the church as "a shopping center for God."

CRIMINAL JUSTICE

Tuck (1979) has provided an insightful analysis of the potential applications of principles of consumer behavior to the criminal justice system. An important issue in this area of application involves the effect of the criminal justice system on criminals. In this light, the (potential or practicing) criminal is a consumer of some product proscribed by law (e.g., murder, rape, stolen property). Deterrence can be understood in terms of attempts to make this product less attractive to the criminal (e.g., increase the price associated with the product, reduce the motivation for the product, mitigate positive feelings for the product), and to enhance the attractiveness of alternative products to the criminal. Much criminological research has been directed toward identifying the determinants of effective deterrence.

The hotly debated penalty of capital punishment has been criticized in some quarters for lacking any deterrent effect (e.g., Wolfgang, 1978; National Research Council, 1978). However, some recent research suggests that capital punishment may, in fact, have a deterrent effect, within limits. Phillips (1980) examined the relationship between weekly homicide statistics in England and the occurrence of, and media attention directed toward, public executions. Phillips' analyses revealed that: the number of homicides decreased substantially during the week before, the week of, and the week after a public execution; however, the number of homicides increased a corresponding amount during the third, fourth, and fifth weeks after an execution. Thus, as Phillips (1980) noted, "the lesson of the scaffold is real, but only temporary" (p. 145). Interestingly, Phillips also observed a significant correlation between the amount of publicity devoted to the execution (the number of column inches devoted to the story in the London Times) and the size of the drop in homicides in the week of the execution. This stands as a demonstration of a significant, short-term relationship between frequency of exposure and product acceptance (where the product being accepted is lawful refraining from homicidal behavior) for this particular nonprofit setting.

Phillips' research suggests that public punishment may exert a deterrent effect in the short run, and that this deterrent effect will be enhanced by making the punishment more public. Serrill (1983) has described a case of judicial punishment that is in many ways unique, and may provide an illustration for this type of effect. Three South Carolina men confessing to the 6-hour gang rape of an 80-pound woman were given a choice between two sentences by Judge C. Victor Pyle: 30 years imprisonment or voluntary castration. This sentencing has been appealed. Certainly, sentencing of this type raises a host of ethical and moral questions, as does capital punishment. However, the consumer psychologist must also view this situation as an opportunity to study the effectiveness of this type of sentencing as a deterrent for this type of behavior in the future. If the appeal is turned down, and if Judge Pyle's sentence is carried out (one way or the other), what effect will this have on the number of rapes committed in that region in subsequent weeks and months? Will the effect (if any) increase as a function of the amount of media attention given to the sentencing procedure?

In addition to the effects of the criminal justice system on criminals, Tuck (1979) suggested that the effects of the criminal justice system on the general population also be considered from the perspective of consumer behavior. For example, Blackwell et al. (1977) described the Expanded Public involvement in Crime Prevention program conducted in Dallas, Texas in the mid-1970s. The theme for this program was "Don't ask for it," and this provided the backdrop for television commercials that delineated simple precautions that the citizenry could take in order to reduce their chances of falling victim to rape, burglary, and so on. Many urban areas have established 3-digit emergency phone numbers (e.g., 911) to be used for reporting crimes. These 3-digit numbers are often plastered on billboards throughout the city, right alongside billboard advertisements for beer and butter beans. Other examples of aspects of the criminal justice system directed toward the general, consumer population are the currently popular "Take a bite outta crime" campaign, and Operation Identification (cf. Fig. 13.3).

ENERGY CONSERVATION

The energy crisis of the late 1970s and early 1980s forced consumers, politicians, and social scientists to become concerned with means of coping with rapidly deplenishing and scarce energy resources. Publications on the application of principles of consumer psychology to the problems of energy conservation began

Latchkey Children:
Young Children at Home Alone

Help me, McGruff . . .
TAKE A BITE OUT OF
CRIME™

FIG. 13.3 Illustration of information directed toward general population in the context of the criminal justice system.

at an average of less than 15 per year before 1974, and increased to 150 per year by 1980 (McDougall, Clanton, Ritchie, & Anderson, 1981). In the 1980s, gas and oil prices have (more or less) stabilized, cars have been made more fuel efficient, and houses have been insulated. Perhaps as a result of these changes, research on energy conservation has levelled off somewhat, although this remains an active and intriguing area of research.

One line of research has involved the study of the relationship between attitudes regarding energy conservation and actual energy conservation behavior. This represents a special case of the attitude–behavior consistency problem, discussed in chapter 8. For example, Heslop, Moran, and Cousineau (1981) found price consciousness to be the only attitudinal variable to predict energy consumption. Highly price conscious people conserved energy to a greater extent than low price conscious people. Neither energy and conservation consciousness nor attitudes regarding social responsibility were related to energy use. In fact, household characteristics and family size were the best predictors of energy consumption. Similarly, Verhallen and Van Raaij (1981) found that attitudes regarding home comfort, energy consciousness, and price consciousness were largely unrelated to energy use, while household characteristics were strongly related to energy use. These researchers recommended that policy makers interested in increasing energy conservation should focus on home improvement rather than conscious-ness-raising.

There are many reasons why pre-existing attitudes seem to be such poor predictors of energy use. The behavior under consideration is very different in many ways from other types of consumer behavior. Unlike many profit-oriented product categories that require a choice between brand A and brand B, energy consumption is usually gauged by a unique type of composite measure. The gas or electric meter reading reflects a number of things in addition to the setting of the thermostat. Even at a given thermostat setting, energy consumption will be influenced by the degree of insulation of the living unit, the living unit's orientation to natural windbreaks, shade, and other living units, current weather conditions and time of day, the age and efficiency of the heating/cooling units, and the operation of alternative heat sources (e.g., solar panels, wood stoves). Research cited in chapter 8 has demonstrated that attitudes, intentions, and behavior will all be more closely related to the extent that attitudes and intentions are on the same level of specificity as the behavior in question. Thus, attitudes toward conserving energy in the home may be very predictive of thermostat settings (a measure that has seldom been used in this research). However, these attitudes may not be very predictive of electric meter readings, with all of the meter readings' peripheral influences.

Even the easy and immediate behavior of setting the thermostat carries with it an unusual blend of immediate, short-term and continual, long-term consequences. Unlike the choice of a brand of soda pop, the setting of a thermostat has the continual and long-lived consequences of cost and health. Unlike selection of an automobile, the setting of a thermostat has the immediate and short-lived consequences of comfort and relief. Thus, the prediction of energy conservation from attitudinal measures seems to involve unusual complexities that continue to challenge consumer psychologists.

Another line of research has involved attempts to gauge the effectiveness of energy conservation programs. For example, in 1979, the U.S. Department of Energy Implemented a Low Cost/No Cost energy conservation program in six New England states. This program involved the direct distribution of an energy efficiency handbook to 4.5 million households, an extensive paid advertising campaign, and public relations activities, such as press conferences and appearances on talk shows. In studying the effects of this program, Hutton and McNeill (1981) observed that the reading of the Low Cost/No Cost energy conservation handbook was positively related to energy conservation, suggesting that the program was (in part) successful. Yates and Aronson (1983) reported a similar analysis of the home energy audit program set up by the Residential Conservation Service.

Psychographic approaches can be just as effective in nonprofit settings as in the private sector. For example, Belk, Painter, and Semenik (1981) developed a psychographic approach that distinguished between consumers in terms of energy conservation-relevant cognitions. Specifically, consumers were categorized in terms of whether they thought the energy crisis was attributable to personal, individual energy use, or to impersonal causes (such as the Organization of Petroleum Exporting Countries [OPEC] and the oil companies). Persons who explained the energy crisis in terms of personal, individual energy use favored (and themselves adopted) the personal solutions of voluntary energy conservation. On the other hand, consumers who blamed the energy crisis on OPEC and the oil companies favored the nonpersonal solutions of government enforced conservation and government pressure on the oil companies. Consider the implications of this psychographic approach. The good news is that energy conservation programs may be effective for that large segment of the population that attributes energy shortages to individual use. The bad news is that energy conservation programs are likely to be ineffective for that large segment of the population that attributes energy shortages to big business. The really bad news is that this latter segment is initially least likely to be engaging in voluntary conservation, and is therefore the group that most needs to develop energy conservation practices.

POLITICAL CAMPAIGNS

The application of principles of consumer behavior to the political arena has a relatively long tradition. McGinnis' *The Selling of the President* (1969), and White's books on *The Making of the President* (1960, 1964, 1968, 1972, 1976) are replete with examples of politicians' concerns for media usage, impression management, persuasion, and other variables described previously. For example, White (1972) described how Franklin Roosevelt cleverly removed Thomas E. Dewey from the stimulus situation for an evening during the 1944 presidential campaign. Roosevelt had reserved a 15-minute segment on NBC Radio, and Dewey subsequently reserved the following 15-minute segment on NBC in order to capitalize on Roosevelt's audience. However, Roosevelt spoke for 14 of his 15 minutes, and left the last full minute of his reserved air-time completely silent. Reportedly, listeners across the country believed that the NBC network had gone off the air after the president's speech, and all of those listeners began scanning the dial for other radio stations. As a result, the millions who had been listening to Roosevelt a minute before were not listening when Dewey came on the air.

Richard Nixon was observed to perform a number of politically motivated acts that served to associate his name with positively regarded representatives from various subgroups. For example, Nixon released from prison Jimmy Hoffa, the convicted former chief of the teamsters. This was followed a few months later by the endorsement of Nixon's candidacy by the 2.5-million member Teamsters' Union. Similarly, Nixon had the visiting president of Mexico "toured" through Chicago, Texas, and Los Angeles, where Latin-American voters might be favorably impressed by Nixon's courteous treatment of the visiting Latin-American dignitary.

Friedman, DiMatheo, and Mertz (1980) provided evidence for the possibility of an intriguing application of some previously considered principles to a political setting. For the month prior to the 1976 presidential election, these researchers collected videotapes of news broadcasters' facial expressions as they referred to Jimmy Carter or to Gerald Ford. Then, 40 observers judged the positivity of each facial expression (with the sound turned off). Systematic patterns were found in these candidate-associated facial expressions. For example, Walter Cronkite and Harry Reasoner showed more positive facial expressions when referring to Carter than when referring to Ford. On the other hand, John Chancellor and Barbara Walters showed more positive facial expressions when referring to Ford than when referring to Carter.

These subtle biases may have been communicated to consumers who tended to watch a particular news broadcast every evening. This possibility becomes especially important in view of the process of vicarious classical conditioning of affective responses, discussed in chapter 6. In that process, the visible pleasure (e.g., the facial expression) of the television character serves as the unconditioned stimulus for a positive emotional response on the part of the television-viewing consumer. As depicted in Fig. 13.4, this sets the stage for the vicarious classical conditioning of positive affective responses toward political candidates that result from repeated exposure to a particular news broadcaster's subtle reactions to the political candidates. For example, the news broadcaster may become conditioned to experience pleasure in response to the candidate's name because the candidate's name is repeatedly paired with an agreeable platform (i.e., positions on important issues with which the news broadcaster agrees). For the consumer/voter watching this repeated association on the evening news, the candidate's name is repeatedly associated with a positive facial expression on the part of the news broadcaster, that elicits a vicarious pleasure response. It should be recognized that while this is happening for Candidate 1 (who elicits smiles from the news broadcaster), the complementary process may be simultaneously happening for Candidate 2 (who elicits frowns from the news broadcaster).

Mullen et al. (1986) pursued this line of reasoning in a study of the 1984 presidential election. Replicating Friedman et al.'s procedure, Mullen et al. found that Peter Jennings showed more positive facial expressions when referring to

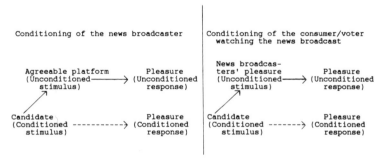

FIG. 13.4 Illustration of the vicarious classical conditioning of emotional responses toward political candidates as a result of news broadcasters' facial expression.

Ronald Reagan than when referring to Walter Mondale (the other two major network newscasters, Tom Brokaw and Dan Rather, did not exhibit any differences in facial expressions for Mondale or Reagan). In a telephone survey conducted in a five-state region after the election, Mullen et al. found that people who watched Peter Jennings were more likely to vote for Reagan than people who watched Brokaw or Rather. This is clearly consistent with the disturbing possibility that a smile might be able to elect a president!

This speculation was anticipated in a chillingly prescient manner by suspense writer Robert Bloch, in his short story entitled "Show Biz" (1959). In this story, an unnamed professor has arranged a secret meeting with the head of the nation's largest advertising firm, in order to propose a means of developing the most effective type of politician.

> When I began to study these things you've mentioned—how people from the entertainment world have gradually infiltrated politics as advisors, producers, technicians; how they've tried to train our politicians and office holders to become like actors. And it occurred to me then—why not use actors? . . . You said yourself that almost any man who starts with a clean record and a noncommittal attitude can be built into a political figure by means of present-day psychological techniques. The trick is to teach him to speak, to handle himself properly when on public display. So why waste time on tired old men or egotistical prima donnas who can't cope with their roles? If politics is show business, why not put the right actors into the parts to begin with? (Bloch, 1959, p. 66)

Incidentally, the unnamed professor is murdered at the end of the story, apparently because the people he was talking to had already begun to implement such a strategy, and they preferred to keep it a secret. It is an interesting, if somewhat fanciful, notion: an effective politician could be produced by starting with an actor who knew how to "play to an audience"!

CONCLUSION

As noted at the beginning of this chapter, these four areas of nonprofit setting application provide only a partial list of the nonprofit applications that are possible. A number of interesting nonprofit setting applications have developed in recent years. For example, Robertson (1971) has extended this type of analysis to the use of health care systems, identifying the types of attributes of a health care system that enhance or impair its use by consumers. Cameron, Oskamp, and Sparks (1977) and Harrison and Saeed (1977) have examined "lonely hearts" newspaper advertisements for dating or marital partners, and have found complementary differences between the advertisements submitted by males and those submitted by females (e.g., females seek financial security and offer physical attractiveness, whereas males offer financial security and seek physical attractiveness (see also interest box, opposite). Pessemier, Bemmaor, and Hanssens (1977) have examined the donation of human body parts, and Burnkrant and Page (1982) have examined the donation of blood, from the perspective of consumer

Interest Box

TLC for DWMs and SWFs

Classified love ads are a booming business

At a few dollars or so per line, they are the natural outlet of the discreet, the sincere and the sensitive, all seeking kindred spirits for meaningful relationships. Classified love ads, once relegated primarily to non-mainstream papers like New York City's *Village Voice* and the sex magazines, are now blossoming almost everywhere. In the ad columns of at least 100 magazines and newspapers, even in dailies like the Chicago *Tribune*, armies of hopeful DWMs and SWFs seek mergers as POSSLQs (translation: divorced white males and single white females wish to unite as persons of the opposite sex sharing living quarters).

Analysts and advertisers seem to agree that love ads are now an important part of the mating game. "Your Aunt Susan isn't going to find anyone for you," complains Philadelphia Businesswoman Cari Lyn Vinci, who has met 25 men by using ads. Adds Edwin Roberts, manager of classifieds for *New York* magazine: "If you talk to people who go to singles bars, you just hear a lot of frustration."

The most successful ads seem to indicate a quivering sensibility or a rakish, humorous personality, perhaps with a naughty hint of "life in the fast lane." The

New York Review of Books often features a mock high-cultural tone ("Man who is a serious novel would like to hear from a woman who is a poem"). Sincere is the lowest-ranking adjective, says Sherri Foxman, author of a new book on the subject, *Classified Love*. "If you write 'Sincere woman seeking sincere man,' you're going to get 25 boring letters." Since standards of accuracy are not always rigorous, the words slim and attractive are not taken literally. Susan Block, a Los Angeles writer, says "the most frequent complaint from men is that the women weigh more than they say. The women complain that the men are flaky."

The recently divorced, along with homosexuals newly out of the closet, use the ads to find quick action. Senior citizens, the handicapped ("I walk with a cane") and those with concerns ("SWM . . . seeks WF WITHOUT HERPES") can come right to the point without hours of social jousting. Once

the natural home of kinks and losers, the classified personals now attract people known to advertisers as "upscale." Even the *Village Voice*, which handles about 50,000 replies to love personals each year, says its audience is "mid-30s, affluent, with many professionals."

Some of the publications do have taboos. The Chicago *Tribune*, which runs love ads Mondays and Fridays, does a brisk business among the divorced, but takes no marrieds. Most large newspapers and city magazines turn down blatantly kinky ads, but a few slip by the censors in disguise. "I love wearing makeup" is a semisubtle hint at transvestism. At the *Voice* almost anything goes. "We allow people to describe themselves fully," says Associate Publisher John Evans, "but we don't allow things like mention of body parts."

A cottage industry is springing up around the ads. Author Foxman runs a classified love telephone line in Cleveland. Entrepreneur Vinci started a similar service in Philadelphia. Author Lynn Davis offers a three-hour workshop in New York City called "Personal Ads, Why Not?" Vi Rogers, editor of National Singles Register, a tabloid published in Southern California with many pages of personals, says the search for love, and not just sex, is producing the boom. "I never realized how many men wanted to get married in Southern California," she says. "Men and women today want the same thing: romance, love and commitment." ∎

(Time, 1983, January 10, p. 65. Copyright © 1983 Time Inc., reprinted by permission.)

psychology. Hyman (1977) and Hankiss (1980) have provided insightful analyses of the techniques of the con artist, who comes to be seen as a very effective type of salesperson.

Extending the concepts and principles of consumer psychology to these and other novel settings provides the consumer psychologist with the opportunity to have substantial input to timely social issues. Of possibly greater importance, these applications and extensions require that the generalizability and the utility of our concepts and principles be subjected to the most stringent of tests. This should be invigorating for the field, and should lead to further refinement of the theoretical foundations of consumer psychology. As the diversity of these areas of application increases, those of us seeking new topics for research are likely to be limited only by the bounds of human interaction and exchange, and by our own imaginations.

Afterword

The reader who has gotten to this point in the text has been exposed to the results of hundreds of studies, which in turn involved the close observation of the behavior of thousands of consumers. How does all of this information contribute to our understanding of consumer behavior?

As the physicist and philosopher of science J. H. Poincare (1908) once wrote, "Science is built up with facts, as a house is with stones. But a collection of facts is no more a science than a heap of stones is a house" (p. 829). In order for the facts to contribute to a science, the facts must be organized into general principles, and the principles integrated into a viable theoretical model. The general model presented in Fig. 1.1 provided just such a framework for organizing and integrating all of this information. As we have progressed through each chapter in the book, we have gained a deeper understanding of a different facet of consumer behavior. Variations in the stimulus situation have been seen to influence the extent to which consumers become aware of the product (chapter 2: Perception), the development of consumers' beliefs about the product (chapter 3: Cognition and Memory), the change of consumers' beliefs about the product (chapter 4: Cognition and Persuasion), the acquisition of associations involving the presence of the product, the use of the product, and various rewards and punishments (chapter 5: Learning), the development of feelings about the product (chapter 6: Emotion), and the development of desires for the product (chapter 7: Motivation). As consumers become aware of the product, develop positive overall beliefs about the product, acquire associations between the use of the product and pleasant consequences, develop good feelings about the product, and develop desires for the product, and as these various effects interact in complex ways, consumers may formulate intentions to buy the product, and thereby engage in the behavior of purchasing the product (chapter 8: Intention and Behavior). This basic atemporal and unidirectional model linking the stimulus situation to behavior was elaborated by a consideration of the feedback effects of behavior, and the variations in the model that can occur over the product life cycle (chapter 9: Behavioral Feedback and Product Life Cycle). This model was further elaborated by a consideration of the effects of acquaintances, friends, and family members on the consumer (chapter 10: The Social Context), as well as by a consideration of the effects of culture, subculture, and social class on the consumer (chapter 11: The Cultural Context). The unique case of sales interactions was examined in detail (chapter 12: Sales Interactions). Finally, applications of principles of consumer psychology to less obvious, nonbusiness realms were discussed (chapter 13: Nonprofit Settings).

Throughout, our goal has been to understand why consumers do what they do. Attempts to reach this goal have answered many questions, but have also raised as many new questions. What are the benefits, if any, of customary (or "psychological") prices, described in chapter 3; do customary prices reveal a truncation in the otherwise linear metric of 'cents,' similar to that discussed in terms of adaptation level theory and assimilation contrast effects? What are the long-term effects of the emotional conditioning described in chapter 6? What are the limits to creating new motives for products, as described in chapter 7? To what extent is the post-decisional dissonance phenomenon described in chapter 9 indicative of a real change in beliefs, and to what extent is it indicative of a concern to avoid appearing foolish; how long-lived are the effects of post-decisional dissonance in real consumer behavior settings? What are the effects of combining and sequencing the various influence techniques used by sales personnel that were examined in chapter 12?

"What influences consumers, and why?" continues to be the ever-ready question of the consumer psychologist. It is our sincere hope that this book will stimulate some of its readers to be caught up in the engaging enterprise of asking this question.

Glossary

Adaptation Level: Some average of the stimulus intensities to which the individual has been exposed.

Adaptation Level Theory: A theory proposed to account for how the same stimulus can be evaluated differently as a function of how similar or dissimilar it is to the adaptation level.

Affect: Emotion.

Aided Recall: A measure of retention that provides minimal prompting. For example, the individual is asked to tell what (product category) commercials they have seen recently.

Anchoring Stimuli: The highest, the lowest, and the average stimulus intensities to which the individual has been exposed.

Assimilation–Contrast Effects: A theory proposed to account for how the same stimulus can be evaluated differently as a function of how similar or dissimilar it is to anchoring stimuli.

Attention: The process of selecting and focusing on only a portion of the available stimulation while ignoring, suppressing, or inhibiting reactions to other stimuli.

Attitude: A general evaluation of some object, comprised of cognitive, emotional, and motivational components.

Attribution Theory: A theory that describes the cognitive processes by which people determine the causes of behavior and events in their world.

Augmentation: In attribution theory, the configuration principle that when a behavior occurs in the face of costs, risks, and sacrifices associated with that event, then that event is more likely to be attributed to internal causes.

Autonomic Decisions: Decisions regarding brand choices in product categories where either the husband or the wife is more likely to make the decision, although the one to make the decision will vary from couple to couple.

Behavior: An act or response.

Behavioral Feedback: The effect of behavior on the internal processes that gave rise to that behavior.

Belief: A potentially verifiable assertion about the true nature of the object of concern.

Cherchez le Creneau (French for "Look for the hole"): In terms of a market space,

174

developing a new brand that is as close as possible to the ideal point, while being as far as possible from competitor brands.

Classical Conditioning (Pavlovian Conditioning, Respondent Conditioning): A model of associative learning in which a response (conditioned response) comes to be evoked by a previously neutral stimulus (conditioned stimulus) that has been repeatedly paired with a stimulus (unconditioned stimulus) that originally elicited the response (unconditioned response).

Closure: The Gestalt perceptual principle that identifies a tendency toward completeness.

Cognition: The processes of knowing or thought.

Cognitive Dissonance: An unpleasant state of tension that results from an inconsistency between cognitive elements. Presumably, the individual is motivated to reduce cognitive dissonance by resolving the inconsistency.

Computer Scan Purchase Diary: Automatic recording of an individual's supermarket buying behavior as the Universal Pricing Code (UPC) symbols are processed by a computerized check-out register. It provides a precise and completely detailed listing of the products and brands purchased by the individual on a daily basis.

Conditioned Response: A behavior or act that comes to be elicited by a previously neutral stimulus by virtue of the association between that stimulus and another stimulus which "naturally" elicits such a response (see Classical Conditioning).

Conditioned Stimulus: A previously neutral stimulus that comes to elicit a response by virtue of its association with another stimulus which "naturally" elicited such a response (see Classical Conditioning).

Configuration Principles: According to attribution theory, principles used to determine the cause of an event when only one observation is available (schema, discounting, augmentation).

Conjugate Lateral Eye Movement (CLEM): Movements of the eyes to the right (inferred to indicate left-hemispheric activities like verbal, analytic, and sequential behaviors) or to the left (inferred to indicate right-hemispheric activities like emotional, imaginative, and spatial behaviors).

Consensus: In attribution theory, the covariation principle that the more other people respond in a given way to an entity, the more likely that an individual's making that response to the entity will be attributed to the entity and not to the individual.

Consistency: In Attribution Theory, the covariation principle that the more consistent an individual's response toward an entity, the more that response will be attributed to the individual or to the entity (rather than making no attribution at all).

Consumer: An individual who uses the products, goods, or services of some organization.

Consumer Psychology: The scientific study of the behavior of consumers.

Consumer Space: The geometric representation of consumers' beliefs about the "ideal" product in a product category.

Context Effects: The influence of the situation in which a stimulus is presented on the perception of that stimulus.

Content: The actual elements contained in a persuasive message.

Continuous Reinforcement: A scheduling of reinforcement in which the reinforcement is provided after every correct response.

Covariation Principles: According to attribution theory, principles used to determine the cause of an event when multiple observations are available (consensus, consistency, distinctiveness).

Cultural Context: The totality of cultural stimulation that influences the individual and his or her social context, including culture, subculture, and social class.

Customary Prices: Prices ending with "9," such as 49¢ rather than 50¢, or $199.99 rather than $200.

Cybernetic Models: General models of consumer behavior comprised of large lists of variables suspected to influence consumer behavior. The variables are conceptualized in a complicated flow of influence that can incorporate influence from one variable to another and then "feed back" to the first variable again.

Demographics: The use of individual differences in sociological and socioeconomic variables to predict consumer behavior.

Dependent Variable: In conducting research, the variable that is measured or observed for variations.

Discounting: In attribution theory, the configuration principle that when there are two or more plausible causes for a given behavior, the likelihood that any given one of them is the sole cause is reduced.

Distinctiveness: In attribution theory, the covariation principle that the more distinctive the individual's response to the entity, the more likely the response will be attributed to the entity and not the individual.

Door-in-the-Face: An influence technique where compliance on a second request is increased by first obtaining noncompliance to an initial, larger request.

Emotion: A state of arousal involving conscious experience and visceral changes.

Encoding Specificity Hypothesis: The retrieval of an item or event from memory can be enhanced by reproducing the context in which the item or event was encoded for long-term storage.

Equity: A state of affairs where each individual's outcomes are proportional to his or her inputs.

"Even a Penny Helps": An influence technique where compliance to a request is increased by making the request appear to be trivial.

Expectation: A readiness to respond in a particular manner.

Extended Family: A family structure where grandparents, parents, and children live together.

Extensive Problem Solving (EPS): The earliest stage of learning how to buy, in which the consumer must construct a new market space for an entirely new product category.

Extinction: The process by which an acquired association is eliminated. Associations acquired through classical conditioning are extinguished by repeated presentations of the conditioned stimulus without the unconditioned stimulus. Associations acquired through instrumental conditioning are extinguished when the individual performs the instrumental response and does not receive reinforcement.

Family of Orientation: The family into which one is born, where one serves as a child.

Family of Procreation: The family created by marriage, where one serves as a spouse and parent.

Fear Appeal: An attempt to arouse a negative emotional response by showing that failure to use the product, good, or service will produce disastrous consequences, whereas use of the product, good, or service will eliminate or prevent the disastrous consequences.

Feedback: When one variable, that has been influenced by a second variable, now exerts influence on that second variable.

Figure-Ground: The gestalt perceptual principle that identifies the perceptual distinction between the figure (which stands out, has good contour, and appears solid and nearby) and the ground (which is indistinct, not clearly shaped, and appears to recede into the background).

Fishbein Multi-Attribute Model: A model that defines the overall evaluation of X in terms of the weighted sum of the beliefs about X, where each belief is weighted by the strength or importance of the belief. This is part of the theory of reasoned action.

Flesch Count: A measure of the readability of written communication.

Focused Self-Report: A measurement of motivation that requires the individual to describe his or her own needs and satisfactions regarding a specific product and selected product attributes.

Foot-in-the-Door: An influence technique where compliance on a second request is increased by first obtaining compliance to an initial, smaller request.

Form: The arrangement and the structure of the elements contained in a persuasive message.

Functional Autonomy: An object or event that was once instrumental to some other goal acquires a value that outlives its instrumentality.

Galvanic Skin Response (GSR): A measure of changes in arousal in terms of changes in the electrical conductivity of the surface of the skin due to changes in the amount of perspiration on one's hands and fingers.

Gestalt: Form, pattern, or configuration.

Global Self-Report: A measurement of motivation that requires the individual to identify broad, underlying motivations.

Husband Dominant Decisions: Decisions regarding brand choices in product categories where the husband is more likely to make the decision in most families.

Impression Management Theory: A theory that holds that the individual tries to manage or control the impressions that others form of him or her.

Independent Variable: In conducting research, the variable that is manipulated or changed in a controlled manner.

Information Overload: Difficulty in information processing that results from an unmanageable amount of information.

Instrumental Conditioning (Operant Conditioning): A model of associative learning in which a response that leads to reinforcement is more likely to be repeated.

Instrumental Response: A response that leads to reinforcement (see Instrumental Conditioning).

Insufficient Justification: The state defined by the performance of a neutral or negative behavior which in turn leads to a neutral or negative outcome; the performance of a behavior for which there is not an adequate outcome or payoff.

Intention: A plan to perform some specific behavior.

Internal Processes: A related series of changes that occur within the individual (perception, cognition, memory, learning, emotion, motivation).

Latency of Response: A measure of retention that indicates how long it takes a person to report recognition of some stimulus.

Learning: The relatively permanent change in behavior as a result of practice or experience.

Limited Problem Solving (LPS): The middle stage of learning how to buy, in which the consumer must locate a new brand in an established market space for an established product category.

Line Extension: An attempt by the manufacturer to enhance stimulus generalization across product categories. The goal is to enhance the likelihood that the favorable responses directed toward the successful brand in the first product category will be generalized to the new or unsuccessful brand in the second product category.

Linguistic Relativity Hypothesis: The assumption that differences in linguistic habits may cause differences in nonlinguistic behaviors, such as thought.

Long-term Store: A relatively permanent and unlimited memory store.

Low-Balling: An influence technique where an agreement is first reached at some specified level of cost for each party, and then the salesperson increases the cost to be incurred by the consumer.

Market Space: The superposition of the product space and the market space. That is, the geometric representation of consumers' beliefs about available brands and the "ideal" product in a product category.

Masked Recognition: A measure of retention that provides considerable prompting. For example, the individual is presented with a commercial to which he or she has previously been exposed minus all audio-visual references to the brand, and is then asked to identify the brand.

Maslow's Hierarchy of Needs: A classification of human needs, arranged in a hierarchy from lower needs to higher needs (physiological, safety, love and affection, self-esteem, self-actualization), with the lower needs being prepotent.

Memory: The retention of information about past events or ideas.

Misattribution: The process of interpreting arousal which has been generated by one source as having been due to another, irrelevant source.

Mere Exposure Effect: The tendency for repetition to lead to more favorable evaluations.

Model: A simple representation of something that is in fact more complicated.

Motivation: A state of tension within the individual which arouses, directs, and maintains behavior toward a goal.

Multiple Store Model of Memory: A model of memory that proposes three related memory storage processes: sensory store, short-term store, and long-term store.

Network Analysis (Sociograms): Sociological methods that graphically represent the patterns of interaction and influence among members of a group.

One-Sided Message: A persuasive message that presents the good, positive points about an issue without mentioning any weaknesses about the issue.

One-Step Flow Model: A model of communication where the manufacturer directs his message to each consumer as an individual.

Operationalization: The principle that the meaning of a term or variable is determined by the procedures or operations used to measure or manipulate it.

Opinion Leader: An individual who engages in oral transmission of product information to other consumers.

Oversufficient Justification: The introduction and then removal of some extrinsic reward decreases the intrinsic motivation to perform a behavior.

Pain–Pill–Pleasure Model: The argument that advertising promotes the notion that any physical or emotional discomfort can be mitigated or cured by taking the appropriate pill.

Partial Reinforcement: A scheduling of reinforcement in which the reinforcement is provided only after a certain number of correct responses, or only after a correct response occurs during a certain interval of time.

Partial Reinforcement Effect: The typical finding that associations acquired under partial reinforcement are acquired more slowly but are more resistant to extinction than associations acquired under continuous reinforcement.

Penetration Pricing: A pricing strategy that introduces a new product at a relatively low price, allowing the product to "penetrate" the market, and then raises the price once the product is established.

Perception: The psychological processing of information received by the senses.

Persuasion: Communication that is designed to change the beliefs of the person receiving it.

Positioning: The location of a product within a product space and/or a market space.

Post-Decisional Dissonance: The arousal of cognitive dissonance through making any nontrivial decision, because one has given up all of the positive aspects of the rejected alternative and accepted all of the negative aspects of the selected alternative.

Price–Quality Relationship: The assumption that higher priced products will be of higher quality.

Primary Motives: Motives that are based on an organism's physiochemical processes, and are considered to be largely unlearned.

Principle of Contrast: People tend to perceive by exception, attending predominately to those stimulus events that represent some difference or change.

Process Tracing Measures: Measures of awareness presumed to reflect ongoing perceptual, information-processing activity.

Product Life Cycle: A general tendency for a product category to grow slowly at first, then to rise rapidly, then to level off, then to begin to decline.

Product Space: The geometric representation of consumers' beliefs about available brands in a product category.

Projective Measure: A measure of motivation that exposes the individual to some vague, incomplete, or ambiguous stimulus, and assumes that important, unsatisfied needs will "project" themselves into the individual's response to the ambiguous stimuli.

Psychographics: The use of individual differences in the internal processes to predict consumer behavior.

Psychological Geography: The identification of geographically defined subcultures that differ in lifestyles, values, and other psychographic dimensions.

Psychological Reactance: An attempt to restore or maintain freedom that the individual feels is lost or threatened.

Punishment: A stimulus that leads to a decrease in the behavior that preceded the stimulus.

Pupil Contraction: Decrease in the size of the pupil of the eye.

Pupil Dilation: Increase in the size of the pupil of the eye.

Reactance Reduction: An influence technique where the consumer is convinced that they are not being subjected to an influence technique, which thereby mitigates psychological reactance.

Reciprocity: The tendency to do to others what they have done to you.

Recognition: A measure of retention that represents extreme discrimination. The individual is presented with the original stimulus material (e.g., a commercial) in its entirety and is then asked whether they've seen it before.

Reinforcement: A stimulus that leads to an increase in the behavior that preceded the stimulus.

Repositioning: Efforts to change consumers' beliefs about a product in a way that runs counter to objective facts about the product.

Retention: The persistence of an experience during a period of no practice.

Rifle Approach: A focused advertising strategy whereby opinion leaders are located and special product-relevant commercials are directed to them.

Routinized Response Behavior (RRB): The final stage of learning how to buy, in which the market space for the product category has been constructed, all available brands have been located within this market space, and the consumers' choices become habitual or "brand loyal".

Sampling: An influence technique where the salesperson gives a small amount of the product to the consumer, and then provides the consumer with the opportunity to purchase the product.

Scanner Cable Television Channels: Using otherwise unused channels on a cable television system, a means of delivering different commercials to consumers on a house by house basis.

Schema: In attribution theory, the configuration principle that there is sometimes a ready-made explanation for an event.

Secondary Motives: Learned motives which are thought to be acquired through classical conditioning.

Self-Perception Theory: A theory that holds that individuals come to know their own internal states partially by inferring from observations of their own overt behavior, and/or the circumstances in which the behavior occurs; and, to the extent that internal cues are weak, ambiguous, and uninterpretable, the individual must rely on external cues to infer internal states.

Sensory Store: A very short-lived type of memory store that holds a very accurate representation of stimulus information for a very short period of time (a second or two).

Serial Position Effect: The common finding that material presented at the end and at the beginning of a message is remembered better than material presented in the middle.

Short-Term Store: The location of current memory processing that can hold unrehearsed information for 30 seconds or less.

Shotgun Approach: A broad advertising strategy whereby product-relevant communications are directed toward all consumers.

Skimming (or Creaming) Pricing: A pricing strategy that introduces a new product at a relatively high price, "skims" off those consumers who are willing to pay, and then lowers the price once the product is established.

Sleeper Effect: The possibility of an increase over time in the persuasive effectiveness of communications from a noncredible source.

Social Class: A subculture defined in terms of the relative levels of social benefits.

Social Comparison Theory: A theory that describes the processes by which people come to evaluate their own abilities, opinions and behaviors by comparing them with those of with other people.

Social Context: The totality of social stimulation that influences the individual, including the real, imagined, or implied presence of others, such as friends, family members, and sales personnel.

Source Credibility: The extent to which a source of a persuasive communication is likely to be believed; due to attractiveness, trustworthiness, expertise, and/or similarity to the recipient of the message.

State Dependent Learning: The common finding that remembering is facilitated when the emotional state during retrieval matches the emotional state during learning.

Stimulus Discrimination: An increase in the specificity of the association involving the stimulus that precedes the response.

Stimulus Generalization: A decrease in the specificity of the association involving the stimulus that precedes the response.

Stimulus Situation: The complex conditions that collectively act as a stimulus to elicit responses from the consumer.

Subculture: A category of people who share a sense of identification that is distinguishable from that of the culture as a whole.

Subjective Norms: The weighted sum of normative beliefs about X, where each normative belief is weighted by the individual's motivation to comply with important others' expectations about X.

Subliminal Perception: The purported result of stimulation that is too weak to reach conscious awareness, but that nonetheless affects behavior.

Syncratic Decisions: Decisions regarding brand choices in product categories where the husband and wife are likely to make the decision jointly.

Theory of Reasoned Action: A theory that holds that behavior toward X results from intentions regarding X, and that intention results from the overall evaluation of X and subjective norms about X.

Time-Compressed Speech: A method of shortening or intensifying radio commercials by mechanically shortening pauses between words and reducing the length of vowel sounds.

Two-Factor Theory of Emotion: The theory that emotional experience is the result of undifferentiated, nonspecific physiological arousal and cognitive cues that are used to interpret that arousal as an emotional experience.

Two-Feet-in-the-Door: An influence technique where compliance on the critical, third request is increased by first obtaining compliance to two initial, smaller requests.

Two-Sided Message: A persuasive message that presents the good, positive points about an issue and also admits some of the weaknesses about that issue.

Two-Step Flow Model: A model of communication where the manufacturer directs the message to each consumer as an individual, and some consumers who do receive and process the message pass the information along orally to other consumers.

Unaided Recall: A measure of retention that provides no cues and represents extreme reconstruction. For example, the individual is asked to tell what commercials he or she has seen recently.

Unconditioned Response: A behavior or act which is "naturally" elicited by some response (see Classical Conditioning).

Unconditioned Stimulus: A stimulus which "naturally" elicits some response (see Classical Conditioning).

Undifferentiated Models: Models of consumer behavior comprised of small lists of variables suspected to influence consumer behavior.

Unilineal Models: Models of consumer behavior comprised of small lists of variables suspected to influence consumer behavior. These variables are arranged in a single, one-way flow of influence.

Unit Pricing: A price-labelling practice where each product's price is stated in both absolute terms and in terms of a price per unit of weight or volume.

Value: A preference or a liking/disliking for the object of concern.

Vicarious Classical Conditioning: The acquisition of a classically conditioned response on the part of an observer who is never directly exposed to the unconditioned stimulus, but who watches as another person is classically conditioned.

Vicarious Emotional Response: Emotional response generated by observing another person's exposure to a stimulus situation that would evoke emotional responses.

Vicarious Instrumental Conditioning: The acquisition of an instrumentally conditioned response on the part of an observer who never received any reinforcement or punishment, but who watches as another person is instrumentally conditioned.

Wife Dominant Decisions: Decisions regarding brand choices in product categories where the wife is more likely to make the decision in most families.

Word-of-Mouth (WOM): The oral transmission of product information among consumers.

References

Ackoff, R. L., & Emshoff, J. R. (1975). Advertising research at Anheuser-Busch, Inc. *Sloan Management Review, 16,* 1–15.

Adams, H. F. (1920). *Advertising and its mental laws.* New York: Macmillan.

Adams, S. (1965). Inequity in social exchange. In L. Berkowtiz (Ed.), *Advances in experimental social psychology* (Vol. 2, pp. 267–299). New York: Academic Press.

Adorno, T. W., Frenkel-Brunswik, E., Levinson, D. J., & Sanford, R. N. (1950). *The authoritarian personality.* New York: Wiley.

Advertising increasing in "non-commercial" uses. (1980). *Advertising Age, 51,* 104–114.

Advertising your church. (1977). *Christianity Today, 22,* 30–31.

Ajzen, I., & Fishbein, M. (1980). *Understanding attitudes and predicting behavior.* Englewood Cliffs, NJ: Prentice-Hall.

Albers, S. (1982). PROPOPP: A program package for optimal positioning of a new product in an attribute space. *Journal of Marketing Research, 19,* 606–608.

Allport, G. W. (1935). Attitudes. In C. Murchison (Ed.), *A handbook of social psychology* (pp. 798–844). Worchester, MA: Clark University Press.

Allport, G. W. (1937). *Personality: A psychological interpretation.* New York: Holt.

Allport, G. W. (1961). *Pattern and growth in personality.* New York: Holt, Rinehart & Winston.

Anderson, J. R., & Jolson, M. A. (1980). Technical wording in advertisements. *Journal of Marketing, 44,* 57–66.

Andren, G. (1980). The rhetoric of advertising. *Journal of Communication, 30,* 74–80.

Arch, D. C. (1979). Pupil dilation measures in consumer research: Application and limitations. *Advances in Consumer Research, 6,* 166–169.

Arndt, J. (1967). Role of product related conversations in the diffusion of a new product. *Journal of Marketing Research, 4,* 291–295.

Arndt, J. (1968). Word-of-mouth advertising and perceived risk. In H. H. Kassarjian & T. S. Robertson (Eds.), *Perspectives in consumer behavior* (pp. 330–336). Glenview, IL: Scott, Foresman.

Asch, S. E. (1955). Opinions and social pressure. *Scientific American, 193,* 31–35.

Asimov, I. (1980). Advertising in the year 2000. *Advertising Age, 51,* 98–102.

Assael, H. (1981). *Consumer behavior and marketing action.* Boston, MA: Kent.

Atkin, C. (1975a). Parent–child communication in supermarket breakfast cereal selection.

In *Effects of TV advertising on children* (Report #7). East Lansing, MI: Michigan State University.

Atkin, C. (1975b). Survey of children's and mother's responses to TV commercials. In *Effects of TV advertising on children* (Report #8). East Lansing, MI: Michigan State University.

Atkin, C. K. (1978a). Observations of parent–child interaction in supermarket decision-making. *Journal of Marketing, 42,* 41–45.

Atkin, C. K. (1978b). Effects of proprietory drug advertising on youth. *Journal of Communications, 28,* 71–79.

Atkin, C., & Block, M. (1983). Effectiveness of celebrity endorsers. *Journal of Advertising Research, 23,* 57–61.

Aycrigg, R. H. (1981). Coupon distribution and redemption patterns. In *NCH Reporter.* Northbrook, IL: A. C. Neilson.

Bacon, J. J. (1974). Arousal and the range of cue utilization. *Journal of Experimental Psychology, 102,* 81–87.

Bagozzi, R. P. (1978). Salesforce performance and satisfaction as a function of individual differences, interpersonal, and situational factors. *Journal of Marketing Research, 15,* 517–531.

Bagozzi, R. P. (1981). Attitudes, intentions, and behavior: A test of some key hypotheses. *Journal of Personality and Social Psychology, 41,* 607–627.

Bambic, P. (1978). *An interpersonal influence study of source acceptance in industrial buyer–seller exchange process: An experimental approach.* Unpublished doctoral dissertation, Graduate School of Business, Pennsylvania State University.

Bandura, A. (1971a). *Social learning theory.* Morristown, NJ: General Learning Press.

Bandura, A. (1971b November). *Modeling influences on children.* Testimony to the Federal Trade Commission.

Bandura, A. & Rosenthal, T. L. (1966). Vicarious classical conditioning as a function of arousal level. *Journal of Personality and Social Psychology, 3,* 54–62.

Bandura, A., Ross, D., & Ross, S. A. (1961). Transmission of aggression through imitation of aggressive models. *Journal of Abnormal and Social Psychology, 63,* 575–582.

Banks, S. (1950). The relationship between preference and purchase of brands. *Journal of Marketing, 14,* 145–157.

Baron, R. A., & Byrne, D. (1977). *Social psychology.* Boston, MA: Allyn & Bacon.

Baron, R. A., & Byrne, D. (1987). *Social psychology: Understanding human interaction.* Boston: Allyn & Bacon.

Barry, H. (1958). Effects of strength of drive on learning and extinction. *Journal of Experimental Psychology, 55,* 473–481.

Bauer, R. A., & Greyser, S. A. (1968). *Advertising in America: The consumer view.* Cambridge, MA: Harvard University Press.

Baumeister, R. F. (1982). A self-presentational view of social phenomena. *Psychological Bulletin, 91,* 3–26.

Bayton, J. A. (1958). Motivation, cognition, learning—basic factors in consumer behavior. *Journal of Marketing, 22,* 282–289.

Becherer, R. C., & Richard, L. M. (1978). Self-monitoring as a moderating variable in consumer behavior. *Journal of Consumer Research, 5,* 159–162.

Belch, G. E. (1982). Effects of television commercial repetition on cognitive responses and message acceptance. *Journal of Consumer Research, 9,* 56–65.

Belk, R., Painter, J., & Semenik, R. (1981). Preferred solutions to the energy crisis as a function of causal attributions. *Journal of Consumer Research, 8,* 306–312.

Bem, D. J. (1965). An experimental analysis of self-persuasion. *Journal of Experimental Social Psychology, 1,* 199–218.

Bem, D. J. (1972). Self-perception theory. In L. Berkowitz (Ed.), *Advances in experimental social psychology* (Vol. 6, pp. 1–62). New York: Academic Press.

Benedict, R. (1934). *Patterns of culture.* Boston, MA: Houghton-Mifflin.

Bentler, P. M., & Speckart, G. (1981). Attitudes cause behaviors: A structural equations analysis. *Journal of Personality and Social Psychology, 40,* 226–238.

Berey, L. A., & Pollay, R. W. (1968). The influencing role of the child in family decision making. *Journal of Marketing Research, 5,* 70–72.

Berlin, B., & Kay, P. (1969). *Basic color terms: Their universality and evolution.* Berkeley, CA: University of California Press.

Berger, S. M. (1962). Conditioning through vicarious instigation. *Psychology Review, 69,* 450–466.

Bernal, G., & Berger, S. M. (1976). Vicarious eyelid conditioning. *Journal of Personality and Social Psychology, 34,* 62–68.

Best food day build up may spurt new coupon usage. (1983, March). *Marketing Communications,* pp. 47–49.

Bettman, J. R. (1979). Memory factors in consumer choice: A review. *Journal of Marketing, 43,* 37–53.

Bierley, C., McSweeney, F. K., & Van Nieuwkerk, R. (1985). Classical conditioning of performances for stimuli. *Journal of Consumer Research, 12,* 316–323.

Bishop, D. W., & Ikeda, M. (1970). Status and role factors in the leisure behavior of different occupations. *Sociology and Social Research, 54,* 190–208.

Blackwell, R. D., Engel, J. F., & Talarzyk, W. W. (1977). *Contemporary cases in consumer behavior.* Hinsdale, IL: Dryden.

Blake, B., Perloff, R., & Heslin, R. (1970). Dogmatism and acceptance of new products. *Journal of Marketing Research, 7,* 483–486.

Blanchard, E. B., & Young, L. B. (1973). Self-control of cardiac functioning: A promise as yet unfulfilled. *Psychological Bulletin, 79,* 145–163.

Blattberg, R. (1980). Ad impact data due for big improvement. *Advertising Age, 51,* 154–156.

Bloch, R. (1959). Show biz. *Ellery Queen's Mystery Magazine, 24,* 1–7.

Bolles, R. C. (1967). *Theory of motivation.* New York: Harper & Row.

Bourne, F. S. (1956). *Group influence in marketing and public relations.* Ann Arbor, MI: Foundation for Research on Human Behavior.

Bower, G. H., Munteiro, K. P., & Gilligan, S. G. (1978). Emotional mood is a context for learning and recall. *Journal of Verbal Living and Verbal Behavior, 17,* 573–585.

Brean, H. (1958, March 31). What hidden sell is all about. *Life,* 104–114.

Brehm, J. W. (1956). Post-decision changes in the desirability of alternatives. *Journal of Abnormal and Social Psychology, 52,* 384–389.

Brehm, J. W. (1966). *A theory of psychological reactance.* New York: Academic Press.

Brock, T. C. (1965). Communicator–recipient similarity and decision change. *Journal of Personality and Social Psychology, 1,* 650–654.

Brodlie, J. F. (1972). Drug abuse and television viewing patterns. *Psychology, 9,* 33–36.

Bruner, J. J., & Postman, L. (1951). An approach to social perception. In W. Dennis (Ed.), *Current trends in social psychology* (pp. 310–343). Pittsburgh, PA: University of Pittsburgh Press.

Buchanan, D. B., & Agatstein, F. C. (1984, March). *Person positively bias in the evaluation of consumer products.* Paper presented at the annual meeting of the Eastern Psychological Association, Baltimore, MD.

Bunn, D. W. (1982). Audience presence during breaks in television programs. *Journal of Advertising Research, 22,* 35–39.

Burger, J. M., & Petty, R. E. (1981). The low-ball compliance technique: Task or person commitment? *Journal of Personality and Social Psychology, 40,* 492–500.

Burnkrant, R. E., & Page, T. J. (1982). An examination of the convergent, discriminant, and predictive validity of Fishbein's behavioral intention. *Journal of Marketing Research, 19,* 550–561.

Burns, A. C., & Granbois, D. H. (1977). Factors moderating the resolution of preference conflict in family automobile purchasing. *Journal of Marketing Research, 14,* 77–86.

Busch, P., & Wilson, D. T. (1976). An experimental analysis of a salesman's expert and referent bases of social power in the buyer–seller dyad. *Journal of Marketing Research, 13,* 3–11.

Butter, E. J., Popovich, P. M., Stockhouse, R. H., & Garner, R. K. (1981). Discrimination of television programs and commercials by pre-school children. *Journal of Advertising Research, 21,* 53–56.

Byrne, D. (1959). The effect of a subliminal food stimulus on verbal responses. *Journal of Applied Psychology, 43,* 249–252.

Cameron, C., Oskamp, S., & Sparks, W. (1977). Courtship American style: Newspaper ads. *Family Coordinator, 26,* 27–30.

Cannon, W. B. (1929). *Bodily changes in pain, hunger, fear, and rage.* New York: Appleton-Century.

Cantor, J., Zillmann, D., & Bryant, J. (1975). Enhancement of experienced sexual arousal in response to erotic stimuli through misattribution of unrelated residual excitation. *Journal of Personality and Social Psychology, 32,* 69–75.

Capella, L. M., Schnake, R., & Garner, J. (1981, November). *The impact of rock group influence upon consumer purchasing decisions.* Paper presented at the annual meeting of the Southern Management Association, Atlanta, GA.

Capretta, P. J., Moore, M. J., & Rossiter, T. R. (1973). Establishment and modification of food and taste preferences: Effects of experience. *Journal of Genetic Psychology, 89,* 27–46.

Cardozo, R. N. (1965). An experimental study of consumer effort, expectation, and satisfaction. *Journal of Marketing Research, 2,* 248–254.

Carey, R. J., Clicque, S. H., Leighton, B. A., & Milton, F. (1976). A test of positive reinforcement of customers. *Journal of Marketing, 40,* 98–100.

Carman, F. M. (1973). A summary of empirical research on unit pricing in supermarkets. *Journal of Retailing, 48,* 63–71.

Cartwright, D. (1949). Some principles of mass persuasion: Selected findings of research on the sale of U.S. war bonds. *Human Relations, 2,* 253–267.

Carver, C. S., & Scheier, M. F. (1981). *Attention and self-regulation: A control theory approach to human behavior.* New York: Springer-Verlag.

Chaves, J. F., & Barber, T. X. (1973). Needles and knives: Behind the mystery of acupuncture and Chinese Manderans. *Human Behavior, 2,* 19–24.

Cheskin, L. (1957). *How to predict what people will buy.* New York: Liveright.

Childers, T. L. (1986). Assessment of the psychometric properties of an opinion leadership scale. *Journal of Marketing Research, 23,* 184–188.

Children's Review Unit, Council of Better Business Bureaus. (1977). *Children's advertising guidelines.* New York: Better Business Bureaus.

Cialdini, R. B., Cacioppo, J. T., Bassett, R., & Miller, J. A. (1978). Low-ball procedure for producing compliance: Commitment then cost. *Journal of Personality and Social Psychology, 36,* 463–476.

Cialdini, R. B., & Schroeder, D. A. (1976). Increasing compliance by legitimizing paltry contributions: When even a penny helps. *Journal of Personality and Social Psychology, 34,* 599–604.

Cialdini, R. B., Vincent, J. E., Lewis, S. K., Catalan, J., Wheeler, D., & Danby, B. L. (1975). Reciprocal concessions procedure for inducing compliance: The door-in-the-face technique. *Journal of Personality and Social Psychology, 31,* 206–215.

Clancy-Hepburn, K. (1974). Children's behavior responses to TV food advertisements. *Journal of Nutrition Education, 6,* 93–96.

Clee, M., & Wicklund, R. (1980). Consumer behavior and psychological reactance. *Journal of Consumer Research, 6,* 389–405.

Coca-Cola turns to Pavlov. (1984, January 19). *Wall Street Journal,* p. 31.

Cohen, J. B. (1967). An interpersonal orientation of the study of consumer behavior. *Journal of Marketing Research, 4,* 270–278.

Coleman, J. S., Katz, E., & Menzel, H. (1966). *Medical innovation: A diffusion study.* Indianapolis, IN: Boobs-Merrill.

Collins, A. M., & Loftus, E. F. (1975). A spreading-activation theory of semantic processing. *Psychological Review, 82,* 407–428.

Coors vs. Coors. (1984, February 6). *Time,* p. 51.

Copulsky, W., & Marton, K. (1977). Sensory cues. *Product Marketing, 6,* 31–34.

Cotton, P. C., & Babb, E. M. (1978). Consumer response to promotional deals. *Journal of Marketing, 42,* 109–113.

Cottrell, N. B. (1972). Social facilitation. In C. G. McClintock (Ed.), *Experimental social psychology* (pp. 185–236). New York: Holt, Rinehart & Winston.

Cowles, J. T. (1937). Food tokens as incentives for learning by chimpanzees. *Comparative Psychological Monographs, 14,* No. 5.

Cox, D. F. (1961). Clues for advertising strategists. *Harvard Business Review, 39,* 160–176.

Craig, K. D., & Weinstein, M. S. (1965). Conditioning vicarious affective arousal. *Psychology Reports, 17,* 955–963.

Crutchfield, R. S. (1955). Conformity and character. *American Psychologist, 10,* 191–198.

Cunningham, I. C. M., & Green, R. T. (1974). Purchasing roles in the U.S. family, 1955 and 1973. *Journal of Marketing, 38,* 61–64.

Darwin, C. (1965). *The expression of emotions in man and animals.* Chicago, IL: University of Chicago Press. (Originally published 1872)

Davis, H. L. (1976). Decision making within the household. *Journal of Consumer Research, 2,* 241–260.

Davis, H. L., & Rigaux, B. P. (1974). Perception of marital roles in decision processes. *Journal of Consumer Research, 1,* 51–62.

Deci, E. L. (1971). Effects of externally mediated rewards on intrinsic motivation. *Journal of Personality and Social Psychology, 18,* 105–115.

Deering, B. J., & Jacoby, J. (1972, November). *Price intervals and individual price limits determinants of product evaluation and selection.* Paper presented at annual convention of Association for Consumer Research.

Deese, J., & Carpenter, J. A. (1951). Drive level and reinforcement. *Journal of Experimental Psychology, 42,* 236–238.

DeJong, W. (1979). An examination of self-perception mediation of the foot-in-the-door effect. *Journal of Personality and Social Psychology, 37,* 2221–2239.

DellaBitta, A. J., & Monroe, K. B. (1974). The influence of adaptation levels on subjective price perceptions. In S. Ward & P. Wright (Eds.), *Advances in consumer research* (Vol. 1, pp. 359–369). Urbana, Il: Association for Consumer Research.

Demby, E. (1974). Psychographics and from whence it came. In W. D. Wells (Ed.), *Life and psychographics* (pp. 1–20). Chicago, IL: American Marketing Association.

Dennis, W. (1957). Use of common objects as indicators of cultural orientations. *Journal of Abnormal and Social Psychology, 55,* 21–28.

Deslauriers, B. C., & Everett, P. B. (1977). The effects of intermittent and continuous token reinforcement on bus ridership. *Journal of Applied Psychology, 62,* 369–375.

Dholakia, R. R., & Sternthal, B. (1977). Highly credible sources: Persuasive facilitators or persuasive liabilities? *Journal of Consumer Research, 3,* 223–232.

Dichter, E. (1962). The world customer. *Harvard Business Review, 40,* 113–122.

Dichter, E. (1964). *Handbook of consumer motivations.* New York: McGraw-Hill.

Dodson, J. A., Tybout, A. M., & Sternthal, B. (1978). Impact of deals and deal retraction on brand switching. *Journal of Marketing Research, 15,* 72–81.

Doerfler, L. G., & Kramer, J. C. (1959). Unconditioned stimulus strength and the galvanic skin response. *Journal of Speech and Hearing Research, 2,* 184–192.

Doob, A. J., Carlsmith, J. M., Freedman, J. L., Landauer, T. K., & Soleng, T. (1969). Effect of initial selling price on subsequent sales. *Journal of Personality and Social Psychology, 11,* 345–350.

Duncker, K. (1938). Experimental modification of children's food preferences through social suggestion. *Journal of Abnormal and Social Psychology, 33,* 489–507.

Duncan, J. W., & Laird, J. D. (1980). Positive and reverse pleabo effects as a function of differences in cues used in self-perception. *Journal of Personality and Social Psychology, 39,* 1024–1036.

Dunlap, B. J., & Rountree, W. D. (1981, November). *A proposed marketing model for religious organizations.* Paper presented at the annual meeting of the Southern Marketing Association, Atlanta, GA.

Eagly, A. H. (1983). Gender and social influence: A social psychological analysis. *American Psychologist, 38,* 971–981.

Eagly, A. H., & Chaikan, S. (1975). An attribution analysis of the effect of communication characteristics on opinion change: The case of communicator attractiveness. *Journal of Personality and Social Psychology, 32,* 136–144.

Easterbrook, J. A. (1959). The effect of emotion on cue utilization and organization of behavior. *Psychological Review, 66,* 187–201.

Eckstrand, G., & Gilliland, A. R. (1948). The psychogalvanometric method for measuring the effectiveness of advertising. *Journal of Applied Psychology, 32,* 415–425.

Edwards, A. L. (1954). *Manual for the Edwards Personal Preference Schedule.* New York: Psychological Corporation.

Ekman, P., & Friesen, W. V. (1971). Constants across cultures in the face and emotion. *Journal of Personality and Social Psychology, 17,* 124–129.

Ellis, M. (1986, January 10). Tired of bull at the meat market. *Herald Journal,* p. 12.

Emery, F. (1970). Some psychological aspects of price. In B. Taylor & G. Wills (Eds.), *Pricing strategy* (pp. 98–111). Princeton, NJ: Brandon/Systems Press.

Engel, J. F., Blackwell, R. D., & Kollat, D. T. (1978). *Consumer behavior.* Hinsdale, IL: Dryden.

Engel, J. F., Fiorillo, H. F., & Cayley, M. A. (1982). *Market segmentation: Concepts and applications.* New York: Holt, Rinehart & Winston.

Engel, J. F., Kollat, D. T., & Blackwell, R. D. (1969). Personality measures and market segmentation. *Business Horizons, 12,* 61–70.

Evans, F. B. (1963). Selling as a dyadic relationship: A new approach. *American Behavior Scientist, 6,* 76–79.

Feinberg, R. A., Mataro, L., & Burroughs, W. J. (1983, May). *Fashion and social identity*. Paper presented at the annual meeting of the Midwestern Psychological Association, Chicago, IL.

Festinger, L. A. (1954). A theory of social comparison processes. *Human Relations, 40,* 427–448.

Festinger, L. (1957). *A theory of cognitive dissonance*. Stanford, CA: Stanford University Press.

Fishbein, M. (1979). A theory of reasoned action: Some applications and implications. In H. Howe & M. Page (Eds.), *Nebraska Symposium on Motivation* (pp. 65–116). Lincoln, NE: University of Nebraska Press.

Fishbein, M., & Ajzen, I. (1972). Attitudes and opinions. *Annual Review of Psychology, 23,* 487–544.

Fishbein, M., & Ajzen, I. (1975). *Belief, attitude, intention, & behavior: An introduction to theory and research*. Reading, MA: Addison-Wesley.

Flesch, R. (1949). *The art of readable writing*. New York: Harper & Row.

Foster, D., Pratt, C., & Schwortz, N. (1955). Variation in flavor judgements in a group situation. *Food Research, 20,* 539–544.

Freedman, J. L., & Fraser, S. C. (1966). Compliance without pressure: The foot-in-the-door technique. *Journal of Personality and Social Psychology, 4,* 195–202.

Frideres, J. S. (1973). Advertising, buying patterns, and children. *Journal of Advertising Research, 13,* 34–36.

Friedman, H. S., DiMatteo, M. R., & Mertz, T. I. (1980). Nonverbal communication on television news: Facial expressions of broadcasters during coverage of a presidential election campaign. *Personality and Social Psychology Bulletin, 6,* 427–435.

Fry, J. M., & Siller, F. H. (1970). A comparison of housewife decision making in two social classes. *Journal of Marketing Research, 8,* 333–337.

Gaedeke, R. M. (Ed.). (1977). *Marketing in private and public nonprofit organizations*. Santa Monica, CA: Goodyear Publishing.

Garreau, J. (1981). *The nine nations of North America*. New York: Avon.

Geen, R. G., & Bushman, B. J. (1987). Drive theory: Effects of socially engendered arousal. In B. Mullen & G. R. Goethals (Eds.), *Theories of group behavior* (pp. 89–109). New York: Springer-Verlag.

Geistfeld, L. V. (1982). The price–quality relationship revisited. *Journal of Consumer Affairs, 16,* 334–335.

Gerstner, E. (1985). Do higher prices signal higher quality? *Journal of Marketing Research, 22,* 209–215.

Gillig, P. M., & Greenwald, A. G. (1974). Is it time to lay the sleeper effect to rest? *Journal of Personality and Social Psychology, 29,* 132–139.

Ginzberg, E. (1936). Customary prices. *American Economic Review, 26,* 296.

Gnepp, E. H. (1979). The psychology of advertising. *Psychology, 16,* 1–6.

Goethals, G. R. (1976). An attributional analysis of some social influence phenomena. In J. H. Harvey, W. J. Ickes, & R. F. Kidd (Eds.), *New directions in attribution research* (Vol. 1, pp. 291–310). Hillsdale, NJ: Lawrence Erlbaum Associates.

Goethals, G. R., & Ebling, T. A. (1975). *A study of opinion comparison*. Unpublished manuscript, Williams College, Williamstown, MA.

Goethals, G. R., & Nelson, E. R. (1973). Similarity in the influence process: The belief value distinction. *Journal of Personality and Social Psychology, 25,* 117–122.

Goethals, G. R., Reckman, R. F., & Rothman, J. (1973). *Impression management as a determinant of attitude statements*. Unpublished manuscript, Williams College, Williamstown, MA.

Goldberg, M. E., & Gorn, G. J. (1978). Some unintended consequences of TV advertising to children. *Journal of Consumer Research, 5,* 22–29.

Goldman, M., & Creason, C. R. (1981). Inducing compliance by a two-door-in-the-face procedure. *Journal of Social Psychology, 114,* 224–235.

Goldsen, R. K. (1978). Why television advertising is deceptive and unfair. *ETC, 35,* 354–375.

Gorn, G. J. (1982). The effects of music in advertising on choice behavior: A classical conditioning approach. *Journal of Marketing, 46,* 94–101.

Gorn, G. J., & Goldberg, M. E. (1980). Children's responses to repetitive television commercials. *Journal of Consumer Research, 7,* 421–424.

Gorn, G. J., & Goldberg, M. E. (1982). Behavioral evidence of the effects of televised food messages on children. *Journal of Consumer Research, 9,* 200–205.

Gouldner, A. W. (1960). The norm of reciprocity: A preliminary statement. *American Sociological Review, 25,* 161–178.

Graham, S. (1956). Class and conservation in the adaption of innovations. *Human Relations, 9,* 91–100.

Granbois, D. H. (1968). Improving the study of customer in-store behavior. *Journal of Marketing, 32,* 28–33.

Green, P. (1980). Huge growth expected in issues/causes advertising. *Advertising Age, 51,* 66–68.

Green, P. E., & Wind, Y. (1975). New way to measure consumers' judgements. *Harvard Business Review, 53,* 107–117.

Greenberg, H., & Mayer, D. (1964). A new approach to the scientific selection of successful salesmen. *Journal of Psychology, 57,* 113–123.

Gregg, V. H. (1976). Word frequency, recognition and recall. In J. Brown (Ed.), *Recall and recognition* (pp. 183–216). London: Wiley.

Grubb, E. L., & Hupp, G. (1968). Perception of self, generalized stereotypes and brand selection. *Journal of Marketing Research, 5,* 58–63.

Gruder, C. L., Cook, T. D., Hennigan, K. M., Flay, B. R., Alessis, C., & Halamaj, J. (1978). Empirical tests of the absolute sleeper effect produced from the discounting cue hypothesis. *Journal of Personality and Social Psychology, 36,* 1061–1074.

Guttman, N., & Kalish, H. I. (1956). Discriminability and stimulus generalization. *Journal of Experimental Psychology, 51,* 79–88.

Haire, M. (1950). Projective techniques in marketing research. *Journal of Marketing, 14,* 649–652.

Haley, R. I., & Case, P. B. (1979). Testing thirteen attitude scales for agreement in brand discrimination. *Journal of Marketing, 43,* 20–32.

Hall, E. T. (1960). The silent language in overseas business. *Harvard Business Review, 38,* 87–96.

Halpern, R. S. (1967). Application of pupil response to before and after experiments. *Journal of Marketing Research, 4,* 320–321.

Hankiss, A. (1980). Games consumers play: The semiosis of deceptive interaction. *Journal of Communication, 30,* 104–112.

Hannah, D. B., & Sternthal, B. (1984). Detecting and explaining the sleeper effect. *Journal of Consumer Research, 11,* 632–642.

Harris, V. A., & Jellison, J. M. (1971). Fear-arousing communications, fake physiological feedback, and the acceptance of recommendations. *Journal of Experimental Social Psychology, 7,* 269–279.

Harrison, A. A., & Saeed, L. (1977). Let's make a deal: An analysis of revelations and stimulations in lonely hearts advertisements. *Journal of Personality and Social Psychology, 35,* 257–264.

Hartley, R. E. (1968). Personal characteristics and acceptance of secondary groups as reference groups. In H. H. Hyman & E. Singer (Eds.), *Reading in reference group theory and research* (pp. 1–36). New York: The Free Press.

Haugh, L. J. (1983). Pass the coupon please. *Advertising Age, 54,* 11–30.

Hawkins, D. (1970). The effects of subliminal stimulation on drive level and brand preference. *Journal of Marketing Research, 7,* 322–326.

Heberlein, T. A., & Black, J. S. (1976). Attitudinal specificity and the prediction of behavior in a field setting. *Journal of Personality and Social Psychology, 33,* 474–479.

Hecker, S. (1981). A brain-hemisphere orientation toward concept testing. *Journal of Advertising Research, 21,* 55–60.

Heider, F. (1958). *The psychology of interpersonal relations.* New York: Wiley.

Heimbach, J. T., & Jacoby, J. (1972, November). The Zaigarnik effect in advertising. *Proceedings of the annual conference of the Association for Consumer Research,* pp. 746–758.

Heller, N. (1956). An application of psychological learning theory to advertising. *Journal of Marketing, 20,* 248–254.

Helson, H. (1964). *Adaptation-level theory: An experimental and systematic approach to behavior.* New York: Harper.

Henion, K. E. (1976). *Ecological marketing.* Columbus, OH: Grid.

Heron House. (1978). *The book of numbers.* New York: Author.

Heslop, L., & Ryans, A. B. (1980). A second look at children and the advertising of premiums. *Journal of Consumer Research, 6,* 414–420.

Heslop, L. A., Moran, L., & Cousineau, A. (1981). 'Consciousness' in energy conservation behavior: An exploratory study. *Journal of Consumer Research, 8,* 299–305.

Hess, E. (1965). Attitude and pupil size. *Scientific American, 212,* 46–54.

Hess, E. H. (1972). Pupillometrics: A method of studying mental, emotional, and sensory processes. In N. S. Greenfield & R. A. Sternbach (Eds.), *Handbook of psychophysiology* (pp. 491–531). New York: Holt, Rinehart & Winston.

Hess, E. H., & Polt, J. M. (1960). Pupil size as related to interest value of visual stimuli. *Science, 132,* 349–350.

Hillman, B., Hunter, W. S., & Kimble, G. A. (1953). The effect of drive level on the maze performance of the white rats. *Journal of Comparative and Physiological Psychology, 46,* 87–89.

Holbrook, M. B., & Lehmann, D. R. (1980). Form vs. content in predicting starch scores. *Journal of Advertising Research, 20,* 55–62.

Hollingshead, A. B., & Redlich, F. C. (1958). *Social class and mental illness.* New York: Wiley.

Horney, K. (1945). *Our inner conflicts.* New York: Norton.

Horowitz, I. A., & Kaye, R. S. (1975). Perception and advertising. *Journal of Advertising Research, 15,* 15–21.

Hovland, C. I. (Ed.). (1957). *The order of presentation in persuasion.* New Haven, CT: Yale University Press.

Hovland, C. I., Lumsdaine, A. A., & Scheffield, F. D. (1949). *Experiments on mass communication.* Princeton, NJ: Princeton University Press.

Hovland, C. I., & Weiss, W. (1951). The influence of source credibility on communication effectiveness. *Public Opinion Quarterly, 15,* 635–650.

How much do consumers know about retail prices? (1964). *Progressive Grocer, 43,* c104–c106.

How important is position in consumer magazine advertising? (1964, June). *Media/Scope*, pp. 52–57.

Howard, J. A. (1977). *Consumer behavior: Application of theory*. New York: McGraw-Hill.

Howard, J. A., & Sheth, J. (1969). *The theory of buyer behavior*. New York: Wiley.

Howell, W. (1976). *Essentials of industrial and organizational behavior*. Homewood, IL: Dorsey.

Hsu, F. L. K. (1970). *Americans and Chinese: Purposes and fulfillment in great civilization*. Garden City, NY: Natural History Press.

Hulse, J. H., Deese, J., & Egeth, H. (1975). *The psychology of learning*. New York: McGraw-Hill.

Husband, R. W. (1953). *The psychology of successful selling*. New York: Harper & Row.

Hutton, R. B., & McNeill, D. L. (1981). The value of incentives in stimulating energy conservation. *Journal of Consumer Research, 8*, 291–298.

Hyland, M., & Birrell, J. (1979). Government health warnings and the "boomerang" effect. *Psychology Reports, 44*, 643–647.

Hyman, R. (1977). "Cold reading": How to convince strangers that you know all about them. *The Zetetic, 1*, 18–37.

Jacoby, J. (1971). A model of multi-brand loyalty. *Journal of Advertising Research, 11*, 26–35.

Jacoby, J., Speller, D. E., & Kohn, C. A. (1974). Brand choice behavior as a function of information load. *Journal of Marketing Research, 11*, 63–69.

James, W. (1890). *Principles of psychology*. New York: Holt.

Janisse, M. P. (1973). Pupil size and affect: A critical review of the literature since 1960. *Canadian Psychologist, 14*, 311–329.

Janisse, M. P. (1974). Pupil size, affect, and exposure frequency. *Social Behavior and Personality, 2*, 125–146.

Johnson, H. H., & Watkins, T. A. (1971). The effects of message repetition on immediate and delayed attitude change. *Psychonomic Science, 22*, 101–103.

Johnson, R. M. (1971). Market segmentation: A strategic management tool. *Journal of Marketing Research, 8*, 13–18.

Johnston, C. (1988). A message from our sponsor. *PC Computing, 10*, 56.

Jones, E. E., Davis, K. E., & Gergen, K. J. (1961). Role playing variations and their informational value for person perception. *Journal of Abnormal and Social Psychology, 63*, 302–310.

Jones, E. E., & Harris, V. A. (1967). The attribution of attitudes. *Journal of Experimental Social Psychology, 3*, 2–24.

Jones, R. A., & Brehm, J. W. (1970). Persuasiveness of one-sided and two-sided communications as a function of awareness there are two sides. *Journal of Experimental Social Psychology, 6*, 47–56.

Kahle, L. R. (1986). The nine nations of North America and the value basis of geographic segmentation. *Journal of Marketing, 50*, 37–47.

Kanti, V., Rao, T. R., & Sheikh, A. A. (1978). Mother vs. commercial. *Journal of Communication, 28*, 91–96.

Kanungo, R. N., & Johar, J. S. (1975). Effects of slogans and human model characteristics in product advertisements. *Journal of Behavior Science, 7*, 127–138.

Kassarjian, H. H., & Robertson, T. S. (Eds.). (1981). *Perceptions in consumer behavior*. Glenview, IL: Scott, Foresman.

Katona, G. (1960). *The powerful consumer*. New York: McGraw-Hill.

Katz, E. (1957). The two-step flow of communication: An up-to-date report of an hypothesis. *Public Opinion Quarterly, 21*, 67–78.

Katz, W. A. (1983). Point of view: A critique of split brain theory. *Journal of Advertising Research, 23,* 63–66.

Kaufman, L. (1980). Prime-time nutrition. *Journal of Communication, 30,* 37–46.

Kelley, H. H. (1967). Attribution theory in social psychology. In D. Levine (Ed.), *Nebraska Symposium on Motivation* (pp. 192–238). Lincoln, NE: University of Nebraska Press.

Kelley, H. H. (1973). The processes of causal attribution. *American Psychologist, 28,* 107–128.

Kelman, H. C., & Cohler, J. (1959, March). *Reactions to persuasive communications as a function of cognitive needs and styles.* Paper presented at the 30th annual meeting of the Eastern Psychological Association, Atlantic City, NJ.

Kelman, H. C., & Hovland, C. I. (1953). Reinstatement of the communicator in analyzed measurement of opinion change. *Journal of Abnormal and Social Psychology, 48,* 327–335.

Kendler, H. H. (1945). Drive interaction: II. Experimental analysis of the role of drive in learning theory. *Journal of Experimental Psychology, 35,* 188–198.

Keyes, B. W. (1980). *The clam-plate orgy and other subliminal techniques for manipulating your behavior.* Englewood Cliffs, NJ: Prentice-Hall.

King, A. (1981, November). *Beyond proposites: Towards a theory of addictive consumption.* Paper presented at the annual meeting of the American Marketing Association, Washington, DC.

King, A. S. (1972). Pupil size, eye direction, and message appeal: Some preliminary findings. *Journal of Marketing, 36,* 55–57.

Kintsch, W. (1970). Models for free recall and recognition. In D. A. Norman (Ed.), *Models of human memory* (pp. 331–373). New York: Academic Press.

Kintsch, W. (1977). *Memory and cognition.* New York: Wiley.

Kirchner, W. K., & Dunnette, M. D. (1959). How salesmen and technical men differ in describing themselves. *Personnel Journal, 37,* 418.

Klein, G. S., Spence, D. P., & Holt, R. R. (1958). Cognition without awareness. *Journal of Abnormal and Social Psychology, 57,* 255–266.

Kling, J. W., & Riggs, L. A. (Eds.). (1972). *Woodworth and Scholsberg's experimental psychology.* New York: Holt, Rinehart & Winston.

Knox, R. E., & Inkster, J. A. (1968). Post-decision dissonance at post-time. *Journal of Personality and Social Psychology, 8,* 319–323.

Koffka, K. (1935). *Principles of gestalt psychology.* New York: Harcourt, Brace.

Kohn, M. L. (1963). Social class and parent–child relationships: An interpretation. *American Journal of Sociology, 68,* 471–480.

Komarovsky, M. (1961). Class differences in family decision making. In N. N. Foote (Ed.), *Household decision making* (pp. 255–265). New York: New York University Press.

Komorita, S. S., & Brenner, A. R. (1968). Bargaining and concession making under bilateral monopoly. *Journal of Personality and Social Psychology, 9,* 15–20.

Konecni, V. J., & Slamenka, N. J. (1972). Awareness in verbal non-operant conditioning. *Journal of Experimental Psychology, 94,* 248–254.

Koponen, A. (1960). Personality characteristics of purchasers. *Journal of Advertising Research, 1,* 6–12.

Kotler, P. (1975). *Marketing for nonprofit organizations.* Englewood Cliffs, NJ: Prentice-Hall.

Kotler, P. (1976). *Marketing management: Analysis, planning, and control.* Englewood Cliffs, NJ: Prentice-Hall.

Kotler, P. (1983). *Principles of marketing*. Englewood Cliffs, NJ: Prentice-Hall.

Kotler, P., & Levy, J. J. (1969). Broadening the concept of marketing. *Journal of Marketing, 33*, 10–15.

Kotzan, J. A., & Evanson, R. V. (1969). Responsiveness of drug store sales to shelf-space allocations. *Journal of Marketing Research, 6*, 465–469.

Kover, A. J. (1967). Models of men as defined by marketing research. *Journal of Marketing Research, 4*, 129–132.

Kozyris, P. J. (1975). Advertising intrusion: Assault on the senses, trespass on the mind—A remedy through separation. *Ohio State Law Journal, 36*, 299–347.

Kroeber-Riel, W. (1979). Activation research: Psychological approaches in consumer research. *Journal of Consumer Research, 5*, 240–250.

Krugman, H. E. (1965). The impact of television advertising without involvement. *Public Opinion Quarterly, 29*, 349–356.

Krugman, H. E. (1983). Television program interest and commercial interruption. *Journal of Advertising Research, 23*, 21–23.

LaBarbera, P. & MacLachlan, J. (1979). Time-compressed speech in radio advertising. *Journal of Marketing, 43*, 30–36.

Laird, J. D. (1974). Self-attribution of emotion: The effects of expressive behavior on the quality of emotional experience. *Journal of Personality and Social Psychology, 42*, 646–657.

Lambert, Z. V. (1975). Perceived prices as related to odd and even price endings. *Journal of Retailing, 51*, 13–22.

Lamont, L. M., & Lundstrom, W. J. (1977). Identifying successful industrial salesmen by personality and personal characteristics. *Journal of Marketing Research, 14*, 517–529.

Lavidge, R. J., & Stiener, G. A. (1961). A model for predicting measurements of advertising effectiveness. *Journal of Marketing, 25*, 59–62.

Lazarus, R. J., & McCleary, R. A. (1951). Autonomic discrimination without awareness: A study of subception. *Psychology Review, 58*, 113–122.

Lazarus, R. S., Cohen, J. B., Folkman, S., Kanner, A., & Schaefer, C. (1980). Psychological stress and adaptation. Some unresolved issues. In H. Selye (Ed.), *Guide to stress research* (pp. 330–350). New York: Van Nostrand Reinhold.

Leading National Advertisers, Inc. (1980). *LNA Advertising $ Summary*. Norwalk, CT: Author.

Leavitt, C. (1961). Intrigue in advertising: The motivating effects of visual organization. *Proceedings of the 7th Annual Conference (Advertising Research Foundation)* (pp. 126–136). Chicago, IL: Leo Burnett Co.

Lesser, J. A., & Hughes, M. A. (1986). The generalizability of psychographic market segments across geographic locations. *Journal of Marketing, 50*, 18–27.

Leventhal, H. (1970). Findings and theory in the study of fear communications. In L. Berkowitz (Ed.), *Advances in experimental social psychology* (Vol. 5, pp. 119–186). New York: Academic Press.

Leventhal, H. (1974). Emotions: A basic problem for social psychology. In C. Nemeth (Ed.), *Social psychology: Classic and contemporary integrations* (pp. 1–51). Chicago, IL: Rand-McNally.

Levy, S. J. (1966). Social class and consumer behavior. In J. W. Newman (Ed.), *On knowing the consumer* (pp. 146–160). New York: Wiley.

Levy, S. J., & Glick, I. O. (1962). *Living with television*. Hawthorne, NY: Aldine.

Liebert, R. M., Sprafkin, J. N., & Davidson, E. S. (Eds.). (1982). *The early window: Effects of television on children and youth*. New York: Pergamon Press.

Loftus, G. R., & Loftus, E. F. (1976). *Human memory: The processing of information*. Hillsdale, NJ: Lawrence Erlbaum Associates.

Lovelock, C. H. (Ed.). (1977). *Nonbusiness marketing cases*. Boston, MA: Intercollegiate Case Clearing House.

Lovelock, C. H., & Weinberg, C. B. (1978). Public and nonprofit marketing comes of age. In G. Zaltman & T. Bonoma (Eds.), *Review of marketing 1978* (pp. 215–240). Chicago, IL: American Marketing Association.

Lumsdaine, A. A., & Janis, I. L. (1953). Resistance to counterpropaganda produced by one-sided propaganda presentations. *Public Opinion Quarterly, 17*, 311–318.

Lynch, J. G., & Srull, T. K. (1982). Memory and attentional factors in consumer choice: Concepts and research methods. *Journal of Consumer Research, 9*, 18.

Macht, M. L., Spear, N. E., & Lewis, D. J. (1977). State-dependent retention in humans induced by alterations in affective state. *Bulletin of the Psychonomic Society, 10*, 415–418.

Malinowski, B. (1953). *Sex and repression in savage society*. London, England: Routledge & Keegan Paul.

Marder, E., & David, M. (1961). Recognition of ad elements: Recall or projection? *Journal of Advertising Research, 1*, 23–25.

Marinho, H. (1942). Social influence in the formation of enduring preferences. *Journal of Abnormal and Social Psychology, 37*, 448–468.

Marshall, G., & Zimbardo, P. G. (1979). Affective consequences of inadequately explained physiological arousal. *Journal of Personality and Social Psychology, 37*, 970–988.

Maslach, C. (1979). Negative emotional biasing of unexplained arousal. *Journal of Personality and Social Psychology, 37*, 953–969.

Maslow, A. H. (1937). The influence of familiarization on preference. *Journal of Experimental Psychology, 21*, 162–180.

Maslow, A. H. (1943). A theory of human motivation. *Psychological Review, 50*, 370–396.

Maslow, A. H. (1970). *Motivation and personality*. New York: Harper & Row.

Massy, W. F., & Frank, R. E. (1965). Short term price and dealing effects in selected market segments. *Journal of Marketing Research, 2*, 171–185.

May, M. A. (1948). Experimentally acquired drives. *Journal of Experimental Psychology, 38*, 66–77.

McCartney, J. (1963, February 25). Drug promotion appeal directed at doctor's ego. *Chicago Daily News*.

McClelland, D. C., & Atkinson, J. W. (1948). The projective expression of needs: In the effects of different intensities of the hunger drive on perception. *Journal of Psychology, 25*, 205–232.

McCrary, J. W., & Hunter, W. S. (1953). Serial position curves in verbal learning. *Science, 117*, 131–134.

McCullough, L., & Ostrom, T. M. (1974). Repetition of highly similar messages and attitude change. *Journal of Applied Psychology, 59*, 395–397.

McDougall, G. H. G., Clanton, J. D., Ritchie, J. R. B., & Anderson, C. D. (1981). Consumer energy research: A review. *Journal of Consumer Research, 8*, 343–354.

McGinnis, J. (1969). *The selling of the president 1968*. New York: Trident Press.

McGuire, W. J. (1969). *An information processing model of advertising effectiveness*. Paper presented at the symposium on Behavioral and Management science in Marketing, Center for Continuing Education, University of Chicago, Chicago, IL.

McGuire, W. J. (1974). Psychological motives and communication gratification. In J. G.

Blumler & E. Katz (Eds.), *The uses of mass communications: Current perspectives on gratifications research* (pp. 412–435). Beverly Hills, CA: Sage.

McGuire, W. J. (1976). Some internal psychological factors influencing consumer choice. *Journal of Consumer Research, 2*, 302–319.

McSweeney, F. K., & Bierley, C. (1984). Recent developments in classical conditioning. *Journal of Consumer Research, 11*, 619–631.

Menzel, H., & Katz, E. (1955). Social relations and innovation in the medical profession: The epidemiology of a new drug. *Public Opinion Quarterly, 19*, 337–352.

Merriam, J. F. (1955). Up and down or all across—How should you stack soup? In H. Brenner (Ed.), *Marketing research pays off* (pp. 237–246). Pleasantville, NY: Printer's Ink Books.

Miller, G. A. (1956). The magical number seven, plus or minus two: Some limits on our capacity for processing information. *Psychological Review, 63*, 81–97.

Miller, N. E. (1948). Studies of fear as an acquirable drive: In fear as motivation and fear reduction as reinforcement in the learning of new responses. *Journal of Experimental Psychology, 38*, 89–101.

Miller, N. E. (1951). Learnable drives and rewards. In S. S. Stevens (Ed.), *Handbook of experimental psychology* (pp. 435–472). New York: Wiley.

Miller, N. E. (1969). Learning of visceral and glanduter responses. *Science, 163*, 434–449.

Miniard, P. W., & Cohen, J. B. (1981). An examination of the Fishbein–Ajzen behavioral intentions model's concepts and measures. *Journal of Experimental Social Psychology, 17*, 309–339.

Mittelstaedt, R. A. (1969). A dissonance approach to repeat purchasing behavior. *Journal of Marketing Research, 6*, 444–446.

Mittelstaedt, R. A., Grossbart, S. L., Curtis, W. W., & Devere, S. P. (1976). Optimal situation level and the adoption decision process. *Journal of Consumer Research, 3*, 84–94.

Mizerski, R. W., & Settle, R. B. (1979). The influence of social character on preference for social versus objective information in advertising. *Journal of Marketing Research, 16*, 552–558.

Monroe, K. B., & Petroshius, B. M. (1981). Buyers' perceptions of price: An update of the evidence. In H. H. Kassarjian, & T. S. Robertson (Eds.), *Perspectives in consumer behavior* (pp. 43–55). Glenview, IL: Scott, Foresman.

Morris, R. T., & Bronson, C. S. (1969). The chaos in competition indicated by consumer reports. *Journal of Marketing, 33*, 26–43.

Morris, R. T., & Jeffries, V. (1970). Class conflict: Forget it! *Sociology and Social Research, 54*, 306–320.

Morrison, D. G. (1979). Purchase intentions and purchase behavior. *Journal of Marketing, 43*, 65–74.

Moschis, G. P. (1976). Social comparison and informal influence. *Journal of Marketing Research, 13*, 237–244.

Moschis, G. P., & Moore, R. L. (1979). Decision making among the young: A socialization perspective. *Journal of Consumer Research, 6*, 101–112.

Moschis, G. P., & Moore, R. L. (1981, November). *A study of the acquisition of desires for products and brands*. Paper presented at the annual meeting of the American Marketing Association, Washington, DC.

Mowen, J. C., & Cialdini, R. B. (1980). On implementing the door-in-the-face compliance technique in a business context. *Journal of Marketing Research, 17*, 253–258.

Mullen, B. (1983). Operationalizing the effect of the group on the individual: A self-attention perspective. *Journal of Experimental Social Psychology, 19,* 295–322.

Mullen, B. (1984). Social psychological models of impression formation among consumers. *Journal of Social Psychology, 124,* 65–77.

Mullen, B., Atkins, J. L., Champion, D. S., Edwards, C., Hardy, D., Storey, J. E., & Vanderklok, M. (1985). The false consensus effect: A meta-analysis of 115 hypothesis tests. *Journal of Experimental Social Psychology, 21,* 262–283.

Mullen, B., Futrell, D., Stairs, D., Tice, D. M., Baumeister, R. F., Dawson, K. E., Riordan, C. A., Radloff, C. E., Goethals, G. R., Kennedy, J. G., & Rosenfeld, P. (1986). Newscasters' facial expressions and voting behavior of viewers: Can a smile elect a president? *Journal of Personality and Social Psychology, 51,* 291–295.

Mullen, B., & Peaugh, S. (1985, March). *Augmentation in advertising: A meta-analysis of the effects of disclaimers.* Paper presented at the annual meeting of the Eastern Psychological Association, Boston, MA.

Murdock, G. P. (1949). *Social structure.* New York: MacMillan.

Murray, H. H. (1938). *Explorations in personality.* New York: Oxford University Press.

Myers, J. H., & Mount, J. (1973). More on social class vs. income as correlates of buyer behavior. *Journal of Marketing, 37,* 71–73.

Myers, J. H., & Reynolds, W. H. (1967). *Consumer behavior and marketing management.* Boston, MA: Houghton-Mifflin.

National Association of Broadcasters. (1976). *Advertising guidelines: Children's TV advertising.* New York: Author.

National Research Council. (1978). *Deterrence and incapacitation.* Washington, DC: National Academy of Sciences.

Naylor, J. C. (1962). Deceptive packaging: Are the deceivers being deceived? *Journal of Applied Psychology, 46,* 393–398.

Nebes, R. D. (1974). Hemispheric specialization in commissurotomized man. *Psychological Bulletin, 81,* 1–14.

Nelson, T. O. (1977). Repetition and depth of processing. *Journal of Verbal Learning and Verbal Behavior, 16,* 151–171.

Nemeth, C. (1985). Dissent, group process and creativity: The contribution of minority influence. In E. Lawler (Ed.), *Advances in group processes* (Vol. 2, pp. 57–75). Greenwich, CT: JAI Press.

A new look at coupons. (1976). *Nielsen Researcher, 1,* 8.

Newman, J. W., & Staelin, R. (1973). Information sources of durable goods. *Journal of Advertising Research, 13,* 19–29.

Newman, J. W., & Werbel, R. A. (1973). Multivariate analysis of brand loyalty for major household appliances. *Journal of Marketing Research, 10,* 404–409.

Newton, D. A. (1967). A marketing communication model for sales management. In D. F. Cox (Ed.), *Risk taking and information handling in consumer behavior.* Boston, MA: Graduate School of Business Administration, Harvard University.

Nisbett, R. E., & Gurwitz, S. (1970). Weight, sex, and the eating behavior of human newborns. *Journal of Comparative and Physiological Psychology, 73,* 245–253.

Nisbett, R. E., & Wilson, T. D. (1977). Telling more than we can know: Verbal reports on mental processes. *Psychological Review, 84,* 231–259.

Nord, W. R., & Peter, J. P. (1980). A behavior modification perspective on marketing. *Journal of Marketing, 44,* 36–47.

Novelli, W. (1980). More effective social marketing urgently needed. *Advertising Age, 51,* 92–94.

Nwokoye, N. G. (1975, November). *Subjective judgements of price: The effects of price parameters on adaptation levels*. Paper presented at annual convention of the American Marketing Association, Chicago, IL.

Obermiller, C. (1985). Varieties of mere exposure. *Journal of Consumer Research, 12,* 17–30.

Olshavsky, R. W. (1973). Customer–salesmen interaction in appliance retailing. *Journal of Marketing Research, 10,* 208–212.

Osterhouse, R. A., & Brock, T. C. (1970). Distraction increases yielding to propaganda by inhibiting counter arguing. *Journal of Personality and Social Psychology, 15,* 355–358.

Oxenfeldt, A. R. (1950). Consumer knowledge: Its measurement and extent. *Review of Economics and Statistics, 32,* 300–314.

Pace, R. W. (1972). Oral communication and sales effectiveness. *Journal of Applied Psychology, 46,* 501–504.

Palda, K. S. (1966). The hypothesis of hierarchy of efforts. *Journal of Marketing Research, 3,* 13–24.

Pallak, S. R., Murroni, E., & Koch, J. (1983). Communicator attractiveness and expertise, emotional vs. rational appeals, and persuasion: A heuristic vs. systematic processing interpretation. *Social Cognition, 2,* 122–141.

Parsons, T., Bales, R. F., & Shils, E. A. (1953). *Working papers in the theory of action.* Glencoe, IL: The Free Press.

Pavlov, I. P. (1927). *Conditioned reflexes.* Oxford, England: Oxford University Press.

Pennington, A. (1968). Customer–salesmen bargaining behavior in retail transactions. *Journal of Marketing Research, 8,* 501–504.

Pessemier, E. A., Bemmaor, A. C., & Hanssens, D. M. (1977). Willingness to supply human body parts: Some empirical results. *Journal of Consumer Research, 4,* 131–140.

Peterson, L. R. (1969). Concurrent verbal activity. *Psychological Review, 76,* 376–386.

Phillips, D. P. (1980). The deterrent effect of capital punishment: New evidence on an old controversy. *American Journal of Sociology, 86,* 139–148.

Plummer, J. T. (1971). Lifestyle patterns and commercial bank credit card usage. *Journal of Marketing, 35,* 35–41.

Poincare, J. H. (1908). *La Science et l'Hypothese.* In E. M. Beck (Ed.), *Bartlett's familiar quotations* (p. 229). Boston, MA: Little, Brown.

Poindexter, J. (1983). Shaping the consumer. *Psychology Today, 17,* 64–68.

Prost, J. H. (1974). An experiment on the physical anthropology of expressive gestures. In M. J. Leaf (Ed.), *Frontiers of anthropology* (pp. 261–289). New York: D. Van Nostrand.

Pruden, H. O., & Peterson, R. A. (1971). Personality and performance satisfaction of industrial salesmen. *Journal of Marketing Research, 8,* 501–504.

Pruitt, D. G., & Drews, J. L. (1969). The effects of time pressure, time elapsed, and the opponent's concession rate on behavior in negotiation. *Journal of Experimental Social Psychology, 5,* 43–60.

Rao, T. V., & Misra, S. (1976). Effectiveness of varying ads style on consumer orientation. *Vikalpz, 1,* 19–26.

Reckman, R. F., & Goethals, G. R. (1973). Deviancy and group orientation as determinants of group composition preferences. *Sociometry, 36,* 419–423.

Reed, O. L., & Coalson, J. L. (1977). Eighteenth-century legal doctrine meets twentieth-century marketing techniques: FTC regulation of emotionally conditioning advertising. *Georgia Law Review, 11,* 733–782.

Reibstein, D. J., Lovelock, C. H., & Dobson, R. D. (1980). Direction of causalty between perceptions, affect & behavior: An application to travel behavior. *Journal of Consumer Research, 6,* 730–376.

Reingen, P. H. (1978). On the social psychology of giving: Door-in-the-face and when even a penny helps. *Advances in Consumer Research, 5,* 1–4.

Reingen, P. H., & Kernan, J. (1977). Compliance with an interview request: A foot-in-the-door, self-perception interpretation. *Journal of Marketing Research, 14,* 365–369.

Religious media's spreading tentacles. (1978). *Christian Century, 95,* 203–204.

Rescorla, R. A. (1967). Pavlovian conditioning and its proper control procedures. *Psychological Review, 74,* 71–80.

Rescorla, R. A. (1968). Probability of shock in the presence and absence of CS in fear conditioning. *Journal of Comparative and Physiological Psychology, 66,* 105.

Resnick, A., & Stern, B. L. (1977). An analysis of information content in television advertising. *Journal of Marketing, 41,* 50–53.

Revett, J. (1975, March 17). FTC threatens big fines for undersized cigaret warnings. *Advertising Age, 46*(11), 1, 74.

Reynolds, F. D., & Darden, W. R. (1971). Mutually adaptive effects of interpersonal communication. *Journal of Marketing Research, 8,* 449–454.

Rich, S. V., & Jain, S. C. (1968). Social class and life cycle as predictors of shopping behavior. *Journal of Marketing Research, 5,* 41–49.

Ricks, D. A., Arpan, J. S., & Fu, M. J. (1975). *International business blunders.* Columbus, OH: Grid.

Ries, A., & Trout, J. (1981). *Positioning: The battle for your mind.* New York: McGraw-Hill.

Riesman, D. (1950). *The lonely crowd.* New Haven, CT: Yale University Press.

Riesman, D., & Roseborough, H. (1955). Careers and consumer behavior. In L. Clark (Ed.), *Consumer behavior. Vol. II: The life cycle and consumer behavior* (pp. 1–18). New York: New York University Press.

Riesz, P. C. (1979). Price–quality correlations for packaged food products. *Journal of Consumer Affairs, 13,* 236–247.

Riley, D. A. (1968). *Discrimination learning.* Boston, MA: Allyn & Bacon.

Riordan, E. A., Oliver, R. L., & Donnelly, J. H. (1977). The unsold prospect: Dyadic and attitudinal determinants. *Journal of Marketing Research, 14,* 530–537.

Robertson, T. S. (1970). *Consumer behavior.* Glenview, IL: Scott, Foresman.

Robertson, T. S. (1971). *Innovative behavior and communication.* New York: Holt, Rinehart & Winston.

Robertson, T. S., & Rossiter, J. R. (1974). Children and commercial persuasion: An attribution theory analysis. *Journal of Consumer Research, 1,* 13–20.

Robertson, T. S., & Rossiter, J. R. (1976). Short-run advertising effects on children: A field study. *Journal of Marketing Research, 13,* 68–70.

Robertson, T. S., Rossiter, J. R., & Gleason, T. C. (1979). *Televised medicine advertising and children.* New York: Praeger.

Rogers, E. M., & Shoemaker, F. F. (1971). *Communication of innovations.* New York: The Free Press.

Rogers, D. (1959). Personality of the route salesman in a basic food industry. *Journal of Applied Psychology, 43,* 235–239.

Rogers, M. (1984, January 16). Selling psych-out software. *Newsweek, 103*(3), 52.

Rogers, R. W., & Mewborn, C. D. (1976). Fear appeals and attitude change: Effects of a threat's noxiousness, probability of occurrence, and the efficacy of coping responses. *Journal of Personality and Social Psychology, 34,* 54–61.

Rokeach, M. (1968). *Beliefs, attitudes, and values.* San Francisco, CA: Jossey-Bass.

Rosberg, J. W. (1956). How does color, size affect ad readership? *Industrial Marketing, 41,* 54–57.

Rosch, E. H. (1975). Cognitive representations of semantic categories. *Journal of Experimental Psychology: General, 104,* 192–233.

Rosenberg, M. J., & Hovland, C. I. (1960). Cognitive, affective, and behavioral components of attitudes. In C. I. Hovland & M. J. Rosenberg (Eds.), *Attitude organization and change* (pp. 1–14). New Haven, CT: Yale University Press.

Rosenfeld, P., Giacalone, R. A., & Tedeschi, J. T. (1981). *Enhancement of courses following preregistration.* Paper presented at the 52nd annual meeting of the Eastern Psychological Association, New York.

Rosenfeld, P., Giacalone, R. A., & Tedeschi, J. T. (1983). Cognitive dissonance vs. impression management. *Journal of Social Psychology, 120,* 203–211.

Ross, L., Greene, D., & House, P. (1977). The "false consensus effect": An egocentric bias in social perception and attribution processes. *Journal of Experimental Social Psychology, 13,* 279–301.

Rossiter, J. R. (1979). Does TV advertising affect children? *Journal of Advertising Research, 19,* 49–53.

Rubin, J. Z., & Brown, B. R. (1975). *The social psychology of bargaining and negotiation.* New York: Academic Press.

Rubin, V., Mager, C., & Friedman, H. H. (1982). Company president vs. spokesperson in television commercials. *Journal of Advertising Research, 22,* 31–33.

Rudolph, H. J. (1947). *Attention and interest factors in advertising.* New York: Funk & Wagnalls.

Russo, J. E. (1978). Eye fixations can save the world: A critical evaluation and a comparison between eye fixations and other information processing methodologies. *Advertising Consumer Research, 5,* 561–570.

Russo, J. E., Krieser, G., & Miyashita, S. (1975). An effective display of unit price information. *Journal of Marketing, 39,* 11–19.

Rust, L., & Watkins, T. A. (1975). Children's commercials: Creative development. *Journal of Advertising Research, 15,* 61–69.

Ryan, M. J., & Bonfield, E. H. (1980). Fishbein's intentions model: A test of external and pragmatic validity. *Journal of Marketing, 44,* 82–95.

Sanders, G. S., & Baron, R. S. (1975). The motivating effects of distraction on task performance. *Journal of Personality and Social Psychology, 32,* 956–963.

Scammon, D. (1977). Information load and consumers. *Journal of Consumer Research 4,* 148–155.

Schachter, S., & Rodin, J. (Eds.). (1974). *Obese humans and rats.* Hillsdale, NJ: Lawrence Erlbaum Associates.

Schachter, S., & Singer, J. E. (1962). Cognitive, social, and physiological determinants of emotional state. *Psychological Review, 69,* 379–399.

Schaninger, C. M. (1981). Social class vs. income revisited. *Journal of Marketing Research, 18,* 192–208.

Schrank, J. (1977). *Snap, crackle, popular taste.* New York: Dell.

Schuller, R. (1974). *God's way to the good life.* Dallas, TX: Keats.

Schwartz, S. H. (1970). Elicitation of moral obligation and self-sacrificing behavior. *Journal of Personality and Social Psychology, 15,* 283–293.

Scott, C. (1976). Effects of trial and incentives on repeat purchase behavior. *Journal of Marketing Research, 13,* 263–269.

Serrill, M. S. (1983, December 12). Castration or incarceration? *Time,* p. 70.

Settle, R. W., & Golden, L. L. (1974). Attribution theory and advertiser credibility. *Journal of Marketing Research, 11,* 181–185.

Shapiro, B. P. (1968). The psychology of pricing. *Harvard Business Review, 46,* 14–25, 160.

Shapiro, D., & Schwartz, G. E. (1972). Biofeedback and visceral learning: Clinical applications. *Seminars in Psychiatry, 4,* 171–184.

Shepard, R. N. (1967). Recognition memory for words, sentences and pictures. *Journal of Verbal Learning and Verbal Behavior, 6,* 156–163.

Sherif, M. (1935). A study of some social factors in perception. *Archives of Psychology,* No. 187.

Sherif, M., & Hovland, C. I. (1961). *Social judgement: Assimilation and contest effects in communication and attitude change.* New Haven, CT: Yale University Press.

Shiffrin, R. M., & Atkinson, R. C. (1969). Storage & retrieval processes in long-term memory. *Psychological Review, 76,* 179–193.

Shimp, T. A., & Dyer, R. F. (1979). The pain-pill-pleasure model and illicit drug consumption. *Journal of Consumer Research, 6,* 36–46.

Shimp, T. A., & Kavas, A. (1984). The theory of reasoned action applied to coupon usage. *Journal of Consumer Research, 11,* 795–809.

Shoemaker, R. W., & Schoaf, R. (1977). Repeat rates of deal purchase. *Journal of Advertising Research, 17,* 47–53.

Shuptrine, F. K., & McVicker, D. D. (1981). Readability levels of magazine ads. *Journal of Advertising Research, 21,* 45–51.

Smith, D., Spence, D. P., & Klein, G. S. (1959). Subliminal effects of verbal stimuli. *Journal of Abnormal and Social Psychology, 59,* 167–177.

Smith, R. E., & Hunt, S. D. (1978). Attributional processes & effects in promotional situations. *Journal of Consumer Research, 5,* 149–158.

Snyder, M. (1979). Self-monitoring processes. In L. Berkowitz (Ed.), *Advances in experimental social psychology* (Vol. 12, pp. 85–128). New York: Academic Press.

Snyder, M., & Cunningham, M. (1975). To comply or not comply: Testing the self-perception explanation of the foot-in-the-door phenomenon. *Journal of Personality and Social Psychology, 31,* 64–67.

Soldow, G. F., & Principe, V. (1981). Response to commercials as a function of program context. *Journal of Advertising Research, 21,* 54–65.

Soldow, G. F., & Thomas, G. P. (1984). Relational communication: Form vs. content in the sales interaction. *Journal of Marketing, 48,* 84–93.

Sorenson, A. W., Wyse, B. W., Wittwer, A. J., & Hansan, R. G. (1976). An index of nutritional quality for a balanced diet. *Journal of the American Dietetic Association, 68,* 236–237.

Spence, K. W. (1956). *Behavior theory and conditioning.* New Haven, CT: Yale University Press.

Spence, K. W. (1964). Anxiety (drive) level and performance in eyelid conditioning. *Psychological Bulletin, 61,* 129–139.

Spence, H. E., & Engel, J. F. (1970). The impact of brand preference on the perception of brand names: A laboratory analysis. In D. T. Kollat, R. D. Blackwell, & J. F. Engel (Eds.), *Research in consumer behavior* (pp. 61–70). New York: Holt, Rinehart & Winston.

Sperry, R. W. (1951). Cerebral organization and behavior. *Science, 133,* 1749.

Sproles, G. B. (1974). Fashion theory: A conceptual framework. In S. Ward & P. Wright (Eds.), *Advertising consumer research* (Vol. 1, pp. 212–245). Urbana, IL: Association for Consumer Research.

Sproles, G. B. (1977). New evidence on price and product quality. *Journal of Consumer Affairs, 11,* 63–77.

Stang, D. J. (1975). When familiarity breeds contempt, absence makes the heart grow fonder: Effects of mere exposure and delay on taste pleasantness ratings. *Bulletin of the Psychonomic Society, 6,* 273–275.

Stang, D. J. (1977). Exposure, recall, judged favorability and sales: "Mere exposure" and consumer behavior. *Social Behavior and Personality, 5,* 329–335.

Starch, D. (1961). What is the best frequency of advertisements? *Media/Scope, 5,* 44–45.

Steiner, G. A. (1966). The people look at commercials: A study of audience behavior. *Journal of Business,* 272–304.

Stern, B. L., Krugman, D. M., & Resnick, A. (1981). Magazine advertising: An analysis of its information context. *Journal of Advertising Research, 21,* 39–44.

Stern, R. M., Farr, J. H., & Ray, W. J. (1975). Pleasure. In P. H. Venables & M. J. Christie (Eds.), *Research in psychophysiology* (pp. 208–233). London, England: Wiley.

Sternthal, B., & Craig, C. S. (1973). Humor in advertising. *Journal of Marketing, 37,* 12–18.

Sternthal, B., & Craig, C. S. (1974). Fear appeals: Revisited and revised. *Journal of Consumer Research, 1,* 22–34.

Stevens, S. S. (1975). *Psychophysics: Introduction to its perceptual, neural and social prospects.* New York: Wiley.

Suls, J., & Miller, R. L. (Eds.). (1977). *Social comparison processes: Theoretical and empirical perspectives.* Washington, DC: Hemisphere.

Sulzberger, A. O. (1981, May 1). Smoking warnings called ineffective. *New York Times,* p. A14.

Summers, J. O. (1970). The identity of women's clothing fashion opinion leaders. *Journal of Marketing Research, 7,* 178–185.

Swinyard, W. R. (1981). The interaction between comparative advertising and copy claim variation. *Journal of Marketing Research, 18,* 175–186.

Taylor, J. W., Houlahan, J. J., & Gabrael, A. C. (1975). The purchase intention question in new product development: A field test. *Journal of Marketing, 39,* 90–92.

Tedeschi, J. T. (Ed.). (1981). *Impression management theory and social psychological research.* New York: Academic Press.

Tedeschi, J. T., Schlenker, B. R., & Bonoma, T. V. (1971). Cognitive dissonance: Private ratiocination or public spectacle. *American Psychologist, 26,* 685–695.

Tedeschi, J. T., Schlenker, B. R., & Bonoma, T. V. (1973). *Conflict, power, and games: The experimental study of interpersonal relations.* Chicago, IL: Aldine.

Tedeschi, J. T., Smith, R. B., & Brown, R. C. (1974). A reinterpretation of research on aggression. *Psychology Bulletin, 81,* 540–563.

Teevan, R. C., & Smith, B. D. (1967). *Motivation.* New York: McGraw-Hill.

Teuber, M. L. (1974). Sources of ambiguity in the prints of Maurits C. Escher. *Scientific American, 231,* 90–104.

Tigert, D. J., & Arnold, S. J. (1970). Profiling self-designated opinion leaders and self-designated innovators through life style research. In D. M. Gardner (Ed.), *Proceedings of the 2nd conference of Association for Consumer Research.* Ann Arbor, MI: Association for Consumer Research.

Tuck, M. (1979). Consumer behavior theory and the criminal justice system: Toward a new strategy for research. *Journal of Market Research Society, 21,* 44–58.

Tulving, E., & Thomson, D. M. (1973). Encoding specificity and retrieval processes in episodic memory. *Psychological Review, 80,* 359–380.

Tversky, A., & Kahneman, D. (1973). Availability: A heuristic for judging frequency and probability. *Cognitive Psychology, 5,* 207–232.

Tversky, A., & Kahnaman, D. (1974). Judgement under uncertainty: Heuristics and biases. *Science, 185,* 1124–1131.

Twedt, D. W. (1961, August). *The consumer psychologist*. Paper presented at the annual meeting of The American Psychology Association.

Ulin, L. G. (1962, July). Does page size influence advertising effectiveness? *Media/Scope*, pp. 47–50.

Valins, S. (1966). Cognitive effects of false heart rate feedback. *Journal of Personality and Social Psychology, 4*, 400–408.

Vaughn, K. B., & Lanzetta, J. T. (1980). Vicarious instigation and conditioning of facial expressive and autonomic responses to a model's expressive displays of pain. *Journal of Personality and Social Psychology, 38*, 909–923.

Veblen, T. (1899). *The theory of the leisure class*. New York: The New American Library (1754 edition).

Venn, J. R., & Short, J. G. (1973). Vicarious classical conditioning of emotional responses in nursery school children. *Journal of Personality and Social Psychology, 28*, 249–255.

Verhallen, T. M. M., & Van Raaij, W. F. (1981). Household behavior and the use of natural gas for home heating. *Journal of Consumer Research, 8*, 253–257.

Vidulich, R. N., & Kaiman, I. P. (1961). The effects of information source status and dogmatism upon conformity behavior. *Journal of Abnormal and Social Psychology, 63*, 639–642.

Vinson, D. E., & Scott, J. E. (1977). The role of personal values in marketing and consumer behavior. *Journal of Marketing, 41*, 44–50.

Ward, S. (1972). Children's reactions to commercials. *Journal of Advertising Research, 12*, 37–45.

Ward, S. (1974). Consumer socialization. *Journal of Consumer Research, 1*, 1–14.

Ward, S. Robertson, T. S., & Wackman, D. (1971). Children's attention to television advertising. In D. M. Gardner (Ed.), *Proceedings for the Annual Convention of the Association for Consumer Research*, pp. 143–156.

Ward, S., & Wackman, D. (1972). Television advertising and intra-family influence: Children's purchase influence attempts and parental yielding. *Journal of Marketing Research, 9*, 316–319.

Warner, W. L., & Lunt, P. S. (1941). *The social life of a modern community*. New Haven, CT: Yale University Press.

Warshaw, P. R. (1980). A new model for predicting behavioral intentions: An alternative to Fishbein. *Journal of Marketing Research, 17*, 153–172.

Wasson, C. R. (1969). Is it time to quit thinking of income classes. *Journal of Marketing, 33*, 54–57.

Watkins, J. L. (1980). *The 100 greatest advertisements: Who wrote them and what they did*. Toronto, Canada: Coles Publishing.

Watson, J. B., & Raynor, R. (1920). Conditioned emotional reactions. *Journal of Experimental Psychology, 3*, 1–4.

Weitz, B. A. (1978). The relationship between salesperson performance and understanding of customer decision making. *Journal of Marketing Research, 15*, 501–516.

Weitz, B. A. (1981). Effectiveness in sales interactions: A contingency famework. *Journal of Marketing, 45*, 85–103.

Wells, W. D. (1975). Psychographics: A critical review. *Journal of Marketing Research, 12*, 196–213.

Wells, W. D., & LoSciuto, L. A. (1966). Direct observation of purchasing behavior. *Journal of Marketing Research, 3*, 227–233.

Wells, W. D., & Reynolds, F. D. (1979). Psychological geography. *Research in Marketing, 2*, 345–357.

White, T. H. (1961). *The making of the President 1960*. New York: Atheneum.

White, T. H. (1965). *The making of the President 1964*. New York: Atheneum.

White, T. H. (1969). *The making of the President 1968.* New York: Atheneum.

White, T. H. (1973). *The making of the President 1972.* New York: Atheneum.

White, T. H. (1977). *The making of the President 1976.* New York: Atheneum.

Whitney, E. N., & Sizer, F. S. (1985). *Nutrition concepts and controversies.* St. Paul, NY: West Publishing.

Whorf, B. (1956). Science and linguistics. In J. B. Carroll (Ed.), *Language, thought and reality: Selected writings of Benjamin Lee Whorf* (pp. 1–40). Cambridge, MA: MIT Press.

Whyte, W. H. (1952). The language of advertising. *Fortune, 46,* 98–101.

Whyte, W. H. (1954). The web of word of mouth. *Fortune, 50,* 140–143, 204, 206, 208, 210, 212.

Wilhelm, R. (1956). Are subliminal commercials bad? *Michigan Business Review, 8,* 26.

Willett, R. P., & Pennington, A. L. (1966). Customer and salesman: The anatomy of choice and influence in a retail setting. In R. M. Hass (Ed.), *Science, technology and marketing* (pp. 126–148). Chicago, IL: American Marketing Association.

Wilson, W. R. (1979). Feeling more than we can know: Exposure effects without learning. *Journal of Personality and Social Psychology, 37,* 811–821.

With 'feeling' commercials. (1981). *Marketing News, 24,* 1–2.

Witt, D. (1977). *Emotional advertising: The relationships between eye-movement patterns and memory: Empirical study with the eye-movement monitor.* Unpublished doctoral dissertation, University of Saarland, Germany.

Witt, R. E. (1969). Informal social group influence on consumer brand choice. *Journal of Marketing Research, 6,* 473–476.

Witt, R. E., & Bruce, G. D. (1970). Purchase decisions and group influence. *Journal of Marketing Research, 7,* 533–535.

Wolfgang, M. E. (1978). The death penalty: Social philosophy and social science research. *Criminal Law Bulletin, 14,* 18–33.

Woodside, A. G., (1974). Relation of price to perception of quality of new products. *Journal of Applied Psychology, 59,* 116–118.

Woodside, A. G., & Davenport, W. J. (1974). The effect of salesman similarity and expertise on consumer purchasing behavior. *Journal of Marketing Research, 11,* 198–202.

Yalch, R., & Bryce, W. (1981, November). *Effects of a reactance reduction technique on reciprocation in personal selling.* Paper presented at the annual meeting of the American Marketing Association.

Yalch, R. F., & Elmore-Yalch, R. (1984). The effect of numbers on the route to persuasion. *Journal of Consumer Research, 11,* 522–527.

Yamanake, J. (1962). The prediction of ad readership scores. *Journal of Advertising Research, 2,* 18–23.

Yates, S. M., & Aronson, E. (1983). A social psychological perceptive on energy conservation in residential buildings. *American Psychologist, 38,* 435–444.

Zajonc, R. B. (1965). Social facilitation. *Science, 149,* 269–274.

Zajonc, R. B. (1968). Attitudinal effects of mere exposure. *Journal of Personality and Social Psychology, 9,* 1–28.

Zajonc, R. B. (1980). Feeling and thinking: Preferences need no inferences. *American Psychologist, 35,* 151–175.

Zborowski, M. (1969). *People in pain.* San Francisco, CA: Jossey-Bass.

Zelinsky, W. (1973). *The cultural geography of the United States.* Englewood Cliffs, NJ: Prentice-Hall.

Zillmann, D. (1978). Attribution and misattribution of excitatory reactions. In J. H. Harvey, W. Ickes, & R. F. Kidd (Eds.), *New directions in attribution research* (Vol. 2, pp. 335–368). Hillsdale, NJ: Lawrence Erlbaum Associates.

Credits

Fig. 7.2e. Reprinted with permission of General Foods Corporation and Grey Advertising Inc.

Fig. 13.1. Illustration courtesy of The Advertising Council Inc.

Fig. 13.2. Reprinted with permission of The Trinitarians.

Fig. 13.3. Reprinted with permission of NYS Division of Criminal Justice Services.

Author Index

A

Ackoff, R. L., 97, 100, 111
Adams, H. F., 20, 140
Adams, S., 155
Adorno, T. W., 129
Agatstein, F. C., 62
Ajzen, I., 60, 107–109
Albers, S., 39
Alessis, C., 53
Allport, G. W., 76, 101
Anderson, C. D., 166
Anderson, J. R., 50
Andren, G., 51
Arch, D. C., 13
Arndt, J., 131, 133
Arnold, S. J., 131
Aronson, E., 167
Arpan, J. S., 140
Asch, S. E., 109
Assimov, I., 112
Assael, H., 64, 83, 92, 120, 131
Atkin, C., 53, 103, 135–137, 146
Atkins, J. L., 109
Atkinson, J. W., 92
Atkinson, R. C., 33
Aycrigg, R. H., 73

B

Babb, E. M., 74
Bacon, J. J., 25
Bagozzi, R. P., 109, 151
Bales, R. F., 134
Bambic, P., 152

Bandura, A., 70, 72, 73
Banks, S., 108
Barber, T. X., 143
Baron, R. A., 49, 123
Baron, R. S., 126
Barry, H., 73
Bassett, R., 157
Bauer, R. A., 16
Baumeister, R. F., 76, 169
Bayton, J. A., 69
Becherer, R. C., 110, 129
Belch, G. E., 55
Belk, R., 168
Bem, D. J., 115
Bemmaor, A. C., 170
Benedict, R., 144, 146
Bentler, P. M., 109
Berey, L. A., 135
Berlin, B., 140
Berger, S. M., 72
Bernal, G., 72
Bettman, J. R., 34, 35
Bierley, C., 64, 65, 83
Birrell, J., 86
Bishop, D. W., 145
Black, J. S., 108
Blackwell, R. D., 4, 6, 7, 131, 133, 164, 165
Blake, B., 130
Blanchard, E. B., 73
Blattberg, R., 112
Bloch, R., 170
Block, M., 53
Bolles, R. C., 91
Bonfield, E. H., 109
Bonoma, T. V., 76, 104, 116, 156
Bourne, F. S., 128

Subject Index